DON'T ASK ME ABOUT MY DAD

For my mum and my sisters

DON'T ASK ME ABOUT MY DAD

TOM MITCHELSON

*An inspiring true story of
a scared little boy with
a dark secret*

HarperElement
An imprint of HarperCollins*Publishers*
1 London Bridge Street
London SE1 9GF

www.harpercollins.co.uk

HarperCollins*Publishers*
Macken House, 39/40 Mayor Street Upper
Dublin 1, D01 C9W8, Ireland

First published by HarperElement 2023

1 3 5 7 9 10 8 6 4 2

A catalogue record of this book is available from the British Library

ISBN 978-0-00-849144-4

Printed and bound in the UK using 100% renewable electricity at CPI Group (UK) Ltd

p142, lyrics from 'I Can See Clearly Now', by Johnny Nash, 1972, Nashco Music Inc
p187, extract from the Daily Echo, 28 Aug 1977, by Ian Tuckey
p291, extract from the Daily Mail, 19 Dec 2019, by Jack Elsom
p292, extract from the Daily Mirror, 21 Dec 2019, by John Siddle

While every effort has been made to trace the owners of copyright material reproduced herein and secure permissions, the publishers would like to apologise for any omissions and will be pleased to incorporate missing acknowledgements in any future edition of this book.

MIX
Paper | Supporting
responsible forestry
FSC™ C007454

This book is produced from independently certified FSC™ paper to ensure responsible forest management.

For more information visit: www.harpercollins.co.uk/green

Author's Note

This is not a novel, though it may read like one. It's not a fantasy, though in places it may seem so. It's not an imagined history constructed to illustrate a genuine horror. Nor is it a 'docudrama', which, to tell a story that's basically true, plays around with the truth, reconstructs, invents, fills in the gaps.

I am doing none of those things here. I'm reporting. This is my true story, the life I lived as a boy, and its effect on my life after that. It is, of course, written from my perspective. I don't always like the person I describe, or approve of my decisions and responses, but I've decided to just be honest and let others do the judging.

All this happened, every scene, every twist and turn, every shock. All the people in this book are real and to the best of my knowledge still alive, save for my dad. The only licence I've allowed myself is where I'm reporting speech. I've sometimes put it in quotation marks to bring it to life, though, while I remember very well what people said, I couldn't swear to every word or phrase. Or not always. Very often I could. Some words are not easily forgotten.

I have used my mum's diaries from the time in question to fill in gaps in my memory and to jog it on other occasions. There is a place for leaps of the imagination, for what might

1

have been or could have happened, but this is not one of those. This is what happened to me, every word of it.

We all have our story to tell. It's just that I didn't know what mine was until recently and, now that I do, I want to tell it to you.

Chapter 1

My dad was dying. Death was in the air and the pallor of his skin. I could feel it in my bones. But I didn't fear it. In fact, I wanted to press fast forward and skip to the last scene. I wasn't going to mourn him. I knew that. I wondered if I'd find myself missing him. I wasn't sure. I suspected I would breathe a sigh of relief. I wanted our forty-year-old relationship to be over.

His trolley was pushed up against the wall in the corridor, along with twenty or so others. The yellowish light flickered down on the blue linoleum floor and the smell of disinfectant and take-away Portuguese pastries pervaded the air. From inside one of the little consulting rooms nearby, two deeply wrinkled women wailed with sadness and, moments before, as I had passed one of the lined-up trolleys, an elderly man, wild eyes shot through with fear, had reached out from the bed and grabbed the sleeve of my jacket, pleading with me, '*Ajuda-me! Ajuda-me!*' Help me, help me.

My dad lay feebly on the bed but some of the colour had returned to his cheeks. I had only been away fifteen minutes – I had been trying to find somewhere to leave his bag – but his relief at seeing me was obvious. He'd been put on a drip and

3

told he would be kept in overnight. He just wanted the surgeons to fix him up so he could get back to his flat and drink gin and tonics.

'Do you have my keys and wallet? I can't find them,' he said.

'Yes, they're in your bag in a locker and the nurse knows which locker it is.'

'What about my hairbrush?'

I surveyed the anarchic scene around us once more as the crying from the old women reached a crescendo. 'I wouldn't worry about it, to be honest.'

He nodded. He was anxious about making his flight back to the UK. He had a hospital appointment in two days' time and now he was asking me to go in search of a doctor to find out if he'd be able to travel. I knew that no one would be able to make him any such promise, but to ease his worries I agreed.

Earlier that day I had visited him in his tiny, filthy studio apartment in a small Portuguese town called Sesimbra. It was obvious he was seriously ill. He could barely stand up. I called the taxi driver, Nuno, the fifty-year-old man who looked like a washed-up Julio Iglesias. My dad had been using him as a personal chauffeur to ferry him to and from the shop, and we got him to drive us to the nearest hospital.

My dad was compos mentis and chatted happily in the car, making jokes with Nuno, who spoke English with the tortured formality of a mistranslated instruction manual.

'St Bernardo is a proficient medical centre and I believe you will receive care that most people would consider satisfactory,' he told us with a less than comforting grin.

My dad had managed to keep his hair during the rounds of chemotherapy, and although he had lost weight he looked good for his seventy-two years. His false teeth gave him a full smile and his blue eyes were sharp and clear. The only physical sign that hinted at the chaos in his life was the sight of around thirty long bristles protruding from his chin and neck that he'd missed while shaving.

He'd moved to Portugal just as his treatment in the UK had ended, and now that he was living abroad, the bladder cancer had returned. I had to carry him from the car, which was surprisingly easy, but it was still difficult to manoeuvre him from the car seat.

Nuno was now standing beside me, and for a moment I allowed myself to be distracted from the grave situation by what he was wearing. A crisp pink shirt under a tight bright-red V-neck jumper, extremely skinny stone-washed jeans and brown suede shoes, which I noticed were different shades of brown.

'Now I have delivered you to the aforementioned place, I can delay myself until I receive information that you can impart to me at a time when you choose,' Nuno said, and then wandered back in the direction of his car.

It was only when I had planted my dad on the beige plastic A&E seat that I noticed his blood was all over my shirt and there were splodges down his trousers. I showed his European health card to the woman behind the desk, paid a €16 fee and then we sat and waited for hours and hours. They brought him a wheelchair and I was able to take him for his frequent toilet visits.

Each time I had to lift him onto the seat and then stand outside, guarding the unlocked door. I could hear his agonised shrieks as he passed urine. Rather than feeling sympathy for his pain, I thought what a coward he was. Why couldn't he swallow his discomfort and desperation? I bet his great hero John Wayne didn't whinge and flail as he died from cancer; more likely he winced and bit his lip and said, 'The big ole C ain't beat me yet.'

Once he'd finished, I'd go back in and help him pull his trousers up, get him back into the wheelchair and then wipe away the blood from the floor with the cheap loo roll you always get in hospitals.

My dad was lost and scared and looked to me for everything. He was a small child again, stripped of his compulsion to control things, and longing for me to rescue him. He was totally absorbed in his own plight and it made me seethe with anger.

He was nothing in this hospital. Just another miserable, toothless old man waiting in line to die, alongside the very people he had always scorned – the helpless. I stayed with him for hours, fetching food and water, talking to him, calming him down and speaking with the nurses in pidgin Portuguese to get information about when he might be treated.

Why was I here after all he had done? Growing up with him was like being in my own war zone, living in perpetual fear of when the bombs would fall. He physically abused and terrified my mother, the only person I had to hold me. He made me cower in a toy store at the age of nine, when we returned a faulty toy, the manager refused a refund and my dad became so aggressive that the manager pushed a panic alarm and called the police. He smashed up the furniture in our home; he screamed with volcanic rage in my eight-year-old face. His criminal viciousness was his defining characteristic. He made my body shake every day of my childhood.

While he committed unspeakable acts downstairs, I paced up and down in my bedroom, pressing my sweaty hands hard together, while my rising panic meant I talked out loud to myself to try to keep calm. When his temper flared a whole world of trouble came crashing down, and yet why was I here after all he had done?

He made me susceptible to a molester, he gave me diarrhoea throughout my primary school years and he made me suspicious of everyone I met. I doubted their motivations and I doubted their kind souls.

He taught me that the world was something to be wary of and made me unsure of my own instincts. I was terrified of becoming him, and in moments I could feel I might. He still lives within me grimly like some battered demon sprite. And I'm fearful of his shadow. The rage, and his blood. There are some moments when he arrives and I want to tear up the whole world with my bare hands, and all I really want is love. I want him away now. Please. Just go.

There was no one else in his life prepared to stay with him in these final days. Nuno, a man he paid, and me, his son, who loved him but hated him too. He was my friend and he was my foe. I jumped to his defence so many times, yet I could have killed him myself. I was bound to him in a way I didn't understand back then.

My first ever memory was of me and him. I was three and pedalling my miniature police car on the way home. My legs worked hard to propel me along, and it was a lot of work for the limited speed. There was a blue siren on the front above the steering wheel and an orange telephone on the dashboard. My dad was walking behind and suggested I call my mum to let her know we'd be home shortly. I held the receiver to my ear and made up a conversation. I was happy and secure. If I saw that scene today from across the street, it would make me smile. A father and son together. Him keeping a watchful eye, making sure I kept to the pavement, joking with me and pointing me in the direction home.

The man on the hospital bed right now was that man too, but I couldn't separate the brute from him. The only thing I was certain of was that I had to be there to see this thing through to the end. I had to be a good son because otherwise what was left?

I could have had a more straightforward life, and my sisters too. What he did to us weighed heavily on me and I couldn't bear to admit the crushing effect it had had. Even now I don't want to accept that is the case, because if I do the sadness won't wash away.

I was conditioned by him. I thought this was what sons did, unquestioning and loyal. Here I was, serving my dues because I thought I owed it to him. I never realised I owed him nothing. I didn't have to give him the time of day, and had I realised that, I could have been free.

I knew what he had done was wrong but I didn't feel it in my heart. I couldn't allow myself to. So I never faced it. I had to believe in the bond between him and me because I felt it. I knew it existed, but it was so contorted with resentment I could neither break nor accept it, so we remained shackled like two quarrelling convicts in a chain gang.

The man in front of me now, lying on a trolley pushed up against a wall, had caused me so much damage, but he was my father. And even nearing forty I still needed him. I needed to extract what good there was and try to forget about the rest. And, although I couldn't admit it to myself, I wanted to be free of him, his solipsism and the chaos he wrought.

But instead I kissed him on the forehead and went in search of a doctor.

Chapter 2

There were eyes on us wherever we went. And a lot of questions. I can still feel the furtive gaze of rubbery-faced shop owners and see whiskery old women waving from shuttered windows. There were affable approaches from smiling waiters, and sun-kissed girls would run out from stone houses to ask us where we were from. I was four years old. I would look up to see scruffy, thin leather belts around old men's waists while having my wavy blond hair ruffled. I hated that, as well as the rough fingers pinching my cheeks, wobbling them affectionately.

It was 1981. My dad quit his job as a newsreader at Radio Orwell, sold our house for £11,000 and led his family out of Essex to the wilds of post-revolutionary Portugal, all in search of a dream: to buy land, set up a campsite and ignite a tourist trade on the south-west coast. We drew attention partly because foreigners were rare in that part of the world back then, but mainly because I had twelve-year-old identical triplet sisters, Emma, Kate and Victoria, who were often dressed in the same clothes because it saved time when shopping, avoiding sartorial arguments.

On closer inspection, the friendly locals would see that my mum had only one hand. This added to the circus-like interest we received. And then there was my dad, side-parted black hair, a full moustache and Buddy Holly glasses. Tall, slim, with a sprinkling of Portuguese. He was quite an imposing man, seeming bigger than he was, although he wasn't small. He was the type of person that made people want to be liked by him.

Once we'd got to know whatever new friends had approached us, we'd clamber aboard our bright orange Volkswagen campervan and drive off down the dusty road, with our trailer carrying all our worldly belongings banging along behind.

The campervan was to become a source of dark obsession for my dad, but I loved having it. There was a Formica pull-out table, a spongy mattress bed-seat, a kitchenette and floral curtains, which required about four or five hard yanks to pull them along the white plastic cord. You could be at home while on the road. My parents would fill a kettle with the dribble of water that came from the shaky stainless-steel tap, heat it up on a gas hob and drink a cup of tea while I'd be playing on the rough upholstery of the built-in seat.

The afternoon we left our small semi-detached house just outside Colchester, I remember only two things. The new house owners arriving as we were leaving, hovering around like customers waiting for a table in a restaurant, and burying my face in the soft cotton of my Winnie-the-Pooh pillow to stifle my tears.

A few hours after we loaded our van onto the ferry at Plymouth we sailed into the Bay of Biscay, where giant Atlantic waves crashed into the boat, wind screamed throughout the cabins and we were flung from wall to wall. 'It's just like *The Poseidon Adventure*,' Victoria said, referring to the film she'd seen the previous week. Plates flew from the cafeteria tables and passengers toppled over, sliding along the floor. My mum took me with her to the toilet, telling me to hold onto a pillar, my arms barely reaching halfway around it, while she went inside the cubicle. There I remained as the floor tilted drastically one way, then the other, until my mum returned.

My dad remained calm throughout, barking orders to my sisters and me about who should stand where, even managing to finish his soup as the storm hit. To me he was like a cowboy from his favourite type of movie. A hard-talking, straight-walking man, not to be messed with. He had even bought a Stetson for our trip. He did lots of things that impressed me. He could drive and I already knew that was one of my life's aims. He had a natural authority that put people into line, and I'd seen him fixing things with a treasure chest of tools, all of which he knew how to use. He paid for things from a brown leather pouch that hung from his belt. Now he was leading us on an adventure into the great unknown.

For the next few weeks we moved around the south of the country, pitching our family-sized tent, looking for land to buy. At night we ate boiled vegetables and salty cod in brightly lit restaurants, where the counters were varnished wood and the whitewashed walls broken by blue tiles. Glass fridges would be full of bowls of chocolate mousse and, after every meal, I'd order one. My cold spoon would plunge into the dessert, and for three or four minutes very little else would matter.

Our days were spent on deserted, pale sandy beaches in the dazzling Portuguese sun, searching for small silver fish in rock pools and being knocked over by the surf. The afternoons smelt of seaweed and salt. We'd take trips to old sea forts or make friends with kids on campsites. I never strayed too far from my mum, who would be grilling sardines or boiling a chickpea stew on a camp stove. My freckled-nosed, bob-haired sisters played in the parks with me before they wandered off together, seeking their own entertainment.

We drove through mountains covered with pine and cork trees, mangy cats staring at us from the roadside. We'd pass heavily burdened donkeys and oxen pulling carts led by short, moustachioed, grizzled men. Once, on an orange-tree-lined road, where the low crumbling houses with faded red-tiled roofs were few and far between, the van came to a forceful halt. Blood and feathers hit the windscreen. A chicken had boldly stepped out to cross the road, as chickens do, got three quarters of the way over, lost confidence or realised it had forgotten something, and made a fatal decision to turn back. We hit it full on. My dad got out, grabbed the dead bird by the neck, its thin, scaly legs dangling beneath, and marched towards a run-down farm by the side of the road, where a dog tethered to a pole was yapping away outside. He came back a few minutes later announcing that the farmer had thanked him, telling him he'd eat it that night.

The rural Portuguese folk looked different to the scrubbed, pasty neighbours we had back home. Their faces would often reveal toothless smiles; their clothes were dusty and I got used to hearing them remark about the weather, '*Muito vento*' – much wind – or shout at the girls, '*Trigêmeos*' – three twins, meaning triplets – like they were giving us information we didn't know.

It's hard to recall things from the first five years of your life. It's hard to say what my emotions were or how I felt about the members of my family, and it's hard to piece together feelings from retold stories or hazy memories and pictures in my head, but I remember my mood. I was happy. It was wild and rough and free, but I half-remember moments of confusion – shuddering flashes when my blithe picture of a child's happy-families world was pierced by something that did not fit that picture. Perhaps we all have such recollections of sudden miseries and discordances, shafts of fear in our childhood, but because things turned out all right in the end, they are later robbed of significance. For me, though, their significance would only grow. Then, they seemed like jarring interludes that soon passed. Now they seem like auguries. Kids don't ask where things are pointing, but only how soon they will be over.

One night, as my mum served what might have been spaghetti bolognaise (I remember Kate teaching me to roll the pasta round my fork to eat it), my dad toppled into our camp table, its legs collapsing completely and the food flying in all directions. Our enamel plates clunked as they hit the floor. Bits of minced meat dripped from the chairs. I didn't know he was drunk back then but the shock stays with me.

A few days later, Emma woke early to the sound of someone breathing heavily at the back of our tent. She called for my dad, who leapt out of my parents' self-contained compartment, hastily pulled on his trousers and disappeared out into the dark. Seconds later there was a commotion. My dad had found a man lying up against the tent, hauled him to his feet, and they'd struggled until the man broke away. My dad gave chase until he saw a rock, which he picked up and hurled at the man, hitting him in the back. Being disturbed in the middle of the night was something I grew used to. This was the first time I recall it happening. The panic I felt as I rushed to understand what was going on. My dad was our protector and it made me feel proud. The next night he slept alone in the campervan, armed with an iron bar, waiting for the intruder to return.

It was as we checked out from that campsite to travel further south that my dad became embroiled in a furious row with a man at reception. The previous night, my mum had tried to call England from the camp's public phone but failed to get through. The receptionist refused to believe she hadn't made contact, telling her she had to pay forty escudos. My mum repeated what had happened and he replied, 'I have to accept your story, but you will not use the phone again.'

My dad, his eyes bulging from their sockets and the veins in his temple pulsating, began remonstrating with the receptionist. I watched on, holding my mum's hand tightly as my dad stormed up to him, pushing his face right up to the receptionist's. A small crowd gathered around the shouting pair. At some point my dad called him an 'ignorant pig' before turning on his heel and walking towards us.

The receptionist rushed towards my dad, jumping on his back. There were jeers from the crowds as my dad fell, rolling over two or three times, his glasses flying from his ears. The dust kicked up from the ground. Several of the onlookers held the receptionist back while my dad brushed himself down. Someone handed him his spectacles. That was the first time I remember being scared.

My dad thought big. As I grew up it would both excite and frustrate me. When he first met my mum, he was starting up his own local newspaper, the *Brentwood Advertiser*. He even asked my mum to be the agony aunt, dishing out advice to those who found themselves struggling with debt or relationship difficulties. It lasted for one month before the creditors were on his case and the final edition was printed.

His entrepreneurial flair had risen again shortly before we left for Portugal, when he had attempted to start a radio station in Colchester. My mum knew he could be charming and persuasive, but the details and the execution would always let him down.

Now we were striking out for a new life in southern Europe. Pioneers riding across the plains in search of gold in our trusty old wagon. We struck a deal to rent an old, battered farmhouse four miles up a dirt track from a tiny village, Bordeira, nestled next to the Atlantic Ocean. Old oak barrels were discarded outside next to a dilapidated pigsty to the side of the house. The surrounding area was remote, wild yellow flowers carpeted the fields around. Apple and peach trees grew among thick brambles and nettles. The house itself was a dirty, white one-storey building with strips of crumbling blue paint around the windows and doors. As we pushed open the rotting wooden door a narrow beam of sunlight streamed into the room. The walls appeared to move. We ventured further inside and saw hundreds of lizards scrambling over each other, heading for the roof rafters. There was a musty aroma around the place, and once the shutters were open, we saw that the floor was littered with shoes, medicine bottles and broken chairs. Two narrow rooms were either side of this rubbish dump; a small kitchen was through the back, which consisted of one large fireplace.

My sisters and I slept on metal-framed camp beds in our dorm-like bedroom while my parents settled in the other room. We set about constructing an outside toilet with bamboo from the nearby woods. I helped my dad dig a giant hole in the ground and we laced the structure with leaves for privacy.

I didn't long for home comforts. The absence of electricity or running water, or a toilet, seemed like a huge game. We were a real-life *Swiss Family Robinson*. My dad sawed wood to make primitive furniture and chopped logs for the fire, cementing him in my mind as a Man of Action. It didn't matter that each plank of wood on the surface of the table was at a different level from the next, meaning putting a glass of water down came with a risk unless I focused hard. At Christmas we put a tablecloth on it, hiding the lopsided top, and then it was like Russian roulette with drinks. I'd get a spark of relief at seeing my glass of orange squash still full but resting lopsided on the table.

I ran free, having close encounters with vipers and mongooses, and I built dens in the woods. We'd purchased a table football game and I would try to persuade one of my sisters into a game. My dad was often out following futile leads for land to buy so we could start our camping empire. It was left to my mum to carry the ice-cold water back up the hill after drawing it from the well.

We didn't go to school, so my mum taught me to read with the Ladybird Peter and Jane books. I became bored of the 'This is Peter', 'This is Jane', 'Peter likes dogs', 'The grass is green' storylines, so I'd write my own about lions and the one lizard who, when the others had scurried away upon our arrival, had stayed and now lived in a crack in the front of the house. He was about five inches long, pale green with small yellow circles, and could be coaxed out with a cut-up bit of tomato.

Once in the open air, he'd remember how much he enjoyed the sun and spend the day lying on a rock soaking up rays.

My dad took it upon himself to teach the girls history, which was his favourite subject. He claimed that he'd passed his exams simply by watching *The Searchers*, starring John Wayne, his favourite movie star. He had grown up in the 1950s on Saturday morning pictures, and Duke was a seminal figure in his life. *The Green Berets* informed his knowledge of the Vietnam War and *She Wore a Yellow Ribbon* told him all he needed to know about post-Civil War America. He saw himself as a Western hero: the unsentimental loner who knows emotions come at a price; who faced down their adversaries in a place where justice was brutal and mercy in short supply. That was his teaching style. He was a harsh taskmaster, with little explaining or tolerance for getting things wrong.

My dad's voice would make me jump. The sudden change in his tone when he became angry would lift me from my seat or make my knees bang together. We'd get lost on the road and he'd blame my mum, calling her stupid, and soon we'd all be crying. I was wary of him. I remember my mum once looking up to the clear night sky littered with stars and saying, once he was out of earshot, 'It's a full moon,' by way of expla-nation. I didn't know what she meant but I was intrigued by the idea of my dad being emotionally affected by the promi-nence of the moon. He'd often say I was a pain in the elbow. On one occasion, after a minor indiscretion, he grabbed me, pulled my pants down in front of the whole family and smacked my bare bum several times. I remember screaming, tears rolling down my cheeks, being consumed with outrage at the humiliation. It was the only time he ever hit me.

Months passed. The £11,000 we'd received from our house sale dwindled away. My dad had made no progress in his search for land and the van had perennial mechanical problems. One day he returned home shaken, without it. As he had driven into a garage to get it fixed, he'd collided with a Fiat, leaving our windscreen shattered, a huge dent in the side and the other driver with a broken leg.

Life was throwing up obstructions and becoming a grind. My sisters, who had turned thirteen, became restless. We were cut off, no school, home comforts or friends. My mum's back gave out after months of carrying water from the well. She and the girls were regularly bitten by ticks, parasites that had to be pulled out with tweezers. After a day trip to Lisbon to see *E.T.*, which I remember clearly because it was in Portuguese, making it hard to follow (the line '*E.T. telefona para casa*' sticks in my head), we arrived home to find large black pigs had ransacked the house and were wandering in and out of our front room like nonchalant burglars. It all got too much. Defeated, we returned homeless, penniless to the UK.

I find it hard to look at photographs of myself from that time. My unknowing five-year-old face framed by my long wavy hair. I am always smiling or holding a toy car or playing on the beach. I didn't understand anything, what lay ahead or what might have been. I was getting to know my dad. He was my hero, and he was about to become my tormentor.

Chapter 3

The image of the dingy whirling-patterned carpet is etched into my mind. It was 1984 and I was seven years old, wearing cheap cotton pyjamas and, as my legs dangled over from the top of the bunkbed, I didn't want to put my bare feet down. I thought there was a strong chance they'd stick to it, like those horrible traps that glue mice to a piece of card. I'd put my socks on first and then climb down the shaky little ladder.

There were around six or seven women living in the refuge with their children and they came from all over Southend. There was a gypsy woman and her young son, a couple of women from the notorious council estates who had hardened Essex accents and swore with relish, and a well-to-do lady who wore expensive jewellery and a horrified look on her face (she went back to her husband after only a few days). A matron-like woman called Margaret ran the place. She had a forthright but caring manner and the innate courage to face down any trouble that might come our way. The place stank of cigarettes. There was a perpetual fog of smoke in the air. The noise was horrible: kids running around screaming, mothers shouting at them to stay still.

Heavy fire doors separated each room; when I went through them they'd swing back fast for a second before a mechanism would click in, immediately slowing the shutting process down to a snail's space. Cheap easy-to-wipe linoleum covered the downstairs floor; health and safety stickers adorned the walls. Laminated signs told us to wash up our plates or make sure we closed the fridge door.

The large communal kitchen was often full of families eating fish and chips from the nearby shop. Then there was my mum, with her peppers and courgettes, trying to ensure we ate as healthily as we could, under the bright fluorescent lights.

I eyed the other children with suspicion. There was general encouragement from all the mothers to make friends, but I didn't want to. I had mates at school, and what did I have in common with these new housemates other than fathers who hurt our mums? I'm sure they felt the same way. There was a TV room that was almost always empty and was an inhospitable place to lounge, with dirty waterproof armchairs and an absence of mood lighting.

The building itself was a huge, gloomy double-fronted Victorian house, right next to the police station. When we arrived, I was reassured by how it seemed like a fortress. If my dad were to turn up, I was pretty sure he'd be put off causing a disturbance by the heavy reinforced door, triple-locked windows and proximity to the police. The comfort of that feeling morphed into sinking gloom when the reality of the house became clear.

Why had it come to this? A woman's refuge in Westcliff-on-Sea. It was as if, once we had returned from Portugal, that volcano of aggression bubbling away within my dad had finally erupted.

My dad landed a job as head of news at Essex Radio and we bought a semi-detached Victorian house in Southend-on-Sea in Essex. Our broken-down, orange Volkswagen campervan sat rusting on the road outside.

In the 1980s large mortgages were handed out with proof of a half-decent salary and a satisfactory smile, so with the help of a small deposit from my dad's parents we were able to pay the £38,000 required to live in a niceish part of town.

Southend has a battered glamour. I'm the first to make a joke about it and the first to defend it from mockery. It's rough, ready, ugly and quaint. It's grand and greasy with fountains and bandstands and fights outside the Wetherspoons. The River Thames runs along it and the cliff tops are calm, but the arterial road drowns out the birdsong. For years the decaying old Royal Hotel on the seafront was a home for the dispossessed.

The pier is what visitors talk about because it's the longest in the world. A Victorian edifice that sticks out more than a mile into the Thames Estuary. The poet John Betjeman wrote, 'The pier is Southend and Southend is the pier,' and there's some truth in that. The pier is to Southend what the pyramids are to Egypt, or the hanging gardens would have been to Babylon. There's no mystery about how it was built or what its purpose was or what engineering feats made it possible; it just came down to a majority decision by the local council in the middle of the nineteenth century.

It always made me laugh when I heard it referred to as a 'pleasure pier' because the last vestiges of anything remotely connected with pleasure – the theatre, the amusement arcades and the six-thousand-seater sun deck – have long since gone. Now the train just tootles up to the end where there is an ice-cream stall and a place to buy tea. But it is the longest pier in the world and it makes Southenders what they are: the people who live near the longest pier in the world.

Southend had nothing of any other significance. There was the UK's central VAT office and what was once the second-biggest Marks and Spencer in the country. Peter Pan's playground on the seafront had dodgems, arcade games, a red and white striped helter-skelter, candyfloss, ice cream and rows of deck chairs lined the pebbled beach. North of the seafront there were some nice houses along the tops of the cliffs, then you got to London Road with an array of Indian restaurants, Chinese takeaways, charity and second-hand shops and chemists.

Nowadays nail bars have added to that mix. As the town spreads out the houses become Edwardian and then there are thousands of prefabs and hastily erected small terraces put up in the fifties and sixties. There are plenty of homes that have been individualised with a bit of pebble-dashing or stone cladding or with a conservatory slapped on the back.

Our house was in a conservation area and my parents were proud of this. It meant no one was going to erect a giant archway on the front of their tiny drive, which was a common occurrence in Southend. Inside there were high ceilings, cracked cornicing and chipped paintwork. The whole house had a run-down feel. At the top there was a small two-room flat and tiny bathroom. This was my sisters' domain. When they moved to that space, it was like they became upstairs neighbours rather than my family.

One of the first things my dad did when we moved in was remove a shower room opposite the downstairs toilet and convert it into a coat cupboard. The only problem was that it was the only shower we had, so for the next ten years we had to restrict ourselves to baths.

To me as a young boy, my dad seemed a highly effective handyman, fixing the car, putting up shelves or knocking up a TV stand. I remember his blue toolbox which opened up to reveal sharp and fascinating things. I loved to help out, passing him screws and being allowed to try to hammer in a nail from time to time.

Flimsy charity shop curtains hung from the windows, apart from the bay window in the front room, where my mum had come by some heavy gold ones, which once drawn at night made sure that whatever occurred inside couldn't be seen. My dad's wobbly table from Portugal had come with us, sitting at the end of the living room.

A large painting of a galleon sailing on a stormy sea adorned one of the walls. All dark blues and crashing waves. My dad had painted it before we moved to Portugal. I hoped one day I'd be able to draw a ship just like him. He was proud of it too, having framed it and putting it pride of place at home. I'd been enrolled in a local primary school and my sisters started at Cecil Jones High School.

My dad began working long hours, often not returning until three in the morning, even though the radio station was less than half a mile away. He would stumble in, falling up the stairs. I'd hear him snoring from my bedroom along the corridor. Delivering the news to the people of Essex seemed a noble pursuit. I was pleased to receive the branded merchandise he'd bring back with him, such as the Essex Radio baseball cap, a satchel and an official Essex Radio leather diary with my initials on the front. Inside was a picture of my dad at a desk in front of a microphone, with a blurb explaining how all the news was gathered and a pull-out map of the motorways of Britain. As I flip through it today, there's a disconcerting picture of Rolf Harris visiting the station and hugging two young kids while they pick up an award for drawing cartoons.

It was my birthday not long after we moved. I received a toy Castle Grayskull, the fortress that He-Man was duty-bound to protect from the evil forces of Skeletor. I'd make my He-Man action figure repeat the words from the opening credits: 'Fabulous secret powers were revealed to me the day I held aloft my magic sword and said, "By the power of Greyskull … I have the power!"' My dad used his connections so the station's star DJ, Tim 'Timbo' Lloyd, wished me happy birthday during his shift, telling the listeners about my present. I found it embarrassing that half of Essex knew what my interests were, but I also liked hearing my full name read out through our Panasonic stereo radio cassette player.

That night I woke to my dad downstairs shouting. I lay there for a few minutes listening out as I stared at the ceiling. The hall light shone into my bedroom through the half-open door. I jumped up, creeping out to stand at the top of the stairs to find out what was going on. He was saying something about an application for a bank card that he needed my mum to sign. I couldn't hear her response, but her voice was different, strained, a higher pitch. He began spewing out hatred, pure, unadulterated rage. My mum was 'a fat cow' and a 'stupid bitch'.

After a few moments I moved down three or four stairs, carefully avoiding the parts of the floorboards that squeaked. I sat down, grasping my legs for comfort and looking at my bare feet on the brown carpet. My body tightened as I heard him cross the room. I shook and pushed the palms of my hands onto my knees to keep them steady.

'Go and hang yourself!' he shouted. 'But sign that fucking form first.'

I sensed he was near her. Then there was a thud and then another, and my mum was screaming. I ran downstairs, pushed open the living-room door to find him bending over her, holding a piece of paper. With his other hand he had her wrist. He was twisting it round. His eyes flashed up towards me through his thick square spectacles, and it caused a break in the attack. He didn't say anything to me but straightened up and walked back across the living room. I took this opportunity to scuttle over to my mum and sit next to her on the sofa. She put her arm round me.

'Go back to bed, Thomas. Your mother is a fucking idiot,' he spat out.

There was no way I was going to leave her side. Somewhere in him, he realised that was enough for the night. He went upstairs. An hour later my mum took me back to bed. We heard the rattling of his snoring, and my mum climbed into bed with me and we held each other in the dark. She explained it away as an argument. Comforted by her presence, I begin to drift off to sleep. A few minutes later I felt the mattress of my single bed lift slightly. I gazed up to see her softly slip out of the room to take her place in the marital bed.

Chapter 4

All of this is hard to write because for almost the entirety of my life, I've never told anyone any of it, ever. I consigned it all to my past. For years after, my mum and I would talk about my dad's behaviour, but only in a general sort of way. 'That was a mad time,' my mum would say, or, 'Thank God it's over now.' A bit like we might talk about bad weather. 'Oh, that was a terrible downpour.'

At the time nothing was ever said about what had gone on. The next morning my dad would just eat toast, grab his briefcase and make his way merrily to work. My mum and I went along with the charade. I was relieved, grateful for the pretence of normality.

He regarded me as a nuisance, I think, with little interest in my requirements, but one weekend afternoon he decided to teach me chess at the kitchen table. The tactical battle and strategising appealed to me, and I picked it up quickly. He was a good teacher too and had a patience with me that I didn't see him have with anyone else. Especially not my sisters. Like any young kid, spending time with my dad was what I wanted most, even if I felt I had to win him round. I think even at the age of seven I made an active choice to engage with him. It felt to me like my sisters had started to retreat from view, to hide away from his monstrous temper, but I wanted the part of him that made jokes and taught me board games, so I worked hard for his affection.

He broke away from our game of logic and sloshed another gin into a tumbler so that it was half full. He got up, yanking the freezer door open, grabbing the ice tray and cracking it hard down onto the kitchen top, causing all the cubes to slide across the counter in different directions. He collected them up and chucked them into the glass, topping it up with a piddle of tonic. My mum was preparing lunch for us, leaning forward over the kitchen counter, using her stump to hold some lettuce in place while cutting it with a knife using her right hand. In between showing me how a rook and king could 'castle' and swap places, he started to make comments about my mum's parents. He said they looked down on him. He was particularly cross about their last visit when, according to him, they'd all but ignored him, especially my grand-mother. Their attitude was a bad influence on me.

Despite my efforts to divert his attention back to the game, it was soon lost to his anger. He stood up to pour more gin, then moved alongside my mum while she buttered bread. He shouted in her face. I got up, hovering nervously behind him, causing him to spin around and pick me up. I was already crying. As I perched on his arm, he started to list all my mum's offences. None of it made any sense to me but he'd been let down, unsupported and her incompetence had damaged us all. 'I'll murder her, she's a bitch,' he told me.

The next moment I was back down on the floor. He started shoving my mum out of the kitchen. 'Get out of the house, you fucker!' he shouted. The memory is clear and a blur all at once. The next thing I recall is that they had both disappeared. I was alone, rushing from room to room, desperately searching for them. I saw the front door was open. I ran out onto the street. I wanted to find someone to help, to intervene, to stop it. I can see myself, straight fringe, bottom teeth missing as the new ones grew, my face serious and hardened. I can feel the concrete of the pavement, hard on my socked feet. I heard screams coming from a little way down the road. He was dragging my mum back to the house, pulling her along by her arm. I looked around and saw neighbours watching from their windows. One or two had come out onto the street. They could see what was happening and yet acted like it was a piece of promenade theatre. The secrets of our house had spilled out onto the road.

I pursued my parents back into the house and my dad slammed the door shut behind us, leaving my mum cowering on the floor.

'I can't stand you – I'll drive into a brick wall at 90 miles per hour,' he said as he stormed upstairs. A feeling of powerlessness stays with me and is one I can't shake. In a way I was like our neighbours, part of the audience of a frightening psychological thriller, but I was so close to the action that I couldn't understand the plot.

My dad returned clutching his car key and said he needed the courage to follow up his plan. I wondered if he meant it. He grabbed the bottle of gin, tossed the cap aside and took a couple of swigs before disappearing upstairs again. This time when he returned, he had a razor, seemingly abandoning the plan to drive into a wall. He stood opposite us and proceeded to make very small cuts into his wrist.

There was a knock at the door. My dad pushed down his rolled-up sleeve and went to answer it. I went to the front room, looked out of the window and saw a police car. I could hear the conversation in the hallway.

'We've had a call about a disturbance at this address,' a policeman told my dad.

'You must have the wrong house,' my dad said.

The constable pressed on. 'Who else is home?'

'Just my wife and son.'

'Can we come in?'

My dad reluctantly agreed, showing the two officers into our front room. He was reasoned and measured but they saw through it. It wasn't hard. They would have seen the fear in my mother's eyes and been suspicious of my dad's quickened breath. The policewoman, seeing how distressed I was, put her arm round me. It was an embrace I'll never forget because it felt like the cavalry had arrived. My dad saw and shouted, 'Get your hands off my son.'

My dad never gave any sign of being afraid or unsure. I sometimes think he must have been terrified of being found out, but it was like his fury overrode such worries. 'I don't want you in my house,' he told them.

The policeman told my mum, 'We can take him away now, but we can't stop him returning tomorrow. It's up to you. Do you want him to go?'

My mum looked desolate, weighing up the responsibility that had been shoved over to her. In that moment she needed respite, however temporary, and she nodded to the policeman. Before my dad left he bent down and hugged me, telling me he would be okay.

I watched from behind the net curtains in our front room as they escorted him to their car, which still had the flashing lights whirling around, casting the surrounding houses blue. He was handcuffed in full view of the street and guided into the back seat. It was frightening and calming at the same time. I knew that nothing else bad would happen today and my body unwound a little.

My mum reassured me that he wasn't going to prison, that he was just going to spend the night in a cell, which to my mind was exactly what going to prison was. I imagined scores of inmates in stripey suits banging cups on the bars of their cells as he was led to his incarceration.

The next morning my dad's parents went to collect him from the police station. My sisters sat on the sofa, not saying anything. I walked obsessively back and forth from the window, all of us thinking about what might lie in wait upon his return.

As we'd gone to bed the night before, my mum had played one of the two mixed audio tapes we'd taken to Portugal with us. A song that soothed me was John Lennon's 'Beautiful Boy', a dreamy, bouncy ballad mixed with ocean waves and triangle pings. My mum said it was her song for me, but the lines I loved most were, '*the monster's gone, he's on the run and your daddy's here*'. I wanted a dad, not a monster.

I wonder now what went on in his house when he was a kid to make him the way he was. If you met him, you might think he was normal. My friends thought he was funny and smart, and nothing about his appearance marked him out as unusual. As he got older he had a touch of Harrison Ford about him. He dressed smart and sounded authoritative, like the newsreader he was. I don't know where he got his voice. His dad was a Geordie and his mum was an East Ender. He grew up in a council house, left school in Essex having failed his A levels, but he sounded posh.

Later, when I was older, he hinted at childhood beatings dished out by his mum with a wooden spoon. He once told me she'd forced him to wear a potato sack as a punishment for something. Whatever had gone on, he felt she'd humiliated him. My grandmother told my mum that occasionally her husband hit her, so I suppose he learned it close-up.

My grandfather had a sparky wit but a harshness running though him. My grandmother was bitter. He'd worked fitting parts to aircraft during the war, while she had worked in a munitions factory. She was tiny, with a pinched face and an eagle-like nose. She was forever placing pound coins in my hand at various times throughout their visits. I wondered why she didn't give it to me all at once. Even as a kid it struck me as needy. 'Here's a couple of quid cos we never see you, darlin',' she'd say, although they seemed to be around all the time. They had both grown up poor. She had eight siblings and spent much of her time gossiping or bad-mouthing family members. She would annoy my mum by popping round unexpectedly, appearing at the door ladened with homemade pies and clothes for the girls. She had a near obsession with my sisters, meaning she and my grandad would often wander about Southend High Street in the hope of bumping into them.

My dad had absolute contempt for them. He barely bothered to hide his scorn. When I was about twenty-five, I heard my grandmother say to him, 'You think you're so much cleverer than me.' He shot back, 'Mother, I've been cleverer than you since I was four years old.' It was such a nasty exchange, but he may have had a point.

My grandparents' Nissan Micra pulled up outside. I watched as they and my dad walked up the garden path. Any hope that a night in the cells would have led to a period of self-reflection evaporated when he walked straight up to my mum and spat in her face. My grandfather simply turned away and sat in an armchair as if nothing out of the ordinary had occurred. My grandmother used this as an opportunity to suggest she go to the kitchen to make my dad ham and eggs because he must be very hungry. When my parents married, my grandmother would share stories with my mum about my dad's erratic, drunken behaviour as a young man and my mum confided in her about his aggressive episodes. Back then she would nod sympathetically, but now she denied her son was doing anything wrong.

I wish someone had spelt out to me that what my dad did was appalling, but instead I seemed to live in a world where it was tolerated and people just shrugged their shoulders and whistled 'Que Sera, Sera'. To some extent I followed suit.

The trip to the police station quietened my dad down for a few days, and I got on with going to school and playing for hours with my action figures, becoming absorbed in my made-up world. I'd use my Mr Spock alongside Princess Leia, as well as the characters from *The Black Hole*, but I'd give them different identities from the ones given by the toy manufacturers. I couldn't tell you any of the plots from my games, but I remember they all involved quite complex interpersonal relationships. They became more than toys, a kind of parallel universe in which to escape, in which I pulled the strings.

My sisters were now fourteen and the distance between us grew. These were the most ferocious years, when a flicker of a flame would soon become a rampant fire. Violence lived in the foundations of our house. The walls shook with the force of slammed doors and the windows rattled with screams. He seemed to come home from work and want to tear everything apart. And he did. He hurled ornaments and vases, cups and bottles across the room to emphasise the points he was trying to make. Kate took to hiding the crockery in upstairs cupboards to make sure we would have plates to eat our food from.

The sound of repeated attempts at getting his key in the front door was enough to set my whole body into a state of readiness. He'd walk in unsteadily and head to the kitchen, uncork the bottle of wine he demanded my mum have waiting, fill a glass, leaving a trail of wine running down the outside, and go and watch Moira Stuart read the evening news.

One day, my teacher took me aside and explained that sports day would have a special guest. The bunting was out, and I joined my classmates in the school field wearing my PE kit and plimsolls. Freshly cut grass flew through the air and occasionally landed on my bare leg, trembling for a few seconds before the wind whisked it off again. The newly drawn white chalk demarked the racetrack and I looked up to see the surprise Mrs Turner had referred to. My dad was sitting at a table in the centre of the sports field, some local dignitary to his left and the head teacher to his right. As the voice of the local news, he had a small-time celebrity status. He was holding a loudspeaker.

At first sight of him, my stomach flipped. He was the loosest of cannons and seeing him interact in my world sent the relative peace that school brought into meltdown. He flashed a smile and made light-hearted quips while the kids hopped around in sacks and carried eggs on spoons. This was my dad, authoritative, popular, charming, a normal functioning person. After a while I relaxed and edgily enjoyed his exalted position and the reflected credit I took. Mrs Turner touched his arm a lot, thanked him profusely and made a joke about him being famous.

Chapter 5

The weekends were harder because he was in the house all the time. One Saturday my sisters were due to race at their athletics club, which was in Basildon, a few miles away. My dad barked at us to get into the shiny Ford Sierra that had come with his job. My seven-year-old brain couldn't determine to what extent he had been drinking red wine, but his eyes were bloodshot. He had a purple line sketched around his lips, like some bastardised glam-rock singer. He put the car in gear and we screeched off down the road. My mum asked him to slow down but he pressed the accelerator harder, taking the bend like he was Ayrton Senna.

He started shouting at my mum for making us late, admonishing her for not being able to give clear directions. Soon we were lost on the outskirts of Basildon, the girls had missed their race and we returned home from our white-knuckle ride.

He crashed around the house, ranting about the trip and pouring a fresh glass of wine before he stomped upstairs to the room he called his office. It was really just a place he went to smoke, meaning the windowsill had a yellowy tint. I didn't go in there much because the smoke hung around, so it was difficult to breathe. His desk was our old camping table, on which sat a grey typewriter. I often heard the clack of his fingers on the keys as he rapidly hammered them in short bursts. Piles of old newspapers and boxes filled with files sat on the floor. The bookshelves were lined with novels by Len Deighton and Ken Follett. There were also a lot of James Micheners that were so thick it impressed me that he had the patience to get through them. He had some old editions of Hornblower novels by C.S. Forester and then hundreds of Sherlock Holmes books and books about Sherlock Holmes. Something appealed to him about the detective's darker side: his associations with the criminal world, his cold, emotionless reactions and maverick tendencies.

He had many of the Richmal Crompton *Just William* books. If he wasn't too pissed, he would occasionally read to me from them before bed, when he would become softer and enjoy my pleasure in the stories. He had read them as a kid. I'd lie down with my head sinking into the pillow, my dad sitting on a chair pushed up close to the bed. I could see the veins in his nose and sometimes feel the warm air from his words. I would be lost in the story, my dad's tantrums a world away. I longed for that peace and closeness. I made it my mission to lure him away from his tempers.

My dad's office was also the room to which he took his mysterious correspondence. Even though he had a job, almost as soon as he took out the mortgage, my dad stopped paying it, along with most of the household bills. My mum made small payments to ward off the creditors from the house-keeping money my dad gave her, but still the financial pressures grew.

One day she agreed with my dad that we should sell the campervan, which was still outside the house, rotting away without an MOT. He gave her the paperwork and keys, and she made a 'For Sale' sign and put it in its window. Within days someone offered us £80. She immediately used the money to prevent court proceedings from the gas board.

That evening, he came back from work and went through to the living room, clutching a rolled-up copy of the *Daily Express*. After a short while he returned to the kitchen, where I was sitting colouring in a picture at the small pine table.

'Where the fuck is the van?' he shouted at my mum, making me literally jump from my seat.

His razor stare bore into her, and I quietly placed my felt tip down. He seemed oblivious to my presence. In that moment everything in my life stopped, my drawing vanished, the entire world outside that room ceased to exist; the bedroom, my toys, my thoughts disappeared. My mouth became dry and I watched, waiting, readying myself with absolute laser clarity. In these moments I would never run, never turn my back. I would just be there.

'Where the fuck is my van?' he repeated.

Mum explained how they had agreed to sell it, how she'd got a good price considering the state it was in and how we needed the money.

He moved closer to her, his face reddening. 'You fucking idiot.'

By now my legs had started to shake and I did a sort of half jig on the spot in an effort to control the adrenaline in my body. Part of the panic was my own inability to react in a useful way.

He grabbed her shoulders and threw her to the floor, slapping her round the head as she kneeled before him and used her arm to shield herself from the blows. The slaps became punches and by now I was circling him, pleading with him to stop.

He grabbed her hair and started pulling her into the hallway, with me trailing in the wake. My mum's legs were kicking out along the floor to propel her in the same direction and lessen the pain. Once they got to the front door he let her go.

'Get it back,' he said. 'Fucking find it.'

I watched as she got to her feet and attempted to compose herself, struggling to open the latch on the door because her hand was shaking so much. She made her way out down the garden path and into the street. I don't know where she went but relative calm came over me as she disappeared away from danger.

I wish I'd had the clarity to hate him, to despise him for his despicable deeds, but I didn't. I just wanted to restore the peace, to lower the temperature, to stop it occurring. I wanted to make it right. There was no time for hatred. This was just the way life was.

My mum was out of the house and quiet descended. My dad and I stood opposite each other in the hallway, both recovering from the violence in our different ways. There was nothing I knew to say. I couldn't admonish him. I can feel a lump in my throat right now. I know what I did next. I went to him and cuddled him, throwing my arms around his neck.

My mum returned, as she always did, and life was quiet for a day or two. It was always the same. She went about scrupulously avoiding things that might set him off, but it was like dancing on a field of landmines. Dinner time would often be the catalyst for one of my dad's tirades. One night he stumbled in from work, affable enough but speaking disconcertingly loudly. He took his suit jacket off and put on his favourite navy-blue army-style jumper, which perpetually had flakes of dandruff on the padded epaulettes. He then headed into the kitchen to pour a large glass of wine from the one-litre plastic bottle he would insist my mum carried back from the local Sainsbury's.

I showed him the flags I'd made of various countries and stuck to lollipop sticks, to which he over-enthusiastically responded for a minute before he asked my mum, 'What's for dinner?'

That question often carried with it a sinister connotation. My eyes darted up towards him to ascertain his mood, or perhaps his state of inebriation. My eyes flashed to my mum.

'Cold meats, pickles and a baked potato,' she replied.

'I'd rather have chips.'

'I've put the potatoes in the oven to bake already but I could do you some oven chips.'

'Oh. Whatever is easier,' he said, heading back down the hall and into the living room to watch *Blankety Blank*. The danger appeared to be averted. I went and joined him, laughing at Les Dawson gurning and cracking jokes to the contestants, who would have to fill in a missing word in a paragraph and match it with the word chosen by a celebrity like Barbara Windsor or Paul Daniels.

The revolving set took away the losers once they'd received their consolation prize of a *Blankety Blank* chequebook and pen, and the winner went home underwhelmed with the star prize, which was often a pressure cooker.

We were both sitting on our green draylon sofa, which my dad had won when he appeared on *Sale of the Century* in the mid-1970s. His aunt had written into the programme suggesting my dad as a participant because he was so good at answering the questions when watching at home. In fact, Nicholas Parsons, the host of the show, was responsible for much of our home decor. My dad had been invited back the next day as the winner of the show, but he told me years later that a liquid lunch had hindered his ability to press the buzzer, so he didn't repeat his success.

When my mum brought in the dinner she'd promised, we sat up at the wonky table we'd brought back from Portugal. My dad took one look at his dinner and said, 'I thought I was having chips.'

I shuffled in my seat and picked up my fork. With my other hand I gripped the green baize tablecloth and ran my fingers along the coarse material. My hands were clammy.

'You said whatever was easier,' my mum answered.

'I'd rather have chips.'

My head started to race with the things I could ask him about to dissipate the tension.

'I'll put some on now,' my mum said, showing no frustration at all.

'Don't bother now.'

I tried to remember one of Les Dawson's jokes that had made us laugh minutes ago to take him back to a moment of levity. My mum sat down. We began to eat our meal, although I was no longer hungry.

'I'm not going to eat this baked potato because I think chips go better,' he said as he prodded it with his knife, pushing it around the plate. 'I like chips best.'

My mum got up from the table, saying she'd put some chips in the oven. My dad and I ate in silence for a minute or so, and then without a word he got up and followed her out to the kitchen. I jumped up and stood in the doorway listening.

'I don't want fucking chips, you stupid bitch,' I heard him snap, followed by a loud clatter, as he knocked the baking tray from my mum's hand and it crashed to the tiled floor. I heard him stomping back up the hall and I shot back to my seat, where I pretended to have been eating all along.

Chapter 6

Even today, if I'm woken by a noise in the middle of the night, I go back to my childhood home. My heart thumps for a few seconds until I realise things aren't the same anymore. When I was small my eyes would flash open. I couldn't be sure if it was a scream or raised voices that had roused me, but it was *something*. I'd wait for a moment to hear if it repeated itself, which invariably it did, and I'd run to the top of the stairs, my legs shaking, listening out for the argument to get physical, which would be when I'd run downstairs and stand in between my mum and dad to try to calm things down. It didn't usually work.

When I was a kid my mum read an A.A. Milne poem that seemed to speak directly to me, although I'm guessing not for the reason the poet intended.

> *Halfway down the stairs*
> *Is a stair*
> *Where I sit*
> *There isn't any*
> *Other stair*
> *Quite like*
> *It.*

I was highly sensitive to any sign of trouble brewing and lived in a state of anxiety. It wasn't just the violence; it was the days and weeks in between. The time when there was peace that was really no peace at all. The perpetual tension of knowing what's coming but never when. I took it upon myself to look after my mum to the best of my abilities, so when the fights occurred I'd draw her pictures and leave them for her to find at the top of the stairs. I knew they made her happy, so I'd draw Winnie-the-Pooh and Piglet or me and her and write that I loved her. I had to keep her spirits up.

To this day I have a recurring fantasy, where as an adult I return home, break down the front door, beat my dad to a pulp, see my younger self sitting on the stairs of our old Victorian house, climb up, reach out, and my younger self jumps into my arms. I carry myself away. I save myself. And it comforts me. And that's what I wanted back then: to be rescued. To feel someone would take care of me, lift me up, hold me, protect me, listen to me, value me and love me.

It wasn't long before my dad started pestering my mum to write to the police inspector and tell him that the night he was arrested had been a misunderstanding and that she would like to withdraw her complaint. She refused. My mum's disobedience sent him into a vicious frenzy: he stormed from the room, the door nearly coming off its hinges as he slammed it shut, sending a tremor across the house. He went out to what we called the conservatory but was actually just an outbuilding beyond the kitchen with a concrete floor and corrugated plastic roof. It was where my dad kept his tools, along with the washing machine and piles of stuff we didn't want in the house.

He returned holding an axe he used to chop wood with when we were in Portugal. He held it over my mum's only hand and told her he would cut her fingers off one by one if she didn't start writing. She began to scrawl but her penmanship was so shaky it was barely legible. I began to hyperventilate, instinctively gasping for air to slow down whatever was happening to my body. How could I stop this? What could I do? Would someone come to help? I begged, 'No,' and, 'Please,' as I stood in front of him, trying to get him to see me, but his eyes were pinned on my mum.

Something clicked in him, or he got tired or maybe he didn't want blood on the floor, but he gave up his plan, leaving the axe propped up against the wall. Emma had been watching the whole thing and she ran upstairs.

The incident convinced my mum she had to act and that's when we left for the refuge. It was 2 November, the day after my sisters' fifteenth birthday (my mum had wanted to wait till their celebrations were over). With no money and no options, my mum went to the police station, leaving me at home with the girls. The officer behind the desk told her that for the sake of herself and her children she must get out. She returned home with a policeman and Margaret from the refuge, and we hurriedly placed some belongings into black bags, fearing my dad might return at any point. As we headed to the front door I turned back and ran to my room. I had forgotten my action figures.

I didn't want to leave my dad but I knew it was the best thing. I didn't know what went on behind the closed doors of other homes, but to me our life wasn't extreme or unusual, it was just what it was: the life we had. The ferocious fighting was our existence.

My dad never played with me or helped me build Lego, which I would have loved, but when things were good we'd watch TV together and he'd encourage me with stories I'd written. When the 1950s *Eagle* comic was relaunched he bought me a copy, telling me about Dan Dare and his arch-enemy, the giant-headed Mekon. He enjoyed sharing things from his own childhood with me.

I had lots of questions and, in the pre-internet days, my dad was my resource. 'Who'd win in a fight between a bear and a lion? How far is Mars? How tall would I grow up to be? Why did the Second World War start?' He never failed to answer. And he never showed doubt, even when my questions got harder. *Now we'd left,* I thought, *I'll have to ask other people.*

We were shown to the room that was to become our base for the next few weeks. My heart sank when I discovered we'd be sharing it with another family. I don't remember anything about them, but I didn't want to make friends. I hoped we wouldn't have to stay there for long. Quite where we were going to end up, however, remained a mystery. My sisters slept on one of the bunkbeds, two of them sharing the bottom bunk and the third on the top. My mum and I cuddled up on another bunkbed while some members of the other family slept beneath us.

I was so close to my mum. The love she gave me was like a blanket that I could feel and pull up all around me. It didn't make me feel calm or stop my legs shaking or the runny tummy I constantly had, but it felt good. Writing this now makes me cry.

A very tall man would turn up every night and hang around on the other side of the street to the house, just staring across. He was mockingly called 'Lurch' by our new housemates. I'd peer out of the front window every night to try to catch a glimpse of his shadowy figure. He was married to one of the women in the refuge. I feared that the windows would be broken, that my dad, or one of the others, would throw a brick through the window. It seemed to me an obvious weak point in the security of the house, and I remember touching the cold panes, tracing my fingers along the frames to see if the glass was extra thick, like bulletproof windows in a president's car.

I kept all that was going on a secret from everyone I knew. How my dad behaved, our change of address. 'What did you do this weekend?' wasn't the most straightforward question to answer. The only person I nearly told around this time was my primary school teacher. One morning my mum dropped me off, but I didn't want to go. I felt I needed to be with her, to protect her, to watch out for signs of danger. When I walked into the classroom Miss Billinghurst could tell something wasn't right. She asked me if I was okay and I couldn't stop the tears from coming. She took me to a quiet corner of the classroom, and the look on her face is with me still. It was so kind and concerned that it made me cry more. Where would I begin? What would happen if I told her everything? It was a mix of shame, fear of what the consequences might be and a sense that I would be betraying my dad. I didn't even know if I should confide in someone. It was too much for me to resolve in that instant. I shook my head. I couldn't muster any words. I had a feeling of panic as the other thirty kids in the classroom took her attention away and she retreated to allow me to pull myself together. *Come back,* I thought. *Please come back.*

A week or so into our stay, my dad wrote my mum a letter. His parents had told him where we were. He explained how everything would be fine if we returned home for Christmas. He expressed his belief that it was a time for family and on balance he thought we were happy. I guess in his mind, for every night spent wielding an axe at his wife in front of his own children, we'd also had fun trips to the cinema, so it all equalled out. It's true, though, those moments of happiness meant so much. Anything normal felt like a bit of paradise or a sign that life might be okay. Only in the last paragraph of his letter did he acknowledge anything about how he had behaved. Without going into specifics he simply said he wouldn't behave in the same way again.

In the little office at the back of the refuge my mum told Margaret about my dad's correspondence. With the air of someone who has seen everything before, Margaret said, 'Yes, well, that's what they do.' She also told my mum, 'And there's always another woman.' To which my mum replied that wasn't the case with my dad.

With Christmas only a few days away the refuge organised a trip to a church service. We weren't a religious family, but in this new life we were inhabiting, here we were. While the vicar talked of love, family and devotion, I noticed my mum sobbing quietly in the corner. I didn't explicitly know it at the time but my mum was in turmoil. Of course she was; she had four kids, no money and a husband she was frightened would kill her. It wasn't just a physical threat – he manipulated her, pressurised her, tormented her too. She was trapped, driven half-mad by the terror. Under his control. Believing the only thing she could do was survive.

After some more platitudes from the vicar, he invited all the mums and kids up onto the stage, where we received presents from the congregation who had been told about our current predicaments. It was embarrassing. I wanted presents handed to me by non-strangers.

Although it was unsettling in the refuge, it was a relief to be there. There were no arguments and my mum felt freer, despite being trapped by her circumstances. She enjoyed the time with the other women: swapping crazy stories about their husbands' appalling behaviour and discussing the pain of the past and their hopes for the future. There was a lot of laughter and crying.

After a number of pleas my mum finally met with my dad in a nearby pub. When she returned she had some news for us: we'd be heading back home for Christmas. I don't remember fully how I greeted this new information. Part of me was pleased that Christmas wouldn't be in this awful place; I hoped my dad would understand that he couldn't continue to behave in the way he had. I wondered if, now that he'd lost us all for a few weeks, maybe he would change. There was so much I didn't understand.

And why did my mum agree? I stayed in that house with her and my dad for another eight years, so it was a decision we lived with for a long time. I wish she'd seen the destruction it caused, the damage it would go on to do, but he tightened his grip on her. In some ways she detached herself from reality, as if she had no control over what was going on, and told herself that she had no choice. After all, how else could she cope with the reality? He didn't even give us financial security. He could barely hold down a job, and as soon as his character became apparent to his employers he would be sacked. It's a sign of the times that in the 1980s my dad threw a male colleague down a flight of stairs and only received a written warning. He once introduced my mum to a work colleague who looked her in the eyes and said slowly, 'You poor, long-suffering woman.' Usually if people say that it's a joke, but he meant it from the bottom of his heart.

Margaret was adamant that moving back was a mistake but she offered no judgement. If that's what my mum had decided then she would support it, or rather she wouldn't try to stop us. There was a nervous ball in the pit of my belly as my dad picked us up. He was smiling and happy loading our stuff into his Ford Sierra, which he had parked on double yellow lines outside the refuge. Emma had a bug of some kind, and while my dad was putting our bags into the boot, a traffic warden wandered by and told him he would have to move the car. 'I have a passenger who is very ill and I'm taking her home,' my dad replied sharply, sending the official into retreat. It wasn't what he said, but the incensed way he said it. Life resumed back at home, and for two days everything was peaceful.

Chapter 7

It was Christmas Eve when my mum, my sisters and I returned an hour late from a day out with my mum's parents. The girls went upstairs straight away to their flat. My mum and I went through to the kitchen. It was small, white paint peeled from the cupboards and the floor tiles were cracked. Our new microwave sat on the counter with a large timer dial and a button that offered you the option of high or defrost. I clearly remember cooking our first pack of Micro Chips. They were disappointingly soggy. Next to that was our Typhoo tea tin, which had a large, foot-shaped dent made during one of my dad's violent rages.

My mum had left out chopped vegetables and meat for my dad's dinner. He was in the middle of cooking them, but something was wrong. 'Where the fuck have you been?' he asked, draining his wine glass and placing it on the counter. His reddened face leaned into my mum's and we knew right away that nothing had changed. There had been no epiphany about the error of his ways.

My mum explained that the train had been delayed, but he wasn't interested. He walked over to the saucepan sitting on the hob. In one rapid movement he threw it across the kitchen, potatoes and boiling water flying everywhere. I was frozen to the spot, standing in front of my mum. My dad said my grandparents were 'pathetic', were trying to undermine him, and that the presents we had received from them would go in the dustbin. The rant continued but with a different subject. Now he was talking about the 'evil whores' from the refuge. They were scum from the gutter and, worse than that, they were lesbians. Quite what riled him so much about lesbians was never clear, but they made the veins in his neck bulge. This went on late into the night until my dad announced that he was going to kill himself.

He went into the living room holding something and sat at the dinner table. I followed him over and sat opposite. I thought if I was there he was less likely to carry out his plan. I didn't know what to say so I just sat with him. He barely acknowledged me but took from his hand an aspirin packet, removed four and swallowed them without water. And that was that. It was awful and confusing at the time, but although I had no experience of being a witness to suicide attempts, I was pretty sure he'd have to at least finish the pack to stand any chance of killing himself. As it was, the only risk was curing a mild headache.

Sometime after midnight my dad decided that I had to go to bed and insisted on taking me to my room. My whole body was shaking but I was still worried that Father Christmas wouldn't come to the house. I believed firmly that he existed and he wouldn't risk manipulating himself down the chimney while he heard all the shouting. My dad couldn't get me to sleep so he left me up there. As soon as he had gone, I went to the top of the stairs and listened to the rest of the fight. At some point in the early hours my mum came up and got into bed with me and we finally fell asleep. Around six, my dad burst into my room and insisted my mum get up. I got up too and this was how our family Christmas began.

It seemed that our trip to the refuge had just been a break away from our uncertain home life, and soon we were back in the habit of waiting for the next explosion. It took him about two seconds to go from calm to furious and we never knew what would flick his switch. If you could play back the moment in slow motion, you'd start by seeing his relaxed countenance, and then the eyes would shift and the brows would furrow – some single thought in his head triggering a thundering response – his face would turn to red, chameleon-like, the veins in his temple would protrude and his eyes would pierce like needles.

One calm, pleasant Sunday afternoon, my dad and I were watching a film called *The Champ*, about a down-on-his-luck ex-boxer and his relationship with his small son. We'd recorded it on our chunky Betamax video recorder, which sat proudly on a shelf next to the TV. It was from a time when buttons were buttons and pressing eject caused an internal whirring followed by a serious mechanical operation. Even then we were beginning to realise we'd made a mistake when choosing between that and the sleeker VHS model, but my dad was adamant that we should stick with it because the quality of the recording was better.

In one scene the champ is arrested by the police and taken away from his boy. My dad was apoplectic. 'That happened to me,' he raged. 'I was carted away in front of my son.' The feeling that stays with me is the seismic shift in mood. The peace was shattered within seconds and then my dad was standing over my mum with his fists raised. That night was long. I was often up until the early hours in the midst of a brutal argument. That evening my dad held me up in front of him, his hot breath on my face, flecks of his spit landing on me, as he told me that my mum was a whore and a bitch. I just hung there in his arms and took it. What else could I do? Later he looked across at me and asked my mum, 'Why is the child still up?' It seemed like the ultimate stupid question.

That night the police were called again. The flashing lights through the net curtains in our front room I'd seen and heard before, but it was no less disconcerting. Would my dad fight the police officers? What would happen when they left? I wanted them to take him away and fix him but sadly that wasn't their job. I don't remember why the police went away that night, but they did. My mum was too scared to press charges, too concerned about what would happen next.

It seemed the prevalent attitude to domestic abuse back in the 1980s was a bit like the Bill Clinton policy towards homo-sexuality in the US army: don't ask, don't tell. Washing dirty laundry in public wasn't the done thing: men hit their wives occasionally, but it wasn't the worst thing in the world. Because it wasn't an issue that existed in any official capacity, the law made very little provision for the requirements of women and children living in those situations. When police were called to an incident it was often referred to as a 'breach of the peace' and these matters were euphemistically called domestic disputes. Women provoked their own abuse. There were no reliable statistics of rates of incidents and no legal protocols on how the police should respond. It was a matter for a husband and wife. Sean Connery was even able to discuss on American television the correct circumstance in which hitting a woman was deemed acceptable. It was okay if 'it merited it'. He went on: 'If you have tried everything else … and women are pretty good at this … they can't leave it alone. They want to have the last word, and you give them the last word, but they're not happy with the last word, they want to say it again and get into a really provocative situation. Then I think it's absolutely right.'

My mum took solace in the little paved garden at the back of the house. There were flower beds along the garden wall. She made a rockery, little mountain plants with pink flowers shooting out between big stones. She collected cuttings of rose and magnolia bushes. It became a haven from the madness.

I never viewed my mum having only one hand as anything unusual. I knew that most other mothers had two, but it didn't bother me and there wasn't anything they could do that she couldn't. She could even tie my shoelaces by looping the string with one hand and pulling through the other end with her teeth. Although she was pleased when I learned to do it myself.

For as long as I can remember she'd made her stump talk to me. The stitches from the operation ran along the middle of the end of where her arm finished, creating a sort of smile on a round face. There is a mole right at the end which gives her arm – or at any rate it did to me at the time – a sort of cyclopic visage. My mum gave this creature a high-pitched voice and an irascible character with a rebellious streak. I decided to call him 'Booby'.

I'd ask my mum to ask Booby whether he'd be willing to come out. I'd then watch as he came alive, moving this way and that from within my mum's sleeve, and asking, 'What does he want? I'm having a sleep. Oh, okay, I suppose I'll say hello.' And then my mum would roll up her sleeve and Booby would pop out, staring me in the face with his mole-eye, demanding to know why I'd disturbed him. I'd roll up with laughter as he grumbled about being cold or wanting to eat some chocolate. I spent hours in conversation with him, telling him about my day or getting his view on my drawings or cardboard box creations. I suppose it was my mum's way of turning her scar into something good. To this day, he's such a part of my childhood that I smile as I write, safe in the knowledge that next time I see my mum I can always get his advice.

I don't recall asking my mum how she came to lose her hand, but she's told me the story many times.

Chapter 8

1961, Essex

She had seen her mother place the letter in a box in the built-in cupboard in their small bungalow in Brentwood, Essex. She waited for her parents to go out then immediately rooted around until she found what she was looking for. The black typewritten words jumped out from the crisp white paper. The address of the hospital was neatly printed at the top of the page and it was dated 29 May 1961. Her eyes went to the paragraph that contained the news.

This is a dangerous condition that she is suffering from, and the danger is that if we delay too long the growth will have spread to other parts of the body and it will be too late. That being so, you will understand that I am anxious to get this operation done if your daughter is to have the maximum chance of survival. On the question of just how much has to be removed, I am afraid there is really no doubt that we can safely leave her only with the wrist remaining from this hand. I know this is a mutilation, but it is the lesser of two evils and I do not really think there is any doubt as to what the choice should be.

The letter was signed by the doctor who had been treating my mum for two years. Her legs almost gave way from under her and she sat down on the nearest chair, methodically folding the letter, putting it back in the envelope and placing the box back in the cupboard, as if it had remained undisturbed. The idea of amputation had never occurred to her.

She was twelve years old when a lump first appeared on the back of her hand and rapidly got larger. A couple of months before, she had been climbing on her bedroom wardrobe and it had toppled over and fallen onto the back of her hand. When she was admitted to hospital for the first time the lump was the size of a ping-pong ball and she had an operation to remove what she was told was a 'ganglion'. My mum didn't know what that was, so she looked it up in a dictionary and found out that it was 'a tumour in a tendon sheath'. This meant nothing to her either, so she looked up what a tumour was and discovered she had 'a swelling or an enlargement'. This made more sense and the doctors matter-of-factly cut the lump away. She had to stay in hospital for six weeks, receiving radiotherapy, which would stop the lump regrowing. Six months passed and the lump returned in the same place, and this time the surgeon cut it out along with one of the bones in my mum's hand.

This left her ring finger floppy and a small scar on her hand. She went back to school, but the same pattern repeated itself. She wasn't worried by these operations. It wasn't long after the Second World War and the nation had learned to live with hardship and trauma. Her parents exemplified the idea of the stiff upper lip and she had no sense that the treatment wouldn't work. She even enjoyed her stays at the hospital in

Whitechapel. She was too old for the children's ward, so she was admitted to the women's ward and was always the youngest patient. The nurses and other patients welcomed her warmly. It was too expensive for her parents to make the journey to visit her daily, so she spent her days helping the nurses arrange flowers, making beds by tucking sheets underneath the mattresses and overlapping the folds to create hospital corners, and taking the patients cups of tea. The other patients' visitors would bring her sweets and comics.

My mum was discharged once more and returned, with her lump, to school. It was at this point that she found the letter. She didn't want to come clean and admit to snooping, so she waited for her mother to tell her the news. She waited. And waited. Weeks went by and nothing was mentioned. They were planning to take half her arm away. Her head was full and the future was frightening. Would it hurt? What would she look like after? How much would it hinder what she could do? Gone would be the days of using a knife *and* a fork. What would people think of her? Would they stare? Would anyone want to marry her? She kept silent. Holding everything within, she moderated her own distress by praying each night to God that the lump would be gone the following morning. Each night she cried herself to sleep knowing the day of the operation was drawing closer.

A few weeks before the date of the operation, her mum told her she would be going into hospital but gave no other information. My mum was desperate to share her torment and fears. Her heart pounded as she drew up the courage she hoped would provoke her mum into revealing the truth.

'Do you think they might take this floppy finger of mine off?'

'I shouldn't think so, darling,' her mother replied, reaching over to turn out the bedside light and leaving the room. Her parents were also experiencing their own turmoil, knowing what lay in wait for their daughter, and perhaps they had figured it was best to deliver bad news late. They knew nothing of my mum's secretly obtained knowledge, and she couldn't admit to prying, so the torment continued.

Shortly after her fourteenth birthday she returned to the hospital and, along with her parents, was shown into the sister's office. The neatly groomed doctor arrived and sat behind the desk as my mum told him in her head, *Go on, get it over with. Just say it.* She clasped her hands together in a tight grip while her parents looked thoughtfully towards the doctor.

'I'm not going to beat around the bush,' the doctor said. 'This is a very serious condition that you are suffering from and I'm afraid that we have no alternative but to amputate your hand.'

My mum had told herself she wasn't going to cry, that like a heroine in a sad film she would just bite her lip and swallow the sorrow. The reality played out differently as she burst into tears. Her parents put their arms around her, and once she had composed herself she asked the only question she had.

'How much of my hand will you take?'

'Just above the wrist,' the doctor said, giving her a visual indication and telling her the operation would be performed tomorrow.

Her parents left straight after the consultation. The hospital wouldn't permit them to be there on the day of the operation but they promised to return the day after. My mum made her way back in silence along the corridor to her bed, where a nurse pulled the curtain around to give her privacy.

After a while my mum conducted a test. She went to the toilet keeping her left hand behind her in an effort to see how she would manage without her hand. She tried pulling sheets of paper off the toilet roll but the whole thing flew across the floor. She peered out of the fourth-floor window to the grey hospital roofs and the lively Whitechapel market, where people were shopping. What if she climbed out of the window to escape? Where would she go and what would then follow? Would she just die quietly in a corner ridden with this disease? Having no hand was preferable to that.

She made her way back to her bed, dazed and overwhelmed.

'Everything all right, love?' asked a jovial fellow patient.

'I'm having my hand amputated tomorrow,' my mum replied before hurrying over to her bed and burying her face in the pillow, rapidly wiping the bonhomie from the woman's demeanour.

My mum's anxiety grew with each passing hour throughout the night. Eventually she drifted into sleep, and when morning arrived she woke and for one blissful moment doubted that any of it was real. Then a flurry of activity began, and she was given an injection, her arm was shaved and she was dressed in a white gown. She began to feel drowsy as she was lifted onto a trolley and the hospital chaplain arrived to say a prayer for her. A few weeks before, she had decided that God was a figment of people's imaginations. Why else would He have failed to answer her prayers? But in that moment, with this official-looking fellow convinced about his direct line to an omnipotent power, she felt humbled and certain of the prospect that there was one last chance for a reprieve. God might come good and pull her out of this hole. She thanked the chaplain for his words.

'You don't need to thank me,' he replied.

Word had got around, and as she was wheeled off the patients gave her comforting smiles and friendly waves. 'Good luck, love,' and, 'See you later, dear,' they said with strained cheerful tones.

My mum's favourite nurse had promised to accompany her to theatre, and held her hand tightly while my mum watched the ceiling move as the trolley was pushed along. The double doors were pushed open and she entered the ante room, where a group of doctors in white masks and gowns congregated. The injection had numbed her feelings but still a slow burn of panic rose within her. The anaesthetist approached, needle in hand, and my mum made one last attempt to prevent the inevitable.

'Please don't take my hand off. Please don't do it.'

'It's all right, dear. You just lie quietly,' he said kindly but having no truck with the emotion. 'I'm going to give you the injection now and I'd like you to count up to ten for me.'

The anguish she felt was brushed away like crumbs on a chair. Like the letter said, it was a mutilation, and now she just had to lie back and accept it. She did as she was told and the needle was inserted.

'One … two … three …'

Too late now. Unless God can—

'Four … five … six …'

She woke hours later with a throbbing pain in her left arm. Her hand hurt. She felt it so maybe …

'They haven't taken my hand away,' she whispered to the nurse, who was still by her side.

'They have, dear,' she said with a firmness to ensure the message would get across. 'It's just the nerves you can feel.'

My mum raised her arm, which was swaddled in bandages. She could see it was shorter than before and thinner at the end, but it still felt like it was there. The nurse gave her pills and she fell into a deep sleep.

The next day her parents arrived. Their relief was palpable when they saw my mum looking bright and cheerful. An hour before their visit my mum had been inconsolable. She was in huge amounts of pain and tearful, but the nurse had patiently explained how worried her parents would be to find her so unhappy and she must cheer herself up for their sake. The nurse dried my mum's eyes and brushed her hair, gave her a wash and propped her up in bed with pillows.

She pulled the performance off and showed her parents that things weren't so bad after all. After three days it was time for the bandages to come off and be replaced with a lighter dressing. The nurse slowly removed them. My mum watched transfixed as each wrap was unwound until the final part of the cloth came away and my mum's stump was revealed. She turned to the nurse and told her, 'It's the ugliest thing I've ever seen.' Although her natural politeness meant she also added that the surgeon had done a very neat job.

It was gone. The job was done. Her hand lay in an incineration bin somewhere in the hospital. The nurse left after a while and she was left to her own devices, to muddle through on her own, disarmed.

Chapter 9

My dad viewed my mum's parents as her collaborators and he implemented a ban on us seeing them. It was my nana whom he reserved most of his venomous hate for. It was always the way. Women were a red rag to his bullish intentions. My nana had always had his number. Right from the moment my mum introduced them. A mother knows, and she did. She was a formidable woman, strict and keen to keep up appearances. She brought out her fine china tea service for our visits, baked flapjacks and rice crispy cakes, and her polyester dresses would scratch my face when I hugged her. She was rigid and firm, in character and physically. She once got knocked off her bicycle and had to go to hospital, where she was kept in for the night. She never even told us until we saw her and the bruises. 'Why didn't you let us know?' my mum asked.

'Well, there's nothing you could have done,' she replied.

They had seen my dad's short fuse burn before, but one day my nana confronted him. 'The way you behave is not acceptable. It has to stop,' she told him. He shouted back, telling them to leave. My nana, sixty-seven, with short white hair and wearing a tight-fitting floral dress, refused. My dad strode over to her, grabbed her left wrist and tried to pull her from the seat. She resisted, keeping her weight back in the chair. My grandad, who was a few years older than his wife and walked with a limp, ever since his imprisonment in a Japanese prisoner of war camp during the Second World War, moved in front of her, raising both his fists in a traditional boxing stance. My dad let out an exaggerated laugh. My grandad stood his ground. The image is etched in my brain. His action poised, moderate, proportionate, silent, noble and strong. And there was my dad, snarling, red-faced, arrogant and bullying an old woman.

'If I find them here again I'll remove them physically,' my dad said, making sure they could hear him as they left the house. From that moment, the times when I saw my grandparents were always clandestine visits to their home. Nana ruled the roost in 'Lodi', their little bungalow in Essex named after the place where they'd met in India. She had moved there with a family, working as their nanny, and he was stationed there with the army. Their relationship was a counterpoint to my parents. It was respectful and loving and they finished sentences to each other with 'my love' or 'darling'. I would bunk off school for the day so my dad didn't suspect that my mum and I were going to my grandparents' house. I'd play board games or go in their shed to find skittles and hula hoops, or watch *Blockbusters* on the television, which my Nana thought 'frivolous'. I suppose it was.

I was fifteen when my nana died. And she died as she lived: stoically. The doctor informed her that she had a tumour and it had attached itself to other organs, meaning she had only days to live.

'Well, that's a bit of a blow, isn't it?' she said, before turning to my sobbing grandad and saying, 'We've had a good innings, haven't we, darling? Thank you for all the happy years you've given me.' He kissed her and called her sweetheart.

She sat up in the hospital bed, getting weaker and weaker, and she would say things like, 'It must be tiring for everyone to have to sit around and wait for me to die. I do apologise it's taking so long.' It was the same attitude that had stopped her talking to my mum about the impending amputation, I guess.

It seemed this side of my family had a generational addiction to keeping schtum about important things. Just like my mum, who had been fourteen when she found the letter to her parents from the hospital, my nana was also fourteen when she stumbled across a hidden document in the loft of her parents' house. It revealed that she had been adopted at the age of four. She took the paper to the woman she had always thought of as her grandmother and was told that every word was true, but that she must never tell her parents she knew. She lived with that secret, while they all lived with the lie.

And in his own way, my grandad shut away the truth in an old box and shoved it in the loft. He had been captured by the Japanese on Boxing Day as Hong Kong fell in 1941, and spent over three and a half years incarcerated in Sham Shui Po, a prisoner of war camp. He experienced the worst of humanity there. He suffered from dysentery, malnourishment, torture and cruelty beyond comprehension, and he remained silent, just like thousands of others.

As far as I know he said only one thing about his time there. He told my mum that the happiest day of his life was seeing from his cell the American tanks rolling into view. Just as he began to talk, my nana walked in with scones and tea. 'Darling, we don't talk about all that, do we?' she said, and with that the ladder to the attic was pushed back up. After she died my grandad took the love letters they'd written to each other during the war out into the garden and burned them all in a bin. Their life together was theirs, their love their own, and once she was gone it had to live on only within him, just like his suffering in the camp.

If life were a graph we'd see the patterns repeat. My mum had found her own cruel prison-camp guard. She was locked in a place where hope of a better life no longer existed. She too was tortured and the prospect of escape was bleak. Perhaps her father's fortitude was an example to her. He had survived and so could she.

My grandad was the quiet assistant to my nana, never raising his voice or forcing home his own views. He died when I was twenty and I treasured the time I spent with him in the last few years, but I sometimes wonder why he didn't do more to rescue his daughter from her tormentor. He knew her anguish, yet he was silent again. Perhaps he felt if he couldn't save himself during the war, why would he be able to save her?

This habit of secrecy, of hiding the harsh reality, had a hold on my family. History does repeat itself, until it's told to stop. My nana kept her secrets, my grandad locked his past away; they in turn hid things from my mum, and my mum ran from the truth too. I took up this trait, like a son might follow his dad's trade (I did that too), lying, keeping the truth at bay.

My mum never sank below the waterline. Just as she'd had to when her hand was amputated, she accepted her lot, her secret life, the violence, the chaos. She kept making the shepherd's pies, pushing the upright hoover round the house and putting away money to buy me a BMX. It wasn't just fear that stopped her leaving; she was so deep in a hole that she couldn't see out.

Her chest was tight, she struggled for breath. She was followed around by the sound of her own heart, constantly letting her know how hard it was working. One afternoon I was kicking a tennis ball up against the wall of the house and playing out different sporting scenarios in my head. I heard a long scream, coming from the house. I rushed inside, through the kitchen and into the front room but saw no sign of a disturbance. I charged up the stairs, finding my mum sitting on her bed. 'What is it?' I asked. 'Nothing,' she said. 'I just really needed to scream.' She seemed okay, so I left and went back to my game, thinking it was odd that she'd cried out and my dad was nowhere to be seen.

She started an English and history A level class at the local college. She enjoyed being taken to different worlds by Scott Fitzgerald's extravagance or discussing the dithering of Hamlet or the use of language in *The Canterbury Tales*. Immersing herself in the poetry of a fourteenth-century author while a tyrant rampaged around her probably wasn't the most practical thing to do, but it gave her a glimpse of a compassionate world where people thought about things, had discussions and respected each other's opinions. There was also a camaraderie within the group, but it wasn't long before my dad became threatened by it. The last thing he wanted was another influence in my mum's life.

She'd been invited to a party by someone from her college class. At the last minute my dad told her she couldn't go and he got into the bath she'd run for herself. She slipped out anyway wearing a glamourous red and black dress, with padding in the shoulders. I told her she looked lovely and she seemed pleased. Her fear of disobeying him hung over her at the party but my mum needed to be part of something else. This small act of defiance was needed; submission to his will didn't work anyway.

At the weekend he would get up around midday and demand my mum cook him a full English breakfast on a Saturday and a roast dinner with trimmings on Sunday, washed down with copious amounts of wine. He'd rant about how disgusting feminism was or how awful the Labour Party were. His politics were hard to pin down. He'd started out as a fully paid-up socialist, lurched over to Margaret Thatcher in the 1980s, and by the end of his life he was an anarchist. My mum would wash up and my dad would watch TV or read the paper, sitting there in his slippers, reeking of stale smoke.

Sometimes my friend Roland, who lived down the road, would come over to play. I'd want my dad to throw us around in a playfight or play football in the park like I'd seen other boys' dads do, but that wasn't his thing. I had met Roland when I was playing alone outside in the front garden. I was constructing a den, using the existing garden wall, a stray bit of carpet that had been knocking around the house, a large bit of MDF, which I used as a roof, and two cardboard boxes. He slowed down on his BMX, which had a red and yellow lightning strike on the saddle, and stared at me as I worked. I asked him what he wanted and he asked if I was a boy or a girl. At the time my hair was quite long but I was still put out by the question. He suggested helping me with my makeshift house, which he did, and we'd often knock for each other since. I didn't like letting him play with my action figures, as that was my world. I didn't want anyone sticking their oar in. But we went for bike rides together.

For my ninth birthday I received a Spectrum 128k computer, which I would hook up to the TV, load my games into the tape deck and then sit there for five or six minutes as the screen flashed multicoloured and a loud screeching sound was emitted. My dad would sometimes join me. We'd sit for a few hours in armchairs, with the computer on the coffee table, right up close to the TV, and play some strategic fantasy adventure game together, in which the character would have to decide whether to drink from the goblet or get on his horse and find another treasure. I longed for those times. My anxiety would increase as the afternoon disappeared and the evening arrived, bringing with it the prospect of unrest.

My parents once hired a builder to knock through a strange oval-shaped doorway that connected the two rooms in the girls' flat and build a proper door. My dad was unimpressed with the work. I remember feeling unease as he announced that he wasn't paying for it and was going to tell the builder when he arrived to finish the job. There was no way this wouldn't end up in a violent confrontation. I rushed out to the garden, picked up as many stones as I could hold in my fists and hid round the side of the house, near an old coal bunker, as he talked with my dad by the front door. My plan was to pelt the builder's head as soon as the fight started.

The leader of my battalion was under attack. It was my duty to defend him. I readied myself for action, like some crazed, dug-in sniper. When I saw the builder calmly retreat down the garden path, I laid down my weapons, baffled and relieved.

According to my dad, it was my mum's fault. She had found this 'idiot cowboy'. He marched through to the conservatory, where the axe was still kept, but this time he took a saw and a shovel, smashing my mum's rockery and all her rose bushes to pieces, hacking out parts of the brick wall that sat behind it too. It wasn't a coincidence that this was the place my mum had made her own. He didn't want her to have anything. Later, after dinner, while my mum was ironing, he kicked the board over, shaking his fist in my mum's face.

He blamed my mum for everything. Once, the little room at the back of the kitchen was broken into, while my mum was in the house. She heard a crash and walked through to see a man making off over the garden wall with my dad's toolbox. My dad railed at her, 'You're fucking useless. You can't even catch a burglar.' I wondered what my mum was supposed to do. Chase him into someone's garden and rugby tackle him into a rose bush?

In fact, his view on practically everyone was that they were useless, but most of his vitriol was reserved for women. The only woman he had any time for was Dolly Parton, whose music he appreciated and wit he admired.

I didn't know it at the time, but my mum was frequently raped once the lights went out. She rarely put up a fight, knowing that it was easier to let him do it than put up resistance that would only result in more bruises. She couldn't sleep for fear he would force himself on her. Night after night it occurred, and if she did refuse, he would scream, 'There's no affection in you. You and your lesbian friends and your mother have destroyed our marriage. I want to make love with you.'

One night he slapped and punched her, twisting her one hand behind her back as far as he could, and when she cried out in pain, he forced himself on her, screaming abuse into her face while he committed his crime. She thought she had to bear this subjugation and violation. I slept five metres down the corridor, pleased that the night had passed off without event, when, in fact, atrocious acts had continued late into the night.

My sisters recall how they once tried to intervene. My dad had repeatedly punched my mum, throwing her onto their marital bed. The girls had rushed to her side and he had pushed them from the bedroom. Once they were outside he told them all, 'This won't take long,' before slamming the door shut.

My mum would relive each violent episode. She seethed with anger and frustration, secretly raging against the injustice of it all. Sometimes she would daydream about his death. If he could simply be wiped off the face of the earth then all our problems would be solved, so she prayed for his demise.

I became pale, gaunt and underweight, a scrawny little wretch. I felt weak. My stomach ached and I always wanted to be at home, where everything would be under my watchful eye. My body revealed my fear. I hunched, half-hugging myself for comfort. I wasn't sleeping or eating anything like as much as I should have been.

When you're a kid you don't *feel* powerless because it does not occur to you that a child could be instrumental in the big things. You know you can be a nuisance; you know that by making a fuss you may be able to get your way in the small things, like ice cream, or making your dad carry you, or not eating your greens. But the big things are just what happen, like the rain, the rising and setting of the sun, the collision of asteroids: things you can't cause, stop or even avoid.

And when you're a kid in a home where violence can erupt at any moment, big, horrible things are a constant worry. An asteroid may hit at any time, in your own living room. You do not really know the cause or even if there is a cause, or when it will start or when it might end.

There were happy times too. Most Saturdays I'd go to the corner shop and pick penny sweets, putting them in a small paper bag. I'd have them after dinner, lining the cola bottles up with fried eggs and shrimps, deciding the order in which I'd eat them. I remember seeing a *SuperTed* show with my mum and just playing with my train set, and these happy times acquired an extra intensity, standing out in my memory, because they were the light when the dark always seemed to be with me, always there in the back of my mind, always a hovering anxiety.

Later, these sharp, joyful memories brought me only sorrow, because they reminded me of what a child's life should be: what mine could have been.

I was made smaller than I actually was. Fearful of interaction, scared of my place in the world, nervous and ill. I was vigilant to the point of obsession: awake to the slightest change in mood, looking for danger, trying to defuse any sign of discomfort, whether imagined or not. I was a compulsive mediator. People's anger obliterated me, and I never exhibited any of my own. I followed my mum's example and acquiesced, longing for normality and peace. I knew that to scream and cry was no use, so I tried to harden myself to be able to act as efficiently as possible when the time came.

Each year, as I grew older, I became more aware of my dad's peculiarity. Each time I met a friend's parents and observed them with their children, I took in a little part of an alternative life. Without fully understanding, I could see there was a different dynamic at play. One where wariness and fear weren't present. I was suspicious of it, wondering why it looked so different. Perhaps their fathers were weak, I thought.

The truth is that I don't know whether I admired my dad back then. I loved him, certainly. I felt scared of him and loyal to the hilt. I looked to him to understand the way the world worked. But the more I followed his strange example, the less I understood.

Focusing was hard. Life seemed to be about surviving, everything else was a distraction. I was unsure of others and their motivations. My mum was a source of goodness and taught me that parts of the world were positive, but my dad made me unsure of my own worth.

At school I dodged the spotlight, instinctively avoiding questions because being observed would send a shiver down my spine. I was frightened that if they scratched beneath the surface, people would find something troubling and I would have to explain things for which I had no words. Conversing without editing my thoughts could expose the things I didn't want people to know. I was protecting my mum, my dad and my own shame.

I became proficient at asking questions. I got on well with adults because they assumed I had an inquiring mind. That was partly true, but my questions weren't for curiosity's sake.

'And what school did you teach at before, Ms Dunlop?'

'Have you ever seen the pyramids in real life, Ms Billinghurst?'

I became good at retaining the information they gave me, so I could follow up my questions – not necessarily straight away, but later, when it might be needed.

'Yes, it has been very hot recently. You must be used to hot weather, though, from your time in Egypt, Miss Billinghurst.'

I frequently asked for days off school. My stomach felt like it was being stirred around with a spoon. I felt responsibility on my nine-year-old shoulders, which slumped forward as I walked. I didn't want to deal with outside concerns when there was enough on my plate at home.

I needed to be with my mum. A bodyguard who couldn't do the job. Home was where I belonged. Perversely, it was where I felt safest. It's why I loved our campervan so much, a place to feel safe while on the road. Home was where I managed my business. I knew the domain, the enemy within, and being away was intolerable. Our home was where my mum suffered but there was a comfort in that. I was afflicted with a need to monitor and scrutinise like an obsessive health and safety inspector, and I was right: when she was alone with him, his rage was unconstrained.

I went to a school camping trip in Danbury, near Chelmsford. It was five days long and everyone in my year was going. When the coach set off, I trudged aboard, my stomach in knots, unable to comprehend my classmates' excitement, despite the Wotsits, bubble-gum, card games and Coca-Cola. They were looking forward to an adventure away from their parents. I sat looking out of the window as the arterial road became a moving blur, gearing myself up to undergo what felt like a prison sentence. Get your head down and get on with it. I felt like a baby but pretended I was as delighted as everyone else.

For most of us it was our first time away from home, a taste of independence, although with six or so teachers in attendance, we weren't running free. What was happening back at home? I was stripped of my ability to react when danger struck.

There were games, campfires, burnt sausages and walks in the sun-dappled woods, but I didn't want to play Robin Hood with the other kids or sing 'Ging Gang Goolie'. Sleeping in a tent with six others, I'd never felt lonelier. After two days we were allowed to call home from a payphone. I told my mum it was dreadful. She was coming along with the other parents on the penultimate day of the camp and I made it clear that I would be returning with her.

My teachers did not sanction my departure. They were determined that I should stay. My mum, who had been won round to my plan within seconds, was persuaded by the teachers that I needed to see it through to the end. It was character-building. I stood with Mr Jameson, the head teacher, with tears streaming down my face, thinking the unthinkable. One more night in the woods. One more night away from home.

Chapter 10

With every new day a fresh dollop of drama would be delivered. I returned from my camp to learn that my dad had lost his job at Essex Radio. It was unclear why or what had happened, but my mum used the phrase 'unreasonable behaviour' when telling me. Losing his job meant our debts started to deepen, but his sudden twenty-four-hour presence in the house also multiplied the possibility of altercations.

The tension reached fever pitch. He sat around watching TV all day, demanding meals, and when his whims weren't catered for he'd grab an ornament and hurl it across the room. My dad signed on and agreed that my mum could take charge of the dole cheque, so she tried to keep the creditors at bay with small payments. We were already thousands of pounds in arrears with our mortgage and the letters stacked on top of the fridge all had red stripes and said, 'FINAL DEMAND'.

My dad refused to help around the house, so my mum continued to struggle back from Sainsbury's. She'd pick me up from school and we'd go along together so I could help carry the bags back. I remember her putting the bags down along the road, rubbing her stump, which was covered in red indentations where the bags had hung, and then reaching down to carry on our journey.

Around this time, I saw the advert with a red phone box for Childline, a counselling service for children who were distressed or in trouble. Esther Rantzen and her prominent teeth frequently appeared on our TV, talking about how kids needed to be protected from abuse. My dad hated her. He said she was a fraud, a self-promotor without integrity. I had no idea that I was the kind of kid who might find the line useful. I now wonder how many other children wouldn't know to call in the first place.

Despite our financial pressures there was cash flowing into the town. The financial boom kept a lot of Southend boys in jobs on the trading floor. The old school tie was out, the striped shirt was in. It didn't matter that you went to Harrow if you couldn't bash the phones. Almost overnight, the bowler hats disappeared, and the hair gel and flash suits moved in. The bosses, who were still old Etonians, looked on in wonder at these flat-vowelled, H-dropping, F-bombing oiks who shouted into their phones late into the night, with only a white-powdered nostril to reveal where they got the energy.

Essex girl and boy jokes were shared in the playground, even if we didn't always get what they meant. Things like: 'An Essex bloke is in an accident and covered in blood. When the paramedics arrive they ask him where he is bleeding from. "I'm from bleeding Romford, mate."' And, 'How do you turn the light off after sex with an Essex girl? Close the car door.' But there's pride in having jokes made about you. It means you're getting noticed. And that's what I wanted to be.

Southend wasn't exactly an optimistic place. It was cynical, slightly down at heel, but with a group belief that you could turn things round. The voices were harsh and the volume loud. The look was flash and work was hard. The culture was conservative and getting told you'd 'made good' was high praise, even sweeter when prefixed by 'poor boy'. What would be the point of the new Audi (lease-buy, naturally) on the freshly tarred driveway of your Thurrock four-bed detached if you couldn't say, 'An' I came from NUFFIN'? 'You think you're better than me?' would be about the worst thing someone could accuse you of.

The town wasn't tolerant of anything that strayed too far off the mainstream. Divorce wasn't a major scandal, but it was definitely frowned upon enough to make people think twice about it. There was a stigma attached to the single mum. If my mum had left my dad, it wasn't as if everyone would be sympathetic. If you were different you'd be bullied, and sympathy would amount to, 'Well, what do you expect?'

Harry Enfield's Loadsamoney was funny because it hit on a character that we all knew. The country was being privatised, greed was good, as Gordon Gekko said, and giant-sized mobile phones, Nintendos and Nike Airs were the aspiration. These weren't our concerns, though.

Around this time, I made friends with a new boy in our class, Jignesh. He didn't have a school uniform when he arrived, so he wore a scruffy grey tracksuit with an image of Rambo emblazoned on the front. He'd moved from Stevenage with his family. Like us, they didn't have much money, and some of the other pupils bullied him because of his cheap clothes and brown skin. We completed a science project together, which was a cardboard garage that had a battery powered light outside. We played football together and argued with his persecutors until the racist slurs abated. He came to ours and he brought a Subbuteo football pitch cloth, which we laid across our kitchen table and flicked the little bases of the plastic pieces till our fingernails ached.

It was my dad's fury directed at an inanimate object that sent a shaft of light onto our lives. My mum had purchased a pretty mahogany dressing table with a mirror for £15 from a second-hand shop. While in the front room I heard sudden loud bangs and crashes coming from upstairs and then my dad's footsteps running out of the house. My mum and I tentatively opened the door to his study. The dresser had been smashed to pieces. The mirror was shattered and glass was all over the floor. Each leg of the table had been broken off. There were chunks of wood scattered about. We had no idea what had caused him to destroy it but we had long since stopped looking for reasons. Despite this being with one of his milder acts of aggression, something about the scene of destruction compelled my mum to act. She rang Margaret from the refuge who came to our house to get us. I remember her saying, 'This is the work of some sort of super-monster.' We hurriedly packed our bags.

We returned to the refuge with heavy hearts but pleased of the respite. Being out of the house gave us hope and momentum, although towards what, we weren't sure. With the support of the refuge, my mum engaged a solicitor who made an application to the courts for my dad to be restrained from molesting, assaulting or harming her in any way. It also stated that he would have to vacate the house and be prohibited from going there.

He wrote to my mum saying he felt ashamed. He missed his family and he would never again repeat his behaviour. He believed he and my mum could be reconciled and, with help, he'd change his ways.

He applied for legal aid and instructed his own solicitor, who put forward their proposal. My dad didn't believe the marriage was irretrievably broken but agreed to leave the family home for three months, only returning to visit us once a week. He undertook to see a psychiatrist and suggested a local vicar to act as a mediator. Why a vicar was chosen I'm unsure. We weren't a God-fearing household. My dad said Christianity was for the needy or old. It was agreed that my dad could visit our home from 1 to 5 p.m. on a Saturday.

Once these details had been worked out, we returned home. I hugged him when he knocked at the door on the first Saturday. He seemed happy to see me after the weeks apart. We went to Peter Pan's amusement park on Southend seafront, where we rode on the dodgems. Me in the driver's seat, him occasionally swinging over a protective arm and swiftly commandeering the steering wheel to avert a crash. He took me to the toy store on the high street and I chose an *A-Team* toy truck. Free from the conflict of home he could just be my dad. To me, this seemed a much better arrangement than before. My mum and dad were never a couple, anyway. Not in my eyes. They were warring factions forced to share living space. This way he couldn't hurt her.

Before he left that day, he placed a letter for my mum on the table which said he'd like to take her out for a meal and would call round at eight o'clock. When he came, my mum sent Emma to the door to decline his offer.

The weekend routine didn't last for long. I was walking home from school with my mum and we passed Albert, the local tramp, who was lying back on his bench, his usual place, swigging from a bottle. He gave us a cheery wave and tipped his trilby in acknowledgement. He seemed to be free of worries and his reddish, jovial glow made me think that if he could get his act together and find a job, he was only one bath away from being my mum's new husband. We turned the corner onto our road and we both stopped in our tracks. Standing right there in front of us was my dad.

'I just want to see my son,' he said.

The line was delivered for maximum emotional impact. I could see through it. Those words spelt trouble and didn't come from a burning desire to be with me. He was here to disrupt.

My dad began to circle my mum, like a wolf with its prey. My mum was shaking and I encouraged her to knock on the nearby vicar's door, in the hope that he could reason with my dad. God wasn't in that day and suddenly my hand was being grabbed, causing me to lurch forward.

'Let's go for a run, Tom. Daddy wants to spend some time with you,' he said. We had already started moving down the road, my legs having to move twice as quickly to match his pace. We passed our house on the other side of the road and the pace picked up.

'We're going to go round the block,' he told me. I was scared of what he might do but never felt he'd hurt me. Everyone else, but not me. In some bizarre way, maybe it made me feel special. We turned the corner. 'Do you play with your *A-Team* truck?' he asked as we slowed down to a quick walk.

Tears had filled my eyes. My breathing was shallow. But I told him I had been playing with it and that I'd built a Lego base for my action figures. Within a couple of minutes we were back and found my mum frantic and relieved at the same time.

'I'll come in briefly,' he said. 'Tom wants to show me what he's built.'

It wasn't sophisticated manipulation, but he seemed convinced it was why he was coming in. He started walking towards our house, taking me along by the hand.

'It's not a good time,' my mum said. 'You shouldn't be here. There's a court order.'

'Thomas is upset. I'll come in for five minutes to see my son's room.' He strode forward, unperturbed.

These surprise appearances became part of our life. He was our stalker, harassing my mum whenever the opportunity arose. He would be there when my mum dropped me off at school, standing at the gate like some nightclub bouncer. I would line up with my fellow pupils and file into the classroom, craning my head to look back at my parents talking by the entrance. I'd see my mum walk off with my dad following behind. Each event hit me in my stomach.

Sometimes he was there at the end of the day too. We'd file out of the classroom and I'd immediately look out towards the gate where all the parents gathered. I'd scan the line, hoping to spot my mum, and only my mum. He'd appear like a ghoul in a horror flick, sending a shiver down my spine. How was it possible to be scared of him and yet want to be loved by him too? The possibility of him lurked around every unseen turn in the road.

At some point the teachers noticed my dad's appearances and the unease it caused. The head teacher, Mr Jameson, took it upon himself to have a word with my dad the next time he turned up. I watched as he approached him, all hushed tones and discretion. My dad was ushered into the office. I watched silently from the end of the corridor. I knew Mr Jameson couldn't solve anything. I was worried my dad would punch him and, if he did, what people would think of me. If they hated him, they knew I was cut from the same cloth. My dad burst out of the office door, which swung back, and Mr Jameson followed, looking dumbfounded but conciliatory. 'Tom, this way!' my dad called out as he left the building. I ran after him.

The vicar my dad had suggested mediate saw my dad and mum separately and together, but seemed defeated by the situation. How could their situation be negotiated? He offered no solutions but did remark to my mum that my dad was the angriest man he'd ever met.

Every Saturday my dad would overstay his allotted time. My mum would arrive to find him sitting in our living room with my sisters and me, lavishing us with attention. One weekday evening, he turned up while my mum was having coffee with two friends. He stood outside the house, banging on the door and shouting through the letterbox to be let in. Emma eventually opened it and he barged into the house, joining my mum and her friends at the table. One of the women burst into tears as he sat with them. He refused to leave, so at midnight my mum, my sisters and I returned to the refuge, leaving him raging at us from the hallway.

We returned to the house the next day and had the locks changed. A few days later a letter arrived from my dad's solicitor saying that my mum was letting out rooms to women from the refuge and my dad was worried for our safety.

He wore her down, like human white noise. When he wasn't filing applications to the court he prowled around outside our home, cajoling, negotiating, blackmailing. Viciousness lurked behind every conciliatory word. He held a knife to her throat and forced her to write a letter to the court agreeing that he could move back in. He half-strangled her to get her to sign it, his hands around her neck, making her a promise: he would kill us all if she refused.

My mum didn't tell the police what he did. She took him at his word. He would have been sent to prison for breaking the court order, but for how long I don't know. Any prospect of escape vanished before it was fully in sight. He moved himself back into the house. I don't know exactly how or when.

If insanity is doing the same thing over and over again and expecting a different result, then we were mad. My mum had long since lost all objectivity. This time a psychiatrist had agreed to evaluate my dad and assist in helping to reunite us.

As a kid I had no choice but to follow my parents' lead. I didn't question the decisions behind my dad's return but the powerlessness I felt grew with every passing month. I didn't blame myself for my dad's behaviour but I became convinced that my role was to moderate it as best I could. I would be the other side of the scale. The angrier he was, the more violent he became; I would attempt to provide the balance required, by showing my mum love and support. I didn't have tantrums or argue over bedtime; I made things as easy as I could. As far as I was concerned there wasn't time for cheekiness or rebellion, so I fitted into a role of acquiescence and mediation.

I despised the things my dad did, but not the man himself. I'd watch his fury rise and try to placate his mood. I was now nine and I saw his rage as an illness, not a fault. You tended to people who were sick and didn't vilify them for their misfortune.

Once we were united again the destruction continued. I was using the area underneath a table in my room to play out mini-dramas with my superhero figures. There was a firm knock at the door and my mum went to answer. I made my way out onto the landing and hovered at the top of the stairs listening and peered over the bannisters when I was sure no one was looking. A female voice was asking for my dad. She said she was from the court. It involved a complaint by a woman who used to work with him. My dad joined the conversation and, although it drifted upstairs as a murmur, I could hear that he had abandoned his usual modus operandi of aggression. He sounded wrongfooted, unsure. The woman handed him some papers before leaving.

This was a new kind of tension, with a different edge. My dad took the papers into the front room and I tentatively made my way downstairs to listen. I could see my parents through the gap in the door. He was sitting at the dining-room table, discombobulated, and it was disconcerting. My mum grabbed the papers and he was pleading for her not to read them, his voice like that of a child begging not to go to school. His demeanour had altered. Most of what followed was unclear to me at the time, but those papers were an affidavit. While in his previous job he had begun an affair. In fact, there was a photo of the woman with my dad and two colleagues on our mantlepiece.

She had become pregnant and wanted to get married, but he'd said he'd never leave my mum. She had an abortion, and the documents listed numerous occasions when he had violently attacked her. The last incident was three days ago. My dad had turned up at her house in breach of an undertaking he had given to a judge to leave her alone, and now she was seeking his committal to prison.

This revelation cowed my dad for a few days. When he was on the backfoot he became infantile, begging for forgiveness, his edges smoothed. He skulked around and started to do the hoovering regularly, which was his way of making amends. I liked the relative peace but my mum was knocked for six. She still had belief in our family, a blind hope that life would settle. She felt the betrayal. He wasn't even our psychopath. He was another woman's too.

Chapter 11

A year or so passed. My dad had taken to wearing contact lenses and shaved off his moustache. He was forty-one now, with greying hair. He surprised the family by coming home with a perm one day, forcing us to stifle our laughs. He had also acquired an Yves Saint Laurent rain mac, which reminded me of film detectives.

A memory comes to me at this time of my mum and me spontaneously dancing around in the kitchen when Freddie Mercury came on the radio singing 'I Want to Break Free'. It's only now that I understand what exactly had gripped us about the lyrics. My mum, flush from dancing with vigour, said as the music finished, 'That's my favourite song ever.'

My parents had their first session with Dr Killala, a psychiatrist who would attempt to understand their problems. My dad performed the role of a rational man seeking reconciliation, but he refused to admit to any violence, making the whole thing a farce. We heard no more about my dad's mistress. He claimed the allegations had been a plot by his former bosses to discredit him. I'm not sure if Dr Killala was the man for the job, anyway. My mum gasped when she met him. He was morbidly obese with wild curly hair and the top button of his trousers left undone. The idea of him having anything to do with the health profession seemed surreal. Halfway through the consultation he got up, adjusted his underpants and left the room to put his video recorder on, making sure he didn't miss the last part of a TV drama.

Years later Dr Killala was struck off for gross professional misconduct. He had been found hoarding huge amounts of porn depicting bestiality, as well as keeping rotting, maggot-infested food in his hospital office. He'd also been found guilty of carrying out a three-year affair with a patient and over-prescribing medicine.

Everywhere I looked the world seemed off-kilter, making my own life seem par for the course. At Christmas the year before, my dad suggested dinner at the dingy-looking hotel at the end of the road. Despite the grubby net curtains and our lack of money, my mum was won over by the idea of not cooking.

Something felt wrong when a grumpy-looking woman in her sixties greeted us at reception. She took our coats, opened a door behind her and chucked them onto a single bed before slamming the door shut. We headed down into the basement, to a dining room where there were two other people sitting at separate tables, staring ahead into the distance. The waitress brought us our food, slopping gravy onto our plates. While my dad argued with her about the absence of a wine list, I tugged on my mum's sleeve to point out that the woman was wearing slippers. Both the other guests started to slump over in their seats.

Growing up, I never felt anyone was luckier than us. Roland's parents weren't even together and he never saw his mum. He'd recently told me how his dad and his 'uncle Gary', who lived with them, had just had a big fight. His dad had taken all of Gary's clothes from the wardrobe and thrown them out of the house, leaving them strewn down the front steps. It seemed to me that everyone's lives were packed with drama.

One calm evening, our new neighbour, Colette, called round, tears streaming down her face and black panda eyes from where her make-up had run. My mum invited her in, and they went through to the kitchen. There had been some argument with her husband, Steve, whom I had seen a few times before, sitting in a deck chair, drinking beer in his garden. A while later, Steve arrived at the front door, unsteady on his feet, slurring his words and looking for his wife. Dried stripes of blood ran down his face and he had deep scratch marks down each cheek. It became clear that Colette had attacked him, and he wore the wounds like an emblem of what he had endured. *How troubled were they,* I thought, *to have to come to our house for a break from the fighting?*

I remember watching *EastEnders*, which seemed to confirm my impression that life brimmed with chaos. The screaming arguments of Dirty Den and Angie were tame by comparison to our own lives. The famous drumbeats at the end of each episode of the soap could have been used as a soundtrack to our nightly dramas.

My sisters became harder to know, our interactions strange and tense. They had a sort of collective verbal tic. If one of them said a word such as 'die', the others would demand, 'Say "live"! Say "live"!' They made noises to show their displeasure at things my mum or I would say. It was a sort of disgusted growl sound that, when they knew we had heard, they would switch to an 'awww' noise, as if we had done something very sweet.

Their exams didn't go well. My dad attributed this to laziness and didn't question the part their home life had played in the results or how his behaviour had affected them. He demanded they study journalism at college, despite their having no interest. My mum explained to him that they needed a minimum of four O levels to get on the course.

'This is the course I want them on, you stupid fucking bitch. I don't care what it says the requirements are, you incompetent cow, you insist they go on it. You lie. You tell them they have four O levels. The thing I can't stand about you is your disloyalty to your family. Why don't you want the best for your daughters?' he screamed at her one evening before storming off to the off-licence to buy a bottle of brandy.

I often wonder what attracted my mum to my dad in the first place, because when I ask her she says she thought he was full of himself and a bit of a dickhead. She was working as a nanny for a family in Kensington when she was nineteen. She came home to her parents with a friend, and a nice local lad called Jeffrey, with fluffy blond hair and a gentle, attentive manner, called round and asked her out.

She explained that she had her friend staying but Jeffrey said he'd bring someone and it could be a double date. When they both turned up she wasn't sure what to make of my dad in his drainpipe trousers and Chelsea boots, boasting about his entrepreneurial flair while driving around in a convertible MG. He stood out from the boy-next-door type she'd met before. His spontaneity and the flash of danger in his eye appealed to her somewhere deep down.

My dad wrote to her after the date and asked her out. She was surprised but flattered. Jeffrey was affronted and felt my dad had stolen his girl, but my dad didn't care about losing a friend. Several months later my mum began to have concerns about her flighty boyfriend, but she found herself pregnant.

'We'll get married, then,' was my dad's response on being told.

Each time my dad landed another job the mood in the house lifted. He'd be out most of the day and our money problems would ease, at least temporarily. He considered himself a newspaper man. After his attempts to set up the *Brentwood Advertiser* he had gone to work for the Associated Press, the *Sunday People* and the *Mirror*. In 1971 he won a local journalist of the year award for his investigation into a drug-dealing doctor. He told me that while covering the story, a henchman of the doctor had thrown a wet sandbag at him from the third floor of a hotel, hitting a metal railing and bouncing onto his head, cutting it badly. He had gone in search of the perpetrator, carrying the sandbag with him, which he launched at the reception desk.

Once, after a tip-off, he arrived at the scene of a crime. The daughter of boxer Gene Tunney had murdered her husband. The walls were spattered with blood. This was the work my dad craved. As I got older, he told me tales of how East End gangsters Ronnie and Reggie Kray had started leaking stories to him to get their side of the story in print. He'd visit them in their nightclub on Bow Road where they'd boast about their legitimate business interests. He got on well with them, thinking them useful and friendly, although he was wary of Ronnie.

Don't Ask Me About My Dad

Fleet Street was his domain. He frequented El Vino, the pub full of pissed newspaper reporters chain-smoking over liquid lunches while their bellies grew over their belts. Women were an inferior species who typed, made tea or got shagged. He told me with a smile how some bars had signs that read, 'No unaccompanied women allowed'. *Mad Men* had nothing on this lot.

His eyes went misty when reminiscing about the bonhomie with his drinking pals, and he saw romance in the old traditions of the printing press. News stories would be typed onto copy paper by the journalist using a manual typewriter, who would triumphantly rip it out of the machine and shout, 'Boy!' A man old enough to be his grandfather would appear, accept the piece of paper and take it to the news desk, where an editor would have a look before giving it back to the old boy to deliver to the subeditors. They would mark it for type size and column width, give it a headline and page allocation and then roll it up, place it in a tin tube, put the lid on it and drop it into one of the pipes at a station on the wall. A vacuum system would propel it to the composing room.

The tin would drop out of the pipe into a cage, and an ever-alert messenger would snatch it up and take it to someone operating a linotype machine. He would retype the story, making the settings that the subs had placed on it. Each line of the story would be separately moulded into a small metal strip from a bucket of boiling lead, heated by a gas jet that hung on the right side of the machine. Solidified, the type would be seized by a swinging arm and dropped into a rack on the operator's left. The dozens of juddering machines, the red glow from the bottom of the lead buckets and the stench of the acrid fumes rising from the liquid metal created a steampunk vision of hell. Men finished their shifts with blackened faces, burns and raw coughs. Later, the moulded type would be fixed to giant rotary presses, which would spew out millions of copies of the day's newspaper.

This time porn supremo David Sullivan had enlisted my dad to launch a downmarket rival to the *News of the World*, called the *Sunday Sport*. It was journalism but only in its broadest sense. How he landed such an important role is a mystery, but he had a flair for persuasion.

Now he was out of the house for days on end, returning only to change clothes, complain about the 'thick idiots' and 'fucking morons' he worked with, and shout at my mum. He was the editor of a national newspaper and the world was finally recognising the brilliance he knew he had all along. The *Sunday Sport* was a bit like the *National Enquirer* with an additional obsession with naked women. My dad boasted about how he introduced a nipple count for each edition of the paper, to make sure they never dropped below a certain number of breasts. He enthusiastically explained his approach: 'Make it good, make it fast, make it up.' And with that, infamous headlines like WORLD WAR TWO BOMBER FOUND ON MOON were born. Other stories included a monkey landing a plane and Hitler really being a woman. My dad, whose personal relationship with the truth was strained, had found his ideal job. He got to lie for a living, and the bigger the lie, the better.

The Independent Broadcasting Authority refused permission for the paper to advertise on television on the grounds of decency, but my dad was delighted when it finally got mentioned on national television, albeit in a joke. The comedian Bob Monkhouse told his audience that a pop-up edition of the *Sunday Sport* was being produced. He then took out a book, opened it and two breasts popped up. Watching on the sofa at home I just felt proud. In my eyes it made my dad legitimate, someone people respected.

My mum knew this benign time wouldn't last. The venture would turn sour, like the others, but she and my sisters still got dressed up for the glamorous launch, held at Peter Stringfellow's nightclub. My mum returned happy with stories of meeting England's World Cup winning captain Bobby Moore, who was also the paper's sports editor, and DJ Tony Blackburn, who had talked a lot about himself. She had also met David Sullivan, but he hadn't impressed her. She said he was small and greasy with a weak handshake.

A few weeks later, things unravelled. My mum answered the phone to a man asking for my dad's car keys to be returned. A letter arrived soon after, which she steamed open. It said the police would be called if my dad didn't return the company car and he had to vacate all property from the Hoxton office by the end of the week. My mum rang the *Sunday Sport* office to be told that he didn't work there anymore. That weekend, my dad came home in the car and left for work on Monday morning. Nothing was said. Another letter arrived, from David Sullivan, saying he thought the job was clearly too much for my dad and he'd been shocked at his lack of business sense.

The truth emerged a week or so later. My parents were arguing in the kitchen. I sat at the table, watching events unfold. He stormed up to me and stuck his face in mine, screaming, 'Mummy wants you to know that your dad doesn't have a fucking job anymore. I'm sure you're disappointed.'

The year of 1987 began with the south-east of England under a foot of snow. The schools closed and I stayed at home for a week, in what was a sort of mini-lockdown. There were fights in supermarkets as customers clashed over the last toilet roll, buses and trains gave up trying to transport passengers and my dad was back at home, smoking in his office. Copies of the *Sunday Sport* were piled up around his desk, the most recent edition revealing how Sarah Ferguson and Prince Andrew had made a secret pact never to have kids.

He suggested we make a sledge to take to the sloping hills of the seafront. We found some offcuts of wood in the conservatory, nailed them together and sandpapered the runners so it would glide through the snow. We made our way, passing giant icicles that hung from the gutters and occasionally broke away, smashing onto the freezing pathways. He pushed me down the little hills and I'd laugh as I whizzed past the trees. It was just how I wanted everything to be, all the time.

Chapter 12

My sisters were like ghosts to me. Ghosts that I shared a home with. I heard them rattle along the hall and glimpsed them through windows, but I didn't know who they were. Because what happened ripped us apart. My sisters clung to each other to protect themselves from a father who treated them with disdain. They didn't learn love from him; they learned derision. When my sisters became teenagers, he was more unpleasant towards them; they withdrew from the family and I watched them vanish, just like ghosts.

Several times I remember him hitting them hard. I returned home from school one day and heard the shouting as I walked down the garden path. Inside I found Victoria with blood all over her face. Emma was screaming in the background. My dad was shoving them both upstairs. 'Don't touch me, you bastard,' Victoria said, and he struck her twice around the face with such cold-hearted efficiency I can still hear the sound it made.

I remember running down the hall towards him, shouting, 'No, no, no, Dad,' as panic took over. Most of all I recall the tone in which he addressed them. It was harsh and scornful. By the time they were seventeen they had started drinking heavily, smoking and self-harming, and they had developed eating disorders.

They'd fight each other. I'd hear crashes and thuds from upstairs and be woken in the early hours by them tripping over or breaking cups. Around five o'clock one morning, my dad stormed out of the bedroom and found Victoria swaying in the hallway. He grabbed the lapels on her coat and pushed her into the kitchen. She slurred, 'Go on, hit me, you bastard. I don't fucking care.' He poured several jugs of water over her head, causing her to slip over again and again on the tiled floor. She screamed in his face. Emma woke up and began pleading with them to stop. I watched from my usual vantage point on the stairs. Victoria eventually managed to stand up and stumbled along the hall, leaving puddles of water on the carpet. I scrambled away as I heard her approach. As she went upstairs she squelched, and water sploshed out from her shoes with each step.

Two minutes later she was back, heading straight out of the front door. My dad belted after her, yanking her back inside as she continued to scream for him to hit her. My mum had joined the commotion by now, and he yelled at her, 'You've done this to your daughter. She's been damaged by your trips to the refuge.'

That night at dinner he said to my mum and me, 'What a nightmare this morning. I hope I don't have to go through anything like that again.'

One afternoon I decided to snoop around the girls' flat. I stood on their landing, listening for signs of movement. When I was sure they were out, I pushed the door open and peered inside. There were unmade beds with cigarette burns on the duvets; empty bottles and crushed beer cans lined the shelves. Mugs brimming with butt ends were on the floor alongside damp towels and piles of dirty clothes. The little kitchenette was covered in grime. The sink was filled with plates and cutlery. Half-eaten food lay on the counter and empty packets were piled up next to the bin. The windows were yellow with nicotine, the walls black with hand marks and the carpet was stained. In the bathroom the toilet seat was broken, the shower curtain covered in mould, and sanitary towels were piled in the corner.

Their bedroom was a symbol of their hearts, I guess: chaotic, neglected and broken. They took their anger out on their surroundings and their own bodies. My dad ruled over them as a tyrant and all they could do was rebel. They threw everything in their power at him but none of it stuck.

My dad told them they were worthless. Once, while they ate dinner, he walked around the table, stopping by each, bending down, putting his face in front of theirs and telling them that they were pigs and they disgusted him. Nothing they did could ever please him.

They looked at me and wondered why I got all the love he had to give. And it's true that I got what there was, even if it was a distorted, mutilated love. Maybe it was because I was a boy, maybe he just hated women. They barely acknowledged me. The rest of the time, if we passed each other at home they'd say things like, 'What you staring at, you little snob?' or, 'When's your voice going to break, pissy?' I began to hate them. Emma once held a knife to my throat and often made threats to kill me.

There was no sibling solidarity in the face of our domestic strife. We became strangers. Inmates in the same prison but suspicious of each other. Where were the three little girls in small-checked dresses, knee-high white socks and buckled shoes, who patiently waited for their turn to hold me?

Emma, Kate and Victoria were born in 1969 from a single egg that split into three, making them identical triplets. The chance of that happening is one in a million. From the moment they were born they were never apart. They took their first breath, first steps, spoke their first words and had their first day at school together. They got ill at the same time and they learned to swim at the same time. They were bridesmaids at the same weddings, met their first boyfriends in the same month and got their first Saturday jobs on the same day. And they experienced my dad's violent tempers. They were eight years older and they were part of an exclusive club to which I did not have membership.

What I knew of them could be written on a Post-it Note. Kate loved Marylin Monroe and put posters of her up on her wall. Victoria liked *The Wizard of Oz* so much she watched it fifty times, and Emma played a cat in the local theatre's panto. They were excellent cross-country runners and consistently took the first three places, in order of birth, in the borough championship.

They once told me a story about how they used their identical appearance to their advantage while at school. When Emma knew she'd fail her maths test, she sent Kate, who was more proficient with numbers, to do it for her. Victoria hated geography so she swapped over with Emma, who was more outgoing and made an effort to answer the questions, earning Victoria much praise. At one stage, word got out to the teachers that they were doing this. Their head of year issued a warning: 'You'd better not try that with me, Kate, because I assure you I can tell the difference.' Unfortunately, she was talking to Emma.

We grew up understanding that the world was unforgiving. Our dad, the person who should have cared for us, showed us that violence and hatred were a way of life and we had to endure it. My recurring fantasy of returning to our family home as an adult and rescuing myself should have included rescuing them. But it didn't because they weren't my allies. They were a neighbouring tribe with an alien culture. We shared the same oppressor, but we were suspicious of each other and only took care of ourselves.

It wasn't always that way. When I was born they couldn't contain their excitement and did cartwheels round the garden. Three eight-year-old girls given what they wanted: a baby doll that actually cried if you dropped it. Emma once told me they wanted mum to have triplet boys so, 'We would get one each.'

I wanted them to protect me, for us to forge an unbreakable alliance, but I had no way of repairing the bridge between us, which crumbled a little more each day. They weren't able to look after me because they couldn't look after themselves. I'd find them lying in the hall, unable to hold my gaze, griping at me because I breathed the same air.

My anger towards them could dissipate in seconds. When I was about eight, I was playing on our street and one of a group of boys, about fifteen, flicked a cigarette at me as they sat on a bench. My sisters were returning from school and saw it happen. I gave the boys an angry stare while they laughed at me for my front. Kate leaned on a wall nonchalantly, Victoria folded her arms and let her satchel drop to the floor, Emma stepped forward, chewing gum, and with a sneer she asked them what their problem was. This triple vision made the boys shift in their seats, their bravado disappeared. They got up from the bench, swearing at us all but walking backwards and lighting more fags to save face. This was my family together, repelling an outside threat. It was the threat from inside that we had no idea how to defend against.

They didn't draw me in as big sisters might. They didn't shield me from the reality of our lives. They ran off and stuck together, and to my mind that was unforgivable. I wasn't going to chase these ghosts; I would stick with what I knew.

Somehow I could make the relationship with my dad work. He might have been a bully, but I could get on with him. I knew he would stab the man that stabbed me, would take an eye for an eye and fight my corner fiercely. If it suited him.

He was something I could work with, and it was, after all, all I'd been given. He was my only dad. I would take what I could, because if I didn't, I wouldn't get anything at all. I needed him, so I gave him my hand and followed his twisted path.

I was now ten and my desire to keep the secrets of our house only increased. As I became more aware that the lives of others were different, my shame of our own grew.

My dad signed on at the dole office, the government resumed paying our mortgage and my mum found a job as a receptionist in a doctor's surgery. Dr McGregor was bald, with small round spectacles and a giant tummy. At the interview he showed no interest in the college courses my mum had taken, but instead asked lots of questions about her missing hand. He then led my mum out of his office into the reception area, where he asked the current receptionist if she could notice anything unusual about her. The young woman made a few polite attempts to guess what it could be, before McGregor triumphantly told her the answer.

McGregor then timed my mum while she put away files, standing next to her with a pocket watch. He admonished her for taking thirty-two seconds for each file, telling her that it should take only nine seconds but he was still prepared to employ her at £2 an hour. The current receptionist smiled weakly.

We didn't socialise with other families. Apart from my dad's parents or occasionally an after-school visit from Jignesh, we didn't entertain. There were no dinner parties or old friends calling round for drinks. Partly it was because we didn't invite anyone, but it was also because people could sense something dark was afoot and their instincts told them not to get close. A friend of my sisters, called Hazel, used to come round for a while, although it didn't last long. I liked her visits. My dad was reined in by her presence and I knew it would be a peaceful night. As she left one evening, she knelt down to the floor, where I was playing with my action figures on the landing, and asked me what I was doing. She talked to me about school and I asked her about her job. Her big smile opened up, revealing a large gap in her top front teeth. Her dark skin was unblemished and she looked me right in the eye. I felt shy in her presence and nervous, like I always was when someone turned their attention to me. She was kind and tender. No screaming, no ridicule. I wanted more of that feeling. Each time she came by after, I'd take my toys and move them to the landing, where she'd have to pass on her way out.

Kate met her boyfriend while working at Pizza Hut and he visited us regularly for about a year. He was a lad from Chester and he made jokes with me when he called round to collect her for a night out. Again, his presence seemed to inhibit my dad's violent tendencies, so the tension eased, at least for a night. We played board games together and he took me to a party with some friends of his who had kids. Did he know what was happening in our house? Had Kate told him? He was always friendly with my dad, so maybe she hadn't. I wanted an older brother, someone to put an arm round me, and when they broke up my heart sank.

The girls, who were now eighteen, started to talk about leaving home, and my mum wondered if she'd ever get out. She told me once that the time might be right when I was eighteen. I nodded in agreement but a feeling I had was growing: *Perhaps we shouldn't be here at all.*

Chapter 13

I failed my eleven-plus, meaning I wouldn't be going to one of the town's two all-boy grammar schools. That test consigned those who failed to an educational dustbin. I wasn't too disappointed. Academia wasn't high on my priorities. There wasn't so much a culture of learning as a culture of surviving at Cecil Jones High School, with only 29 per cent of kids getting five GCSEs or more at the time.

I said goodbye to my friend Jignesh, who was off to one of the other comprehensives in the area. My new friendships seemed to be largely based on who I knew from my old school. We spotted familiar faces on our first day and, scared of this new place with much bigger kids, drifted over to form a huddle in the playground. Boys hung out with boys and girls with girls.

I was scared of the world, fearful of stepping into the unknown, but I arrived on my first day with a determination to get through whatever lay in store. The school was a low 1970s utilitarian building on a busy arterial road. The surrounding area was an empty stretch of brown belt. There was a private hospital, some sort of scout hut and then our school. From the front the school was in two blocks. On the left-hand side, the assembly hall, reception and head teacher's office.

Behind them, rising slightly higher, was the sports hall. On the right was the drama studio, music room and cafeteria, and behind that the science labs, common rooms and humanities classrooms.

In the centre of all this was what we called the quad, grey and concrete with tough evergreen plants under the windows of the classrooms. There were square kneecap-height slab benches, and dividing the quad was a thick wall that had some bricks missing and others protruding. The one attempt at architectural flair. Right at the back of the school was a huge field that stopped at the farmland beyond. Eventually they built a Waitrose next door. Some of the kids would go there to shoplift at the end of the day. There were about fifteen hundred students. If you wanted to be anonymous, maybe this wasn't a bad place. Most of the pupils were from the surrounding council houses, but a fair few, like me, were bussed in from further afield.

There was a hardness to some of the kids there and a few only came in a handful of times a year. One dumpy, spotty boy once brought in a crossbow, telling us that one arrow could penetrate twelve people if they lined up behind each other. I'm not sure I ever saw him again.

There were lots of suspensions, often for uniform or decorum violations. One boy was expelled for having his head shaved, which made the local paper. There were a smattering of pupils with behavioural difficulties, and there was a bit of cannabis floating about, some drinking, quite a bit of fighting, especially on the roundabout after school, and a lot of pissing about in lessons. If my friends are anything to go by, most of the kids ended up having careers in the police, nursing or as teachers. This was the end of the time when you could expect to get a decent job without necessarily going to university.

The teachers were a mixed bag. Some were disciplinarians, exploding at the smallest indiscretion, others were phlegmatic and maintained control by being well-liked. There was a shambolic chemistry teacher who had trouble getting kids to line up outside his classroom in readiness to go in. Often it would be twenty minutes into the lesson and he'd still be trying to get the kids in single file. Once inside it was basically an indoor playtime with the added danger of Bunsen burners. There was Miss Quinn who taught physics and insisted to the class that it was the sun that orbited the earth. She marked homework by wandering around the classroom at great speed, peering briefly into our notebooks to see if there was something on the page. We quickly worked out that as long as we showed her some writing, she'd give us a giant red tick.

Mr Carter was the affable German teacher with an over-sized moustache and the world-weary manner of a man who perpetually loses at the betting shop. There was a rumour that he'd once thrown a badly behaved student out of the first-floor window of his classroom. Years later I asked him if it was true. He was non-committal but said if it had happened, it was from the ground floor. Also in the language department was Mr Gharbi, a former featherweight boxer from Algeria who taught us French. He was conscientious but easily distracted. 'Who'd win in a fight between you and Frank Bruno?' we'd ask. He couldn't stop himself. His eyes would flit towards the work on the blackboard before he'd sit down on the edge of his desk and begin: 'If we disregard his obvious weight advantage, purely on boxing terms I think I would have knocked him out in round seven.' He'd then proceed to analyse his hypothetical opponent's abilities for the next hour. I still can't speak French.

I was liked by most of my fellow students. The teachers said I was quiet and it was true, I didn't talk much in class. I was shy but with my friends I'd liven up. My birthday was at the end of July, which made me one of the youngest in my year, so I was physically smaller than a lot of the other kids. The prospect of being asked questions in class, whether I knew the answer or not, would send me into spasms of fear, and if a strict male teacher shouted at the class, my legs would begin to tremble. In some classes I excelled, but only if I liked the teacher. When I had Mr Webster for geography I regularly scored highly in the tests. He gently mocked his students: 'I'm sure it impresses your parents, Liam, when you fail to listen to a word they say and flick bits of chalk across the room at home. I'm sure they are delighted with the endless possibilities for your future and the hope of what you may become, but here I'd like you to pay attention and use your hands for writing down the answers, you little git.'

Mr Ullmer was new to the school. He was pudgy, wore big silver-framed glasses and his hair was thinning. He often wore a thin black jumper stretched too tight over a white shirt. He was different to the other teachers. I remember the first time I saw him. I'd been at school for about a year when he arrived, and he caused a strong reaction when he got up to address us at assembly and explain that he was the new drama teacher. We'd never seen anyone like him before. He was confident, posh, enunciating very clearly when he spoke and using camp hand gestures to make his point.

I was dreading the thought of doing a drama class, but once I started, Mr Ullmer encouraged my attempts at performance. I was quietly chuffed. I went to see him and his office door was ajar. I tentatively knocked. He turned round in his chair and said, 'Yes, come on in, sit down.' He pointed to the lounge chair, next to his. 'What can I do for you?'

His office walls were adorned with mementos of his achievements. There were local press cuttings from previous productions at other schools, a framed photo of him graduating from Oxford. On the shelves there were brightly coloured files with laminated, printed labels saying 'drama sketches' and 'Improvisation!' There were several black, gold, red and white Venetian masks with feathers attached peering down from the walls. Stage-fighting swords, wooden muskets and dressing-up hats were jammed into boxes, and multicoloured paper, Pritt Sticks and Sellotape crammed onto the shelves.

I got straight to the point. 'I want to make a film. A jokey documentary but a bit like *The Cook Report.*' *The Cook Report* was a popular TV show where a trench-coat-wearing reporter went round doorstepping people and confronting them about their bad behaviour. It only occurs to me now what I found appealing about this show. He was calling out the ills of the world in a way I wish I could have done in my own home. 'I wondered if I could borrow the video camera?'

Ullmer pulled a pensive face for a second before breaking out into a laugh. 'Well, I'm sure you can, but do you know how to use it?'

I told him I already had a cameraman.

'Right, who's that?' he said, swapping over his crossed legs.

It was my friend Ho, whose Chinese parents owned a chip shop near where I got the bus to school. This seemed to cast some doubt on my proposal.

'I don't know him, so I'll have to meet him. I don't just lend the camera to anyone. It's very expensive.'

I reassured him that we could be trusted and asked if I could use the drama studio to film the following week.

'Yes, I can make sure I'm around to keep an eye on things.'

The following week the camera was waiting for me. I played the investigative reporter while my friends were the dodgy owners of a comically disgusting restaurant. We finished, my friends left and I stayed to pack things up. I crammed the camera and its cables into the case, closed the lid and went back to the office to drop it off.

'How did it go?' he asked.

'Very well. There's a bit more to do, though.'

'We can arrange another time.' Mr Ullmer rummaged through some papers on his desk. 'Now, some exciting news! I've found this competition for you to enter the film in.'

I scanned the form, trying to understand the rules. It hadn't occurred to me to try to win something for my work. I was pleased that he thought my idea might be good enough. I thanked him.

'You must make sure it fits the requirements. No more than ten minutes. By the way, is someone picking you up?'

I told him I planned on walking home. 'Where do you live?' Mr Ullmer asked, loosening his tie, rolling up his sleeves to reveal simian-level hairy arms and placing his hands on his hips. When I told him he replied, 'That's near me, I can give you a lift. You'll just have to wait till I finish up here.'

The walk home took about an hour, so I gratefully accepted his offer. I sat reading as he busied himself with papers and trundled back and forth from the drama studio. We were the last people to leave the school apart from the caretaker, who gave us a cheery wave as we made our way to Mr Ullmer's car. Our family hadn't had a car for a couple of years, and I got a buzz from riding in the front seat of Mr Ullmer's souped-up Vauxhall Astra. The engine had a kick and the tartan upholstery seemed quite sophisticated.

It was awkward sitting in the front seat with this adult I barely knew, but he asked me a lot of questions which filled any silence. I didn't want to tell him my dad was unemployed so I lied, saying that he worked for a radio station in Surrey. I told Mr Ullmer how he had started the *Sunday Sport*, which made him raise his eyebrows. I said I wouldn't be choosing drama GCSE when the time came but I'd been enjoying the classes.

'Why not, then?'

'I like art, so will probably do that instead.' I didn't add that in my view, like pretty much everyone else's, drama was for girls or gay people and my dad called it a Mickey Mouse subject, which was not a good thing. Mr Ullmer gave a wry smile and began making strange little thoughtful noises, variations on the 'hmmm' sound, as I spoke.

He launched into an earnest defence of drama, describing it as the very essence of life. 'It's an expressive art, Tom. It conveys so many ideas and thoughts. The author D.H. Lawrence said "all art is didactic".'

'What does that mean?' I asked.

'It teaches you something, a moral lesson.' He told me how his students' marks were the highest in the school. 'You should take GCSE drama,' he told me. 'You'd do very well. You have to ask yourself, *What are you going to get more out of?*'

Apart from winning two prizes at primary school, one for a poster about picking up litter (I drew a lot of penguins holding bits of bottles and fag packets) and the second for a story I'd written about a detective, with lots of stolen jokes like 'I slept like a log, I woke up in the fireplace', I'd never received any compliments about my work.

He drove very slowly while he spoke, giving his driving about as much attention as you might to eating a packet of crisps. I became more concerned about the queue of cars building up behind us than the conversation we were having. Several times he turned so late, without indicating, that it would cause a driver behind to beep their horn.

We got to the end of my road when he pulled the car over. 'It's just down the other end,' I said.

'Ha! You can walk the rest. Don't be idle,' he said, so I thanked him as I got out, thinking it was petty to leave me five hundred metres away from home.

He wound down the window. 'If you need to use the drama studio at lunch time tomorrow feel free,' he said. 'I can give you the keys if I'm not there, but you must keep them safe.'

In a school where a lot of the teachers had a sort of *can we really face doing this shit again?* attitude he provided a counterpoint. He announced big, ambitious school productions and persuaded the grumbling headmaster to agree to his plans.

His first production was *Oh! What a Lovely War.* They used pyrotechnics, special effects, blood capsules – and the overall impression was impressive. Mr Ullmer persuaded a number of kids who wouldn't have touched a proscenium arch with a barge pole to take part. Even my friend Kane, who would later join the military because he loved guns so much, took one of the minor roles.

The drama department was Mr Ullmer's kingdom. School rules were there to be flouted, or at least the ones that didn't matter. He would drive his car into the quad, leaving it there all afternoon, meaning students had to walk round it on their way to lessons. He interrupted other teachers' classes with noise from his own and he would ride roughshod over kids' timetables to get them to complete their dramatic endeavours. Other teachers would look peeved as he pushed past them in the dinner queue. He drank industrial levels of Diet Coke and I'd often see him walking though the cafeteria demolishing an iced bun.

He was mocked by some of the pupils for his superior voice, his expanding tummy and the frequent demands for kids to 'stop pratting around' (which was the extent of his swearing), but all of a sudden I felt I had someone who was taking me seriously in my life, looking out for me; someone prepared to help.

Chapter 14

Even when we had money, we never had money. When my dad was in work it would blow around us, like a bank vault blown up with dynamite, and the pound notes would dance tantalisingly in the air before they went the way of the wind.

My dad's default setting was to be at war. He couldn't pay a bill, even if he had cash in his pocket. His modus operandi was to try to fuck the world at every opportunity. British Gas weren't a utility to provide us with heating for an agreed sum; they were a faceless corporation who deserved to be taken advantage of. Bob Hoskins appeared in BT ads and in a gruff cockney voice would say, 'It's good to talk.' My dad agreed but thought talk wasn't just cheap, it had to be free.

I thought all letters came with a thick red line across the top and that final notices were just the start of a negotiation. I bought into his idea that these companies were cons. I admired my dad's fight against the system. The parents of other kids paid their way, but that was because they were spineless and had the hearts of cowards. They wouldn't shake their fists and rail at injustice, unlike my dad, who never stopped.

After months of non-payment, the Electricity Board insisted on installing a meter in our house. We'd take the key to the local shop and put £10 of credit on when we could afford it.

Shortly before this happened my dad told us all, 'They'll never cut it off. It's a human fucking right. It's like food or water, you have to have it.'

We hadn't paid the water bill either, so I hoped he was right. My mum told him, 'Yes, but you have to have money to get food, water and electricity or you go without.'

This was the kind of logic that really got to him. It was as if my mum was insisting that a Second World War bomber really had been found on the moon. 'No, no, no! You have to have it, you stupid cow. They can't take it away.'

The letters about non-payment of rates and arrears on the mortgage piled up on top of the fridge, wedged in between our butter dish and a pot of pens. All the time my dad demanded wine and cigarettes or complained that there wasn't enough meat in the shepherd's pie.

My mum wrote me notes to get out of PE because I didn't have any trainers. I begged her to tell them it was because of an injury. I had to quit a local football team because I couldn't afford any boots. I was disappointed to miss out, but my biggest concern was the shame. It all felt so embarrassing and I hid our situation from the world. I went to the local phone box only to find it occupied by Albert the tramp, who had fallen asleep inside. I didn't want to wake him, so I continued up the road to the next phone, where I called the coach and lied to him, saying that I wasn't interested in football anymore.

We were saved by my mum's wages and the twenty quid she got from the girls, but we always had to count out our bus fare before leaving home. My mum and I spent many cold, rain-soaked evenings waiting at depots for delayed buses, or hanging around station platforms after our train was cancelled.

Sometimes we'd get off a stop early, where we knew there were no ticket barriers. I recall the ache in my legs as we trudged along Southend High Street, past the red, white and blue stripes of C&A, loaded down with Sainsbury's carrier bags.

My dad coerced my mum into playing his cat and mouse game with creditors. She became the co-signatory on many loans, which were often secured against the house to pay off other debts. He'd harass her for days until she acquiesced. Credit cards, bank overdrafts, arrears of the mortgage and unpaid bills meant we were drowning in debt. My mum explained to me once, 'You can't borrow from Peter to pay back Paul,' and for a moment I thought to myself, *Shit, do we owe money to them as well?*

My dad seemed to glide through these economic travails with the concern someone might show over borrowing an egg from a neighbour. It's possible that he lay awake at night tormented by the net closing, but I don't think so. There was a button in his brain he could switch off, making all consequences disappear. Two smartly attired young men from First National Bank called round, inquiring about the £15,000 loan we'd stopped paying. My dad invited them in, assured and affable, pretending it was all a silly oversight. They wanted to agree a £600-a-month repayment scheme, and my dad nodded and smiled like he had the loose change in a drawer. Once they'd gone, he wrote to the bank accepting their proposal of £200 a month. He reasoned that this would cause several weeks' delay. He muddied the water like a dodgy oil refinery.

His real expertise in life was prevaricating and wearing down officials. Whether it was poll tax notices or credit card debts, he'd head out to the civic centre and find an argument for an extension or go to the library to research a legal loophole. This would allow him to find some minor fault in the behaviour of the creditor, so we could get an adjournment from a judge. Our phone was cut off but he caused such a fuss with BT that they allowed us to have incoming calls only.

My mum's job gave us a lifeline, but the doctor's surgery wasn't exactly a break from the madness of home. She discovered that Doctor McGregor had been splitting the flu vaccine in half, giving each patient half the dose they should have received. This meant he administered double the vaccinations for half the cost. She checked the bins, finding fifteen empty packets of vaccines for the thirty patients he'd seen. McGregor asked my mum to help maintain the garden out the back of the surgery, and asked his partner Doctor Patel if he could bring in his secateurs. My mum told him firmly that she had enough of her own gardening to do, but he just laughed and said, 'Then you're an expert, you can be in charge.'

Mum was confronted daily with heroin addicts, poverty and depression. She'd often see women in the waiting room with black eyes and split lips. She'd know their stories before they shared them with her, which they frequently did. A medical rep once told her how she had escaped her abusive husband the previous year. My mum revealed a little of her own situation and the woman told her, 'When you leave, which you must, you can come and stay with me for as long as you need.' There's nothing like someone else having lived the same experience to understand the help required.

Often patients would prefer to speak to my mum rather than the doctor about their ailments. A shoeless obese woman in a tight-fitting dress who was bleeding from both ears told her of her struggles with drink. She'd kicked her drugs habit but was still working as a prostitute. She had brought her little girl to the surgery, who had a cough.

Albert would turn up regularly, high on prescription drugs, drunk on vodka and looking grubby. He'd plead for some diazepam and regale her with incoherent tales while trying to tap dance and sing. He once came into the surgery carrying three roses and asked my mum for a rubber band. She found one and he struggled to put it round the stems but eventually managed. 'These are for you. I picked them from the church yard,' he told her.

We listened to my dad's half-baked fantasies about his next venture. 'This time next year we'll be millionaires,' was Del Boy's line to his dopey brother, Rodney, in the sitcom *Only Fools and Horses*, and it was a line uttered regularly by my dad, without irony, when faced with the TV conking out or the roof leaking. He'd grow furious if we didn't embrace his schemes with the same enthusiasm he did. He'd spend half our social-security money on printing or faxes or train fares to London, convinced he could buy the rights to *Doctor Who* and make a film starring Michael Caine. He planned to relaunch *Eagle* comic, raking in thousands, and he was sure that a letter he'd written to a financier would result in a £100,000 invest-ment to start a new national magazine. My mum would listen patiently for hours as he detailed his plans. The more I heard him fantasise and saw how our situation never changed, what good I did see in him chipped away. I still wanted to spend time with him – we made jokes together, he helped me with my homework – but my frustration grew.

His powers of persuasion did once get him £12,000 from a businessman to start Basildon's own morning television show on a cable network. He presented it himself and enlisted Bobby Moore to front a local sport segment. It was cheap and poor quality but lasted six months. He'd bring home video tapes of him interviewing *Hi-de-Hi!* actress Su Pollard or discussing town planning with a local councillor, and insist we made approving noises. There was something I admired about his never-say-die attitude. Oblivious to reality, he'd forge ahead, believing a pot of gold was within his grasp. He had an uncanny ability to ride out of town unscathed, leaving a trail of disasters in his wake. In a funny way he convinced me that dreams could happen, even if they usually turned into nightmares.

The violent episodes reduced in frequency but the threat was always there. As I turned fourteen I began to see that my dad wasn't quite the smooth operator he pretended to be. The lies and inconsistencies in his stories became more apparent to me and his abuse of my mum made me seethe. He had told me (perhaps for his own amusement) that Sherlock Holmes was a real historical figure and the books that lined his shelves were factual accounts of the famous detective's cases. I repeated this to my English class, and the kids all laughed. Our English teacher told me this wasn't the case but I insisted I was right. My dad was an expert on the man, and he should know. I had never held my own in such a public way before, so when my dad later told me it wasn't true I felt betrayed by him. Far more betrayed by that lie than anything else I had witnessed.

I opted for GCSE drama, making more videos under Mr Ullmer's watchful gaze. I formed a sketch group with my new best friend, Ian. He was diffident, kind and didn't walk but shuffled. He had curly hair and big eyes that widened when he made a joke. We made each other laugh with a shared wariness of the world around us and we put revues on for other students. Mr Ullmer provided the rehearsal space, props and advice. He made himself available at any time of the school day and told me I was talented and smart. He said he'd not met a student like me before, one who was so mature and funny.

He made much of having gone to Oxford University and how he had mixed with the cream of the crop. I later discovered that he'd done a teaching certificate there for a year and it wasn't an actual degree. He had lots of letters after his name, which he made sure were on all his correspondence. He was obsessed with his own status. He boasted about how he had been on television when studying in Canada and was a published author of two drama books, which turned out to be cheaply produced pamphlets containing drama exercises. He said I needed to learn to think, question and analyse, and he'd teach me to do all three. I started to construct myself, to some extent, on the ideals he aspired to.

We'd spend ages talking in his car while he gave me a lift home. We had private jokes. He once ate my pack-lunch sandwiches when I left them by mistake in his office. 'Touch my sandwiches again and I'll smash your face in,' I told him in jest, and he squawked with laughter. After that he'd always threaten to eat anything left unattended. He'd often treat himself to an iced bun from the school cafeteria. 'You should cut down on the buns,' I told him once, pointing to his large belly. He agreed that when he bought one, he'd buy me one too, so I didn't make him feel bad about it. We shook on it. He would let me in on staff-room gossip, telling me who his subordinate in the drama department was dating. 'What's Miss Durham's first name?' I'd ask, for no reason other than it gave me some sort of power to know the teachers' names.

I'd started to get interested in politics. I'd watched a tearful Margaret Thatcher be shunted out of Downing Street and the political drama gripped me. I was able to follow the news because my dad always found the 30p necessary to buy the *Daily Express*. Once I scrawled on the back of my maths text-book who I thought should be in the new cabinet. 'Who do you vote for?' I asked Mr Ullmer.

'Well, that's a very private question,' he said. 'It's an anonymous poll for a reason.' It wasn't long, though, before he started revealing lots of private information to me.

He'd park down the road from my house where we'd talk about my future plans, politics and religion. I told him my parents fought and my dad was difficult, although I left the details out. He'd refer to the strong friendship we were building and say it had taken him by surprise. He told me he held me in the same regard as his other, older, established friends. I felt valued and humbled that this educated adult invested so much time in me.

Other teachers might not understand our unique, close friendship, he explained, so even though he wanted to spend more time with me outside of school, we'd have to wait until I was sixteen. I should stay on at school and take performing arts A level, he said. He offered to help me with the other

A levels I would take, saying he knew the teaching wasn't always of the highest standard, but he'd make sure I got the support I needed.

I had someone fighting my corner and it made me feel secure. Sometimes I'd hear other students remark, 'You're his favourite,' or, 'Ullmer loves you,' but I didn't care. When they were standing in the quad getting wet at break, I was sitting with my feet up in his office eating my packed lunch.

Chapter 15

1969, Essex

The doctor had agreed to call round to my mum and dad's council flat in Hutton to deliver the news. A tinny version of 'Honky Tonk Women' by the Rolling Stones played out from the radio perched on the windowsill in the hallway.

My mum, who was seven months pregnant, opened the door to the neat-looking medical man who exclaimed excitedly, 'Have I got some news for you!'

When my mum found out she was pregnant, she and my dad had married hastily. He was twenty-three and she was twenty-one. It was just the done thing. At this stage my dad had never hit my mum, but he was frequently rude, demanding and dismissive.

'What?' asked my mum, not in any mood for games.

'It's not twins,' the doctor said, fixing her with a firm gaze.

A couple of weeks before, she was sure she had felt simultaneous kicks on either side of her tummy. She was getting bigger at an alarming rate and was seriously worried that she might explode. She'd gone to the doctor who'd told her, 'In all my years of professional practice, Mrs Mitchelson, I've never had a patient blow up.'

He added that it was very unlikely to be twins, offering the possibility that 'you probably got your dates wrong, dear' as a way of accounting for her size. Upon her insistence he gave her an X-ray and told her he'd call round with the results on his way home from work. Now he was standing in front of her, smiling.

'What is it, then?' my mum asked.

'Triplets,' he beamed and opened his hands in a ta-da! gesture. His smile evaporated when he saw my mum turn deathly pale.

'Three?'

'Triplets,' he repeated, having another go at a smile.

My dad was in bed after a night shift, so my mum left the doctor at the door and ran into the bedroom. 'I'm going to have triplets.'

My dad, drowsy from being woken, replied blankly, 'Triplets, that's good,' and pulled the blankets over his head.

She turned round to find that the doctor had entered the flat and was now hovering around the bedroom door. 'It's triplets,' my mum said to no one in particular. The doctor nodded his head enthusiastically and rummaged around in his leather holdall, eventually producing the X-ray, which he held up to the light. Her size, the back ache, the discomfort, the constant trips to the toilet, everything fell into place. Her baby didn't have three legs; she had three babies growing inside her.

'My guess is two boys and a girl,' said the doctor. My mum ignored him, still grappling with the prospect of a ready-made multiple-child family and all that would entail. 'Well, congratulations, anyway,' he said with a hint of disappointment that his surprising news hadn't been more gleefully received.

He left the X-ray on a table before sticking his head round the bedroom door again, where my dad was sitting up, staring at the ceiling with his mouth open. 'Poor man!' the doctor said as he saw himself out.

The next day, with a premature birth inevitable, my mum checked into hospital. After a couple of uncomfortable nights lying awake, the pain became unbearable. My mum called a nurse. The sister, who happened to be a nun, arrived, took one look at her, called for a trolley and told my mum in an authoritative manner, 'The babies will be here within the hour.'

They wheeled her into the delivery room, which immediately filled with doctors and students. The sister asked rhetorically, 'It is all right if people watch, isn't it? Good for the education. We've not had a triplet birth here in years.' My mum wasn't enamoured with the idea of scores of people lining up to watch this intimate moment in her life, but she was past caring.

My mum yelled out, 'Bloody hell!' as another excruciating contraction occurred, then she apologised to the sister, remembering that it was a sin to swear in front of nuns.

'I'll get you something for the pain,' the sister said, and returned a short while later with two paracetamol. Disappointed, my mum necked the pills and began to push. At 10.25 a.m. my mum heard the sister pronounce, 'It's a girl,' and handed her a tiny baby, whom she cradled to her chest. She knew her name. 'Emma Louise,' she said softly to her first child. There was no time for sentimentality, as my mum had to start pushing straight away. Emma was taken from my mum's arms and whizzed off to an incubator. Thirty minutes later Kate Elizabeth arrived. My mum's warm glow of motherhood was broken as she heard the sister shout, 'And another!' and she got back to pushing. She'd almost forgotten there was another one to come. Within sixty seconds the sister exclaimed 'It's a girl. Three girls!' Victoria Jane was handed to my mum for a brief cuddle before she was taken, along with Kate, out of the ward.

And with that the show was over. The onlookers left and within seconds it was just my mum alone, without an audience or her babies. My dad, who had arrived just before the birth but stayed outside, came in to see my mum. They didn't say much but just grinned at each other in shock, the enormous responsibility that had been delivered sinking in.

In the evening, once she'd been stitched up, she hobbled along to the premature baby unit. Pressed up against the viewing glass, she took a good look at her new family. She thought they looked like three little dolls. Lovely long, firm legs, no wrinkles or marks. She longed to hold them.

'One in a million,' a passing doctor, who had heard about the multiple birth, said.

'Excuse me?'

'The triplets. They are identical. It's a one in a million chance.'

It hadn't occurred to my mum that they'd look the same. This meant the same fertilised egg had split once and then again, whereas multiple births usually result from separate eggs.

As she made her way back to her bed, she passed all the other mothers in the unit and for a few minutes felt rather superior. She'd managed to push out three whole babies, not just one mite. Over the next few days telegrams, letters and cards arrived, and she had a request played for her on the Jimmy Young radio show. A man from the *Evening Standard* arrived and took their photo, and in the article my dad is quoted as saying, 'I had wanted a boy, but three little girls will do just fine.'

My mum was sent home after ten days, but the babies remained in hospital. Every day she travelled up on the bus to wash and feed them, holding their fragile bodies as she pinned their nappies together with her one hand. It was Victoria who first accompanied my mum home, having reached two kilograms, the weight designated as safe. Kate came the next day and Emma was allowed home three days after that. They each wore little name tags on their wrists, which was the only way of telling them apart, aside from the differing-sized belly buttons. My mum soon began to differentiate them by the way they smiled or the sound of their gurgles.

Once my mum had her brood at home, she set about a creating a routine. Cow & Gate, the formula-milk company, wrote to my mum, offering free baby food for the first few months. My dad's reluctance to pay the bills meant creditors were already knocking at the door, so it was a welcome financial boost.

An administrative error meant that Heinz sent three large teddy bears the week of the birth, and then a further three bears the week after, and another three arrived seven days after that. My mum wrote a letter to the company saying please stop sending bears. They replied enclosing the postage for six bears to be sent back.

Friends knitted jumpers and gave babygrows, and she was delighted to receive a £66 maintenance grant, which she used to buy a reconditioned washing machine to launder the hundreds of nappies. Soon the girls were sleeping through the night, comforted by one another and falling asleep altogether in a big cot. One morning my mum forgot to put the water outlet from the washing machine into the sink and it flooded the flat, water seeping through the ceiling of the flat downstairs. That night she listened to the care-free neighbours party until 4 a.m., blaring out Pink Floyd in between complaining about her.

Leaving the flat after sterilising the bottles, preparing the day's food, doing the housework and then washing, feeding and dressing the girls took a long time. The flat was on the second floor so my mum would walk down the concrete stairwell cradling one baby at a time. She'd put the first one in the pram and then return for the others. The pram in question was for twins, and she would push it with her one hand and rely on the kindness of strangers to help her get on and off buses. That wasn't the only problem that going outside presented. There was so much interest in the girls that she would be stopped at least ten times on each trip by curious passers-by asking what their names were, or how on earth she managed.

Once home she would put them in the bouncing cradles, prepare dinner, feed them and get them to bed. She'd watch the black and white TV until my dad came home, although more often than not she'd go to bed alone.

Don't Ask Me About My Dad

As soon as my parents knew they were having triplets they had put their names down for a bigger council flat. After seven months they were given a ground floor, two-bedroom property. The buildings were three storeys high with concrete steps and parked prams inside the lobby. They were perpetually full of children playing games and bouncing on space hoppers on the grass outside.

By now the girls were eating solid food, and my mum would line them up in a row to feed them cereal, taking it in turns to give them a spoonful. When she gave them the bottle, she would feed one, propping the other two babies up against pillows. She could then lean over and burp the ones not feeding when required. She'd make sure to cuddle each of them separately, so no one got left out. They grew healthily and happily and were charming toddlers whom she'd often hear giggling in the bedroom together. My mum would go in to find all the sheets from the beds stripped, the windows wide open and pillowcases tossed onto the muddy grass outside.

My dad was doing shifts for Associated Press and should have been home at 11 p.m., but frequently wouldn't return till 3 a.m. My mum would ask where he'd been but he'd snarl back and fall into bed. She told herself he was struggling with the responsibility of parenthood. He was only twenty-five and had been landed with a ready-made family. He refused to do anything around the house, although a couple of times he gave the girls their bottle before leaving for work. My mum's concept of marriage was like a lot of people's in the late sixties: the man earns the money and the woman looks after the kids. But she still found his uninterest harsh.

As she lay in bed one night waiting for him to return, she was startled by a loud knock on the door. Two bobbies greeted her with the news that my dad was in hospital after falling from a moving train carriage. They offered no other information, and once my bruised dad came home he added nothing further.

She discovered letters stuffed into drawers from the bank, saying he was overdrawn. The household bills didn't get paid, but if she asked about it he'd snap and say he'd take care of it. Clipboard-carrying men in Marks and Spencer suits would peer through the windows or bang on the door, asking for payment or threatening to cut off the utilities. My mum got used to appeasing them with small amounts from the family allowance or the housekeeping money my dad gave her.

My dad's mother obsessively called round unannounced. She'd come laden with gifts. My mum told my dad it was getting too much.

'Well, tell her to fuck off, then,' he suggested. 'I don't like either of them. I certainly don't want them to visit. My father showed no interest in me at all, and my mother threatened to kill herself. What sort of person does that in front of a six-year-old boy?' His hatred of them never stopped him asking them to bail him out just before the gas was cut off.

The next time his mum called by, my mum, desperate for some time alone and with the girls asleep, didn't answer the door and instead lay silently on the lounge floor until her unwanted visitor departed.

My dad kept increasingly irregular hours but insisted that my mum had dinner ready. She'd keep it hot in the oven and when he arrived in the early hours, would take it out for him.

'I don't want dinner now, you silly cow,' he'd say, but if she didn't have it ready he'd scream at her for not caring.

Shirts were ironed, food was cooked, beds were made. The girls were just something he lived with. It became clear to my mum that she had made a mistake of the largest proportions, but her days were so full it was hard to know what to do.

Marriage was forever and single mums were bad. Disapproving glances carried weight and the judgement of others won out. What would she be swapping this life for? Maybe he'd change. Perhaps he was stressed or overwhelmed. Besides, she reasoned, most of the time it was just the four of them.

In the mid-1970s my parents moved to the small semi-detached house near Colchester where I was to be born. I wasn't planned. In the late autumn of 1976, at the age of twenty-nine, my mum missed her period. Seven years on from the birth of the girls, the last thing she wanted was more responsibility. My dad was horrified, insisting that she went to see the doctor to get some pills to prevent my arrival. The morning-after pill was a few years from being developed, but she made an appointment regardless. The doctor took a deep breath. 'There are no magic drugs for your predicament. I'm surprised you think there are. You can probably get an abortion on the National Health,' he informed her, and added, 'as long as you are sterilised at the same time.'

My mum couldn't go through with it and, as my dad refused to discuss the situation, like a lot of things in his life, it went unacknowledged. She'd managed to raise the girls without his help, so she could do it again.

It wasn't until a few months had gone by that my dad, after drinking a litre of wine, exploded: 'I don't want any more fucking kids. It will be an unwanted child. Do you get it? I will have nothing to do with it. Do not expect anything from me, you fucking stupid bitch.'

My mum told him that I was coming regardless. He slurred his words, his eyes boring into her. He pounded his fists on the dining-room table, and my mum threw a glass of water over him. He lurched into action, charging at his pregnant wife and striking her twice around the head before overturning the dining-room table. It was the first time he ever hit her. I read about this attack recently in my mum's diaries and, while not much can shock me when it comes to my dad, the thought of him hitting her while she was pregnant felt like an attack on me too.

My mum was relieved the girls hadn't woken to question the noise and the wrecked front room. She hadn't told them the news but soon she would be unable to hide it. They were thrilled when she eventually told them and, perhaps aware of my dad's indifference, took care of my mum the best they were able to. Unlike her uncomfortable first pregnancy, she began to welcome the changes in her body. Her friends told her she looked great: shiny and rosy-cheeked. She felt like a giant mother cat who could purr with satisfaction.

There was a month to go when my dad mentioned my arrival again. But this time he had softened. He took the girls to school and did the washing-up. A few days before, the doctor had confirmed that I was only one baby, not three, so maybe some of the pressure lifted.

If I had been an easier pregnancy, I was a harder birth. My mum experienced excruciating contractions, the agony of which was partially alleviated this time with pethidine. The cord was wrapped round my neck, meaning there were moments when I might have been strangled before I popped out. Unlike when my sisters were born, my dad was in the room for my birth and was delighted that I was a boy, if somewhat underwhelmed by my looks. He told my mum I looked like a squashed lemon. I had a big nose and a flattened chin. The consensus was that there were prettier babies.

The girls were delighted, taking it in turns to cuddle me, and my mum spent hours looking at me. I slept a lot and the doctor said I was 'a perfect specimen'. Once my chin developed people even said I was cute. Before I was taken home, my dad cleaned the house and put the girls in nice dresses. Three months in we had a family holiday in Wales, where I laughed for the first time, when Emma blew her fringe up over her forehead.

My dad took an interest in me that had been absent with the girls. He changed my nappy, held me and took me for walks in my pram. He was acting like a father.

Chapter 16

Just as the forest comes to life at night with animals embold-
ened by darkness, our house was most alive in the early hours.
I was now fifteen and my dad's booming voice would wake
me, shattering the sleepy silence in a second. These days the
arguments were often about my sisters. The night before my
geography exam I heard footsteps hammering around in
my parents' bedroom. I got up and listened at my door. 'It's
disgusting behaviour. I will not accept it. Emma is a selfish
bitch,' my dad wailed.

Victoria had been the first to leave home, working double
shifts in a restaurant and buying her own flat, and Kate had
eventually made her own way out too, hooking up with a former
bouncer who ran a video shop, but Emma still lived with us.

My mum shouted back, 'Maybe it's because she has
witnessed your behaviour all her life.' My heart banged against
my chest. What was she thinking, throwing wood on the fire?
We'd always lived with our heads down, placating, constrain-
ing any instinct to challenge him.

'What are you saying, you poisonous bitch?' he shrieked.
'Don't you dare lay this at my door, you ugly, fat cow. You
should be ashamed of the way your daughters behave. That

fucking refuge ruined them. To think you tried to get *me* thrown out of my own home.'

My mum hit back again. Her voice clearer, stronger than usual. 'Yes. Yes, I did. And why do you think that was, you stupid bastard? You attacked me and raped me.' It was as if my mum had taken a truth serum.

Recently, I'd noticed that my dad would be disconcerted when confronted. I stepped back into my room as he emerged from theirs. He made his way along the hall, pulling his dressing gown to his body and yanking the cord around his waist.

My mum continued: 'You have no insight into what you've done. Why don't you take responsibility?'

He moved faster, running from the truth like a frightened deer. The verbal onslaught continued. 'I'm no longer prepared to keep quiet. I don't want to live like this,' my mum hollered from the bedroom. I hovered around for ten minutes before experience told me that the night's events were probably over and I could return to bed.

Late at night, my mum and I would spend ages discussing in hushed tones the crazy things he had said or done. I encouraged my mum to leave him. I had few answers to the practical difficulties we would face but I knew they had no future together. I no longer viewed him as the Big Man. I could see him for the fool he was. I was embarrassed by not having a car, not being able to make phone calls and not having a holiday. I'd begun to wonder why we didn't do the normal things that other families did. I was fed up of having to make up lies to see my grandparents. Where were our family friends? I wanted my dad to be able to buy me things like trainers and an electric guitar. I wanted our house not to be falling apart. I was envious of some of my friends, who had kitchens with sleek appliances and didn't get stuff from charity shops.

Mr Ullmer seemed to know how the world worked so maybe my dad didn't have a monopoly on that knowledge. I can't remember now what the argument was about, but one afternoon my dad said something unfair to me before storming off to his office. A bolt inside me wriggled loose and the nut fell off. I charged down the corridor after him, stood in the doorway and watched as he lit a cigarette, surrounded by all the old boxes filled with files from the various jobs he'd lost.

I shouted at him the same word I'd heard him use over and over again since I was five years old. Now I was fifteen and it seemed about time.

'You're a cunt. You're such a cunt.' I spat the words out and stood there waiting for his reaction. He stood up, open-mouthed in disbelief.

'I've never let anyone speak to me like that,' he said, and sat back down to contemplate his next move. I didn't hang around, heading off down the hall, half-expecting him to chase me. He didn't.

Later that evening he came downstairs, my insult obviously still bothering him. Looking indignant, he addressed my mum: 'Thomas was incredibly rude today. Did you hear what he said? He called me a cunt.'

The word filled the air with expectation. I was sure my mum would have hated me using the word, but she showed no emotion. 'Oh,' she replied.

'That's it, is it?' He stood there for a moment, bewildered by her apathy. Sensing he'd find no sympathy, he turned away sharply. Once I'd heard the door to his room slam shut, I felt the need to explain.

'Well, he is,' I told my mum.

'I know,' she sighed.

My dad was home all the time, so we inevitably spent more time together. He helped me with my maths homework and encouraged me as I tried to learn guitar. He introduced me to his favourite songs, such as Johnny Cash's 'Ring of Fire' and 'Folsom Prison Blues', from which the lyric 'I shot a man in Reno just to watch him die' would make him laugh out loud each time. I learned to play them with him singing along. He'd tell me stories of bar-room brawls and bravado. He once battered two men in a car park using the element of surprise, a kick to the groin and a well-timed punch to the bridge of the nose. He told me about how he had fought off three attackers with a broken milk bottle, which left a puddle of blood, milk and glass in the street. No one was around to challenge his world view. I lapped up these stories believing he'd delivered just deserts.

We owed more than £90,000 overall, and with my dad running out of tricks, a final eviction notice was served and we knew it was a matter of weeks before we'd lose our house. My mum had told my dad that she was going to Cornwall with her friend Jan for a week. It would be the first holiday she'd had in years and it became a running source of tension. The night before my final GSCE exam, I heard them arguing in their bedroom. I crept along the hallway to listen outside.

'We can't afford your stupid holiday,' my dad said.

'I'm using the money my dad and sister sent me,' my mum told him.

'You are not going.'

'I am.'

I stood there silently, my muscles twitching. How dare he forbid her from going away. Who did he think he was?

'Over my dead body,' he said. I heard a slap followed by my mum screaming. I turned the handle and stepped inside. He was sitting up in bed, leaning over my mum. He had grabbed her wrist and was twisting it. She continued to scream.

'Let her go,' I told him. To my surprise he did. My mum sprung back up and hit him in the face. My stomach did a somersault.

'I'm going to fucking kill you,' he blurted out, swinging his hand at her head. 'I will break your back, you bitch.' He leapt at her.

Without realising, I had been waiting for this moment. Waiting for years to grow big enough to defend her. At fifteen I was small and skinny, but I launched myself at him, securing my arm around his neck and pulling him into a headlock. I felt his hands pulling at my arm, so I squeezed harder. 'You little bastard,' he cried as he flailed around.

I began to pull him off the bed, but his legs gripped around my mum's head. Somehow, years of being ready for anything, observing his every step, allowed me to anticipate his movements. I ducked away from his punches and squeezed harder. With my free hand I began to pull at his leg and leaned back with all my body weight so his grasp on my mum weakened. She wriggled free. My dad and I fell from the bed with me still holding onto him.

My mum stood up, her nightgown ripped.

'Get out,' I said. I wanted her away from him. She stood there, frozen to the spot. Her face white. She was worried about what would happen next. 'Leave,' I said again. I knew he couldn't break free. 'I'll be fine.' I adjusted my hold.

'Bastard,' he blurted out. His face was puce with either anger or lack of oxygen.

My mum ran. I heard the front door shut, leaving me and him tangled on the floor. I'd have to let him go at some point. And then what? He was calling me a traitor. I changed tack, loosened my grip slightly and pretended to cry. He placed a conciliatory arm on my shoulder, patting me gently. When I was sure my mum would be far enough away I released him.

He dragged himself to his feet, grabbed his dressing gown, which was draped over a chair, and stormed downstairs. I wandered out of the bedroom and met Emma on the landing. She showed me a bread knife hidden under her jacket and shared with me her plan to kill him. Emma, my dad and I milled around the house until my mum returned an hour or so later. I quietly told her of Emma's plan and she set about persuading her to put the knife back in the kitchen drawer. The four of us sat at the kitchen table. I told my dad that my mum should go to Cornwall. He looked at her, his eyes pulsating, and said, 'You caused these scenes when the girls did their exams and now you're doing the same with Tom.'

I'd forgotten I had an exam in the morning but such things didn't seem to matter. He looked lost. It was as if the chaos he wrought was no longer making sense to him. He changed the subject from the holiday, telling us that when she got back we'd start looking for another house to live in. This was met with silence, the lunacy of the idea suddenly tangible. Another family home, a fresh start, all of it was impossible. This was our opportunity to escape.

The next day my mum left for Cornwall. I walked out with her onto the street. Her body was badly bruised. When I hugged her she winced. I saw my dad watching us from the bedroom window, scowling.

The fight the night before had unnerved my dad. He knew that any more violence from now on would involve me and my mum. We had no plan, no money, but we were going to leave. The eviction date had given us something to aim for. We had made our choice.

When my mum returned we began to explore what a new life would look like. We called in at the refuge, discovering that, due to the complicated benefits system, we would qualify for housing benefit and social security, providing my mum worked fewer hours at the doctor's surgery. We would need to find a month's deposit for a flat. My mum began to tell friends she was leaving and found a wealth of encouragement. My grandad gave us the deposit.

My mum raised the possibility with my dad that they should split up. He scoffed at her idea as impractical. Later, my mum received a phone call from her friend Jan and was talking to her when my dad came into the kitchen. He started banging the cupboard doors and stage whispered, 'Bloody trouble-making dyke.' My mum replaced the receiver, telling him that the impending eviction would be a good time to go their separate ways.

'If you ever take Tom away from me, I will kill you. I mean it. I will kill you,' he told her.

'Your threats don't bother me,' my mum told him, while shaking.

'I'll bloody your nose for you, you silly cow.'

This was my mum's last attempt at reasoning. She opened her own bank account, giving her parents' address, and then, like the prisoners from *The Great Escape* secretly getting rid of dirt from the tunnel they were digging, we began removing my mum's possessions from the house, storing them with her friends.

The day after my sixteenth birthday she would leave the house and stay with Jan until we found a place to live. In the meantime I would remain with my dad. That was my choice. I didn't want him to be alone. If I didn't show care for him then what would he have? He didn't have friends like normal people. I had to be there to manage his reaction, to make sure he didn't go after my mum. I didn't want him to think I didn't love him.

Despite everything I had seen, that's how I felt. I owed him. I don't even know if it was love. Our blood ties held us together and I wanted my dad. I took all I could that was good and didn't know you could break away, or what that would feel like. If I never saw him again I would miss the parts of him that I needed, but I wouldn't miss the pain.

After a trip with my parents to the cinema to see *Jurassic Park*, my mum went to the supermarket, spending £50 on provisions for my dad. We had no doubt about the course of action, but we didn't know when we would be living together. My mum told me her mother had appeared to her the night before in a dream, sitting at the end of her bed. She'd asked if it was really her and my grandmother smiled a warm, rosy smile before disappearing. The night-time apparition convinced my mum that her mother was sending her strength to go through with the plan.

The following morning my mum wrote a letter to my dad telling him the marriage was over, which she planned to post later that day. She left a £10 note on top of the fridge and told him she'd be staying over at her dad's.

It was as if I had done my part. My mum was going to escape, and although the future was uncertain, she would be better off than ever before, away from my dad. The unknown was frightening but the relief poured out as I realised a chain had been broken. I hugged her goodbye as she went to work. She told Theresa, the girl who worked in the chemist, she had left, and Theresa threw her arms around my mum. Despite having no money herself, she gave my mum £10 to put towards her new life. At the end of the day, Doctor Patel handed my mum £30 and Jan picked her up in her car, taking her to her home in Maldon.

That night my mum and Jan sat in the garden with the tape deck playing a mixtape. Slowly over the course of the evening, aided by glasses of wine, the cool summer air and the breeze rustling through the trees, relief overwhelmed her. She felt elated. Jimmy Cliff started singing and she looked up to the early evening sky, taking in his lyrics.

> *I can see clearly now the rain has gone. I can see all obstacles in my way.*
> *Gone are the dark clouds that had me blind. It's going to be a bright, bright sunshiny day.*

Don't Ask Me About My Dad

I'd only seen my dad cry once. It was in 1986 while watching Ronald Reagan address the American public after the *Challenger* space shuttle disaster, where the seven-strong crew were killed when the shuttle exploded just over a minute after take-off. Reagan delivered the lines like the actor he was, for maximum impact:

> The future doesn't belong to the fainthearted. It belongs to the brave ... Nothing ends here. Our hopes and our journeys continue ... the crew of the space shuttle *Challenger* honored us by the manner in which they lived their lives. We will never forget them nor the last time we saw them, this morning as they prepared for their journey and waved goodbye and "slipped the surly bonds of earth" to "touch the face of God."

I wondered how a man so cruel could be moved at all. Maybe it was the talk of the pioneering spirit. The exploits of those astronauts touched him the same way Western movies did, in which the protagonists braved new frontiers. He saw himself as being cut from the same cloth as the astronauts. His entrepreneurial adventures always ended up the same: a disaster.

This was another ending. I knew the letter was going to drop through the letterbox that morning so I stayed in my room until I could be sure he had read it. When I went down my dad was sitting quietly in the armchair.

'You mother has left,' was the first thing he said.

'I know.'

'Oh, you knew about it, did you?' he said, stung by my secrecy.

I nodded.

'The last two years have been very stressful, they would be for anyone. Losing the house is hard. I can understand your mum's disappointment.'

Did he really believe what he was saying? Did he think their relationship was ending because the house was being repossessed? He took no responsibility for what he had done, so he looked elsewhere. A solitary tear rolled down his cheek. I felt no sympathy. How could I understand a man who cried over losing a person he seemed to despise? But I was unable to separate myself from him. When he hit my mum I turned to him for comfort. I was part of him, and he was part of me. Invisible bonds held me to him everywhere I turned, like being caught in a spiderweb. To hate him, and only hate him, would be to hate myself. I protected him – us.

Each day my mum and I would meet and view properties. She wanted out of Southend. The prospect of bumping into my dad in the supermarket held no appeal. The fresh start needed new surroundings and we figured that, while he might walk twenty minutes to harass her, twenty minutes and a bus ride might well put him off.

The homes we saw were grotty, musty smelling and unfurnished. We were dispirited by the small flats above takeaway shops with ripped net curtains and damp walls, then we came across a little house on an estate twenty miles from Southend. The owner welcomed us in, showing us the newly fitted kitchen, a nice, plush pink carpet and a living room with long blue-and-rose-coloured curtains with giraffes, fishes and birds in the pattern. They were nicer than they sound. A full-length window looked onto a peaceful garden.

The owner told us how his last tenants had trashed the place and he was looking for people to treat the house with respect. My mum gushed, telling him what a beautiful home he had, promising to cherish the property. She'd been worried about telling him we were on housing benefit, fearing he'd think badly of us, but he gave a generous smile and said it was better for him because at least he'd know the rent would be paid. He warned us that he had more people to show the house to, and we left feeling that we'd had a glimpse of a different life but that it would likely disappear.

Jan suggested to my mum that she meet with a friend of hers, an ex-bouncer. He had apparently offered to warn my dad off us. My mum and I discussed the prospect. The ex-bouncer had said he'd threaten to break his legs, but honour dictated he'd have to do it if my dad defied him. After mulling it over we both agreed that a criminal path might lead to more trouble than it promised to solve. Later, my mum received a call telling us the house was ours and very suddenly our future looked brighter.

I kept all this secret from my dad. He settled seamlessly into a life without his wife. The house was now only a few weeks away from repossession, yet he carried on watching television and reading the paper. He made dinner for us both each night, which we'd eat while watching a *Mike Tyson, Baddest Man on the Planet* VHS tape. My dad would explain how Tyson managed to annihilate his opponents so quickly but compared him unfavourably with Muhammad Ali. At least with boxing the violence was contained to the ring. The Marquess of Queensberry rules, the weight divisions, the gloves and a referee made me wish all violence could be managed and controlled.

After a few days he announced that he was going out to win my mum back. I knew this wouldn't involve flowers and a serenade, so as he left the house I ran to the phone box, put 10p in the slot and called my mum at work to warn her. I followed him from a discreet distance, watching as he entered the building. I found out later from my mum that he burst in, insisting in front of the waiting patients that she return home. She told him again that the relationship was over. Doctor Patel came out from his consultation and told my dad this wasn't the time or the place. When it became apparent this didn't bother my dad in the least, he closed up the surgery, ushering the patients out of the door.

From my vantage point I saw a small group of infirm-looking people shuffle out of the surgery. Doctor Patel opened the door to his Ford Sierra and my mum and Theresa, who had been delivering prescriptions, got in. My dad stormed out from the surgery and stood behind the car, preventing their escape. Doctor Patel remonstrated with my dad across the bonnet of the car before going back into the surgery, saying he was going to call the police.

My dad seized this opportunity to berate the women in the car. He started screaming at Theresa, who was sitting in the back, calling her a 'tarty, bleached blonde dyke'. He thumped the roof of the car with his fist, screaming at my mum, 'We need to talk – your family is falling apart.'

He circled the Sierra like a lion at a safari park. 'How can you put this burden on your son?' he asked.

Doctor Patel returned, announcing that the police were on their way. My dad, realising his time was up, hurled abuse at him, kicked the car and walked away abruptly. I hid behind a tree as he passed.

The police were there in seconds. I walked hesitantly towards the car, where my mum and Theresa were talking with them. Theresa was shaking and her face was pale. 'My God. He is a madman,' she told the police.

A few days later I told my dad that my mum would be collecting her belongings from the house. 'Sure thing,' he said with a shrug of his shoulders, but I had learned that nothing was ever that simple.

My mum arranged a van and came with Jan who, fearing what lay in wait, had brought with her three male friends, who were hovering around the vehicle. I had been watching out for them and went to meet them on the street. My dad appeared at our front door, clutching an iron bar and menacingly hitting one end of it into the palm of his hand.

'No one is entering my property,' he announced. The men shuffled their feet, considering what they had got themselves into.

'Your gorillas can fuck off,' he told my mum. The stand-off went on for a few minutes. I tried to reason with my dad. 'Can you let them come in because some of the furniture is heavy.' He stared through me. Eventually someone must have called the police because the flashing lights of a panda car soon appeared.

A young police officer with a phlegmatic manner and an ironic eyebrow surveyed the scene. These were the moments my dad lived for. In his eyes he was standing his ground, against the odds, fighting for justice. He was Gary Cooper in *High Noon* fighting the bad guys, although the dialogue was mostly effing and blinding at the would-be moving crew.

The copper instructed him politely, 'Please lower the iron bar, sir.' He then turned to my mum and asked ironically, 'So, why are you leaving him?'

The young cop explained that there was nothing he could do about my dad holding a weapon on his own property. Emma was crying and sitting on the garden wall, so I suggested I go in and bring stuff out. My dad nodded and, not wanting him to give it a second thought, I darted into the house to begin the moving job.

'You're a bunch of scum,' he told everyone.

I made several journeys back and forth, carrying what I could. I saw that my dad had gone over to Emma, draping his arm across her shoulder, talking calmly, intently to her. It was all a charade. The policeman asked my mum for my dad's first name. 'I refuse to keep calling him sir,' he said.

Eventually the job was done. My mum was driven off, the policemen got back in their car, and my dad and I headed back into what used to be our family home.

Chapter 17

2018, London

My heart beats slowly. If I am lying down and doing nothing, it settles at a steady pace of about forty-eight thumps every sixty seconds. Now, I'm sitting on a metal bench by a sleek glass lift in a very busy St Pancras station, spooning yoghurt and granola into my mouth. I don't measure it, but if I had to guess, I'd say my heart rate is around fifty-five beats per minute. The only real difference from normal is that I can *hear* it, as if it's the bass drum in an orchestra.

I'm not hungry but I haven't eaten for hours and I know I need the energy, so I finish the food, place the tub in a bin and check my watch. It's 5.15 p.m., quarter of an hour to go before I meet him. My friend Pete had suggested coming with me and observing from a distance, in case he was needed, but I'd said no. Part of me would have liked the comfort but this is something I have to do alone. I get in the lift. It's one where the doors are in no hurry to close, so people keep pressing the button over and over again. An old man in a suit, who has been driven half-mad by the twenty-second wait, stares at me and spits out, 'Modern technology!' I guess he's referring to the design because lifts must have been around a long time before he was born. The doors shut and we're transported smoothly to the next floor.

'Finally!' he says with a shake of the head and rushes out. I enter the Booking Office, the bar on the site of the railway station's old ticket office. I'd felt that what I was about to do deserved some sort of grand location, and with the giant cathedral-like ceiling, intricate Victorian brickwork and elongated bar, St Pancras fitted the bill. The size of the building and resulting space between the tables would mean any conversation could be relatively private.

I sit in one of the big leather armchairs and order fizzy water. I'd like a beer but I don't want to numb my senses. Other customers' voices echo around the big hall but still I can hear, *Lub-DUB*, *lub-DUB*, as the valves of my heart do their job. I'm not dreading what I'm about to do, nor am I looking forward to it. Given the chance I'd rather be somewhere else, but I don't have that choice. I have never been surer of anything: I have to deal with this face to face.

I had tried the police; that wasn't going to work, so it was down to me. The experience I went through had defined me, shaped me in ways that I was still trying to make sense of. This meeting was a big deal. It was twenty-seven years overdue. I had to keep a cool head.

I had played out this scene in my mind: once I'd said my piece I would stand up and lean over the table menacingly. 'One more thing,' I'd whisper, then I'd swing back my fist and bring it crashing down on the bridge of his nose. Nothing more. I'd stop at that point. I wouldn't pull him from his seat and fill him in with the steel-capped boots I'd purposefully worn. I'd just leave him, bloodied, clasping his nose and sobbing like the coward he was.

I had to be cleverer than that, but I wasn't sure how I'd react to what he said. I knew there was a rage inside me that would flare up at the slightest provocation. I was scared of that. I had led him to believe that this was going to be a catch-up, an amiable drink. He had the impression we were friends. I wanted him to know I saw things very differently now. The smartest thing would be to continue to lull him into a false sense of security and approach the subject like I was reminiscing fondly, but that was beyond me. I didn't want to be here any longer than I had to be.

At 5.43 he walks into the bar and looks around. My heart thumps louder as the valves open and close a little harder. I reckon it's up to about seventy beats a minute. I watch him for a few seconds. He imperiously ignores the maitre d' and she follows in his wake, asking if she can help him. He's hugely fat and there are beads of sweat all over his face, causing his wired spectacles to slip down his nose. He pushes them back.

'I'm here,' I say loudly and firmly. This causes him to turn around, and he breaks into a thin-lipped smile and begins to chortle. This strange unprovoked laughter is his most recognisable habit. It's been five years since I've seen him, at a party to celebrate his MBE for services to education, and he's now in his late fifties and the hair has all but gone from the top of his head; just a few over-long wispy curls remain. For a split second he looks unsure when I don't get up or offer him my hand, but he takes the seat opposite and the chortling continues. I'm not sure what he's saying, something about his teenage son.

151

'Yeah, how's that going?' I ask. I don't listen to his response but mentally prepare myself for what I'm about to do. I reach into my pocket and take out my phone, making out that I'm being polite and switching it off to give him my full attention. I tap the sound recorder icon, press record, check to see the timer start and place it on the table with the screen face-down. He's none the wiser. I come straight to the point.

'I wanted to talk to you about something.'

His bonhomie evaporates. 'Yes,' he says, straightening himself up in his chair. My tone is stern and I imagine he thinks I'm going to ask his advice about something serious.

'Our friendship,' I say.

'Ah-hum.' He looks me straight in the eye. I guess there aren't many moments when you're about to say something that'll blow the lid off someone's life.

'What do you make of it looking back now?' I ask. The colour drains from his face. He actually looks like someone whose chickens are coming home to roost. He doesn't speak for about thirty seconds and my heart ceases to bang with the same ferocity. It's back in its slow rhythm, normal. The hard bit is over; the power has switched.

'Interesting question,' he mumbles as he shifts in his seat. I say nothing.

Throughout my whole life I've always believed that you shouldn't wallow in things. What doesn't kill you makes you stronger and other people have far worse things happen, so don't moan about it. But I had thought that the man in front of me was looking out for me, putting a fatherly arm around me, while my own dad rampaged at home. Now I had a very different view.

Chapter 18

My dad was always in the green baize armchair. One half of it had faded from the sun that shone through the balcony doors. Over the years, the carpet where he lay his feet began to wear away. A glass of red wine was always within reach. He sat there throughout the day and into the evening watching American legal dramas or reading Ken Follett novels or the *Daily Express*. At the weekend that would change to *The Times* and the *News of the World*.

When our house was repossessed, he found an expensive flat overlooking the Thames Estuary in Southend. There was no way the benefit department would agree to such a large monthly rent, but he worked out that if he came off the dole and signed back on once he was living in the flat, the rules meant the government would take over the payments. He bullied his parents into giving him a deposit, signed a rental agreement and then went back on social security. Radio 4 was the soundtrack to his new flat. He only ever turned it off when *Woman's Hour* came on or the *Afternoon Play*, which he couldn't stand. There were no rugs, no trinkets on shelves, just my dad's books and two photos. One of me at twelve years old playing my guitar, the other a professional picture of the girls when they were sixteen, all in stripey T-shirts and smiling for the camera. The walls were magnolia, unadorned, and there was very little furniture.

It hadn't been the plan, but I began to spend a lot of time with him there. I had just turned sixteen, started the sixth form at Cecil Jones High School and my mum's new house was a forty-minute bus ride away, then a twenty-minute walk. All my friends were nearby and I had recently met my first ever girlfriend, Vicki.

Vicki was in my sketch revue group. I'd written loads of comedy sketches with my friend Ian, and we'd approached the local theatre, promising to pack it out with pupils from school, all paying £2.50 a ticket. Our first show had sold out and now we were producing our second. Mr Ullmer drove us everywhere, did the lights, lent us props and gave us notes on our performance. A friend introduced Vicki to me, telling me she'd be up for being in the show. She looked like a young Rosanna Arquette, with shoulder-length blonde hair. She listened when people spoke but wasn't afraid to say what she thought. She had poise and seemed very grown-up for her seventeen years, driving herself round in a Citroen 2CV.

I had written a sketch that involved a character with two heads, requiring the actors to wear one set of clothes between them. I cast myself and Vicki in the roles. We'd climb into an oversized woollen pullover, taking it in turns to push our heads through the neck hole. Our bodies were pushed close together. The sketch wasn't any good but there was no way I was cutting it from the show. We fell in love as we rehearsed and sat on Southend's cliff tops in the evening, holding hands, kissing and planning our future adventures.

Mr Ullmer lived near my dad and offered to give me a lift each morning. I stopped staying with my mum as much and spent most of my time at my dad's flat. Free from the constant tension of our old house, my dad and I started to form a new bond. I could relate to him without having to hate him every day. Now I was older he became more interested in me, and I lapped it up. He could just be my dad, although we weren't like father and son. He became my formidable friend.

One afternoon we were sitting on the balcony. There was loud music coming from next door and an old woman with a blue rinse, wearing a duffle coat, shouted up to us from the street below. 'You should turn your music down,' she said, although we could barely register her frail voice.

In a flash my dad leapt up from his seat and screamed at her, 'It's not our music, you fucking ignorant witch.'

The woman stumbled back on her heel. It took her a moment to register her offence. 'I've never been spoken to so rudely by anyone before,' she proffered.

'Well, you can't get out much,' my dad said, returning to his seat, looking proud.

He was my boisterous flatmate to drink and watch television with. He wanted to hold court, commanding people's attention, but no one was around to listen apart from me. He'd lecture me about why climate change wasn't anything to worry about: 'The earth's temperature has always gone up and down. That's why there was a bloody ice age. And then it got hot again and melted.'

My mum was no longer there to buy TV licence stamps, and there was no way he would pay the yearly fee. Even if he'd had the money, he wouldn't have given it to the BBC. 'There's nothing on. I don't watch *EastEnders* and I'm not paying ninety quid for *Songs of Praise*.'

He enjoyed his run-ins with the licensing people, arguing at the front door with them. 'You're beaming signals into my home,' he'd say. 'If you don't want me to receive them, stop sending them.' After a while they stopped chasing, having obviously put him down on the system as 'leave well alone'.

I found it all amusing. He wanted to tear up any form of authority, answering to no one. He was his own man, fighting the system, and I admired it. He was an anti-parent. He wouldn't ask, 'Have you eaten?' or suggest I go to bed; I could do as I pleased. It was like handing me the keys to a Ferrari and saying just bring it back in the morning. He did once ask me what I liked for breakfast. I told him I was fond of Müller fruit corner yoghurts. After that he stocked the fridge with them every time he went to the supermarket, safe in the knowledge that he'd sorted my dietary requirements. He never questioned my choices or asked me what time I'd be back.

My friends' mothers and fathers were tame by comparison, but this made me feel pleased to have the father I did. He stood out from the crowd. Vicki's parents were quiet and unassuming. They had polite discussions at the dinner table, held down jobs and paid their way. I was sure it was because they didn't realise that what they should *actually* be doing was standing up against the system.

I never thought back to his treatment of my mum. It was too painful to revisit but it simmered away inside. I look at it now like an open wound that bled and covered everything I touched, but I had no way of tending to it.

One morning, he tried to give advice to me on a personal matter. I'd been going out with Vicki for a few months before I summoned up the courage to ask him a question while watching a recorded TV show.

'Would it be okay if Vicki stayed over?' I said, taking the opportunity that the television commercials afforded to broach the subject.

'Yes. That's fine,' he replied, immediately going on to ask if I'd fast forward the rest of the ad breaks.

It had obviously been playing on his mind because weeks later he closed the *Daily Express*, folded it over once and placed it on the coffee table. 'I think I should talk to you about sex,' he said.

'Okay,' I replied. I stopped eating my yoghurt and pushed it across the table. By now Vicki had stayed over several times, so I wondered where this was going.

'You should have sex whenever you get the opportunity,' he told me without looking me directly in the eye. 'And don't worry too much about condoms.' And that was it. He picked the paper back up and began doing the crossword.

My mum understood the practical reasons why I stayed with my dad, although I look back now and know she was hurt. She wanted me with her in her new home to begin our second life.

I went every couple of weeks for a few days, often taking with me a CD to play on her new hi-fi. The prospect of my dad harassing her dwindled away. She surrounded herself with friends, taking a thrill from her independence. She left the doctor's surgery and took shift work for a care agency, making sure to carefully budget for every expense. A couple of thousand pounds left to her by an aunt allowed her to take driving lessons, she joined a social club that went on day trips and she looked after the house with the pride of an owner.

She visited my sisters occasionally, but they wanted to get on with their own lives the best they could. They were seemingly content to be with each other. I saw them sometimes but we were all angry and we had no way of untangling the past. Kate, it seemed to me, hid away from the outside world and Emma raged against it. She was treated in a psychiatric ward for a bit but the help there didn't seem to fit.

I couldn't quite see it at the time, but my mum had been broken. Her spirit had been pummelled. It showed in the way she held herself. She set about making arrangements with a quiet, diligent focus. She was trying to repair herself.

Maybe part of me felt I had done my bit with my mum. I'd taken care of her, as much as I could, and now I had a freedom to follow my own desires, shaking off the responsibilities that weighed on me. My dad, with his pioneering spirit, became more attractive. My world was opening up and there he was, telling me anything was possible.

I was cagey, secretive and mistrustful, but these were the last things I wanted people to know. I worked hard to show people I wasn't like that. It was as if it was wired into me. I was on edge, waiting for the fight to happen or the person I was with to attack me. I constructed someone to keep people at bay. When *Four Weddings and a Funeral* came out in 1994, people thought I looked like Hugh Grant, so I started playing up to this. I even worked out that I could get laughs by feigning awkwardness and mimicking the type of jokes in the film.

I perfected this act. Why not slip into someone else's identity when you don't have your own? A lot of the hard work had been done for me.

I threw all my effort into charming people, making jokes and showing sympathy for their plights. I watched their reactions, analysing what worked and what didn't. I wasn't aware of it at the time, but I was full of nervous energy. If I sat down, I'd soon be up. It was as if I couldn't manage what was going on inside, so I moved around with the feeling, putting it to use.

The first time Mr Ullmer took me on a trip was straight after my parents separated, in the summertime before school started. I had just turned sixteen. He was taking me to see the head of drama at his previous school, who he said had been a guiding light in his career. It was clear that he saw himself in a similar role to her, providing me with a steady, sage influence.

I wore my best shirt and smart jeans with a suit jacket, which hung too loosely on my gawky frame. I was looking out for him at the window when I saw him pull up. He had a habit of honking his car horn to let me know he was there. It was embarrassing and I worried it would bother the neighbours. I rushed to put on my shoes, but he'd already beeped three times.

I peered through the open car window. 'Can't you get out of the car and knock?' I asked.

This brought about a huge belly laugh. As I was about to get in, he edged the car forward, forcing me to follow after him. Just as I reached the vehicle, he did it again, causing him to giggle more.

We sped off on our way to Kent for our lunch appointment, stopping on the way for snacks and Coca-Cola. I complained when he started to eat my food too. This caused him to make a clucking sound to drown me out, until I relented and let him finish the crisps. We met the friendly, if, after the build-up, underwhelming woman, and afterwards he showed me around his old school, pointing out the hall, the location of his successful productions. He ended up busying himself with scores of errands and we didn't leave until the light was lost.

Once we were on the road Mr Ullmer said he was tired and it was too late to get home, but we could stay in a flat, which I think was either his old home or a friend's.

'We can take our time, relax,' he said. 'Let's leave tomorrow. Stop on the way. We could even go to the cinema.' The plan took me by surprise but sounded fine. Eating out and cinema trips were rare occurrences, and I didn't want to pass up the opportunity.

As soon as I walked into the flat, it was obvious no one lived there. It was basic, small, with few windows. The ceilings were low and there were no lightshades covering the bulbs that hung down. It felt like a police safe house. We had stopped off to buy pizza and beers, and Mr Ullmer went through to the kitchen to find plates. I pushed open one of the doors that led off the front room, discovering a pokey bedroom with a double bed. It made me do a double take like Groucho Marx and I scanned the property to see that I hadn't missed another room. Mr Ullmer walked back in, carrying two glasses and two plates.

'There's only one bed.' I said, turning round again to show him the bedroom.

He didn't miss a beat, putting the plates on the table and dividing up the pizza. 'Do you want any pepperoni?' he asked, his mouth already full with his first slice.

I repeated myself.

'And?' he asked, like it was the most normal thing in the world. 'We'll both sleep there.'

'We can't share a bed.'

'Well, I'm not sleeping in the bath.' He laughed.

I stood there for a minute without saying anything, looking at the small two-seater sofa. 'I'll sleep there, I guess.'

He switched to reassuring mode: 'Oh, come on. I'll be on my side, you on yours. It's not a problem.'

People didn't sleep in the same bed together unless they were a couple. The thought of it horrified me. I'd only ever slept in a bed with my mum before. It felt like an intimate thing to do.

'There's nothing wrong with two good friends sharing a bed. What's the matter with you?'

'It's weird.'

'Only because you're uptight. Neither of us are gay. We need to stay somewhere. We might as well both get a good night's sleep. Stop being so neurotic.'

I had known him for three years, so even though the prospect made me squirm I accepted his rationale. I had no idea that this thirty-three-year-old man held a position of trust and shouldn't have been talking teenage boys into sleeping in a bed with him; he was my friend. When it was time for bed, he undressed in front of me, stripping to his boxer shorts and taking out his contact lenses, which he put in a pot on the bedside table. I remained clothed, climbing into bed beside him.

'Thomas! You can't sleep in your trousers. Dear me! You'll be uncomfortable.'

I didn't argue but pulled back the quilt, got up and took off my jeans, holding them up in front of me so he couldn't see my pants. I climbed back in the bed, dropping my jeans on the floor.

'You really don't have to keep your shirt on. It'll get creased.'

I ignored this suggestion, turning away. I moved so near to the edge of the bed, I felt like the bus in the last scene of *The Italian Job*, almost falling off the cliff. The thought of his skin touching mine made me shiver. I wasn't fearful of what might happen; I just couldn't shake my feeling of deep unease. He turned out the light and I lay there, eyes open, in the dark. It was only one night. I carefully avoided contact with him, but it got harder as the night wore on. He was asleep but kept edging closer. Sometimes he'd stir and his foot would brush mine. I woke up in the early hours to find his arm resting on my shoulder, so I wriggled free.

And that was it. We got up, went out for breakfast and no harm had been done. He dropped me off at my mum's in the late afternoon. I knew that sleeping in the same bed would sound weird so there was no way I was going to mention it to anyone. As he drove into the estate I saw Emma slumped against the house. She was due to visit, and I knew she was drunk. Like a screwball comedy I tried to distract Mr Ullmer from seeing her, moving my head from side to side to cover his view. He drove off and I wandered over to the front of the house. I turned the key, dragging Emma into the house like I was shifting a bag of spuds.

Chapter 19

We pulled up outside his flat, right next to the Southend cliff tops, and I grabbed my school rucksack, which had a luminous-green footprint design, and got out. I had bought the bag from the PE teacher who used to flog them discreetly out of the back of his Ford Fiesta. He had sold so many it had become the unofficial school bag, on the backs of scores of boys. The headmaster must have been under the misapprehension that it was a fashion craze sweeping the place.

I made my way into Mr Ullmer's flat. There was a subtle musty smell. Someone needed to open all the windows and let some air in. It was a nice place, though. The living room had an urbane feel with antique armchairs, neat little wooden side tables, fancy lamps and a church pew up against one wall. Academic books lined the shelves and expensive-looking vases and ornaments were dotted around. The walls were covered with photos of him and his friends performing amateur theatre shows and framed certificates from various universities.

I had grown tall, and I was skinny and parted my longish hair into curtains. I pulled the strings at the top of my bag and reached in to get my English textbooks. I took out my trainers, my Tupperware lunchbox, containing an empty sandwich bag, an apple core and a Penguin wrapper, and rummaged around until I spotted the copy of *Macbeth*.

I was scared of one of the English teachers. He made you read aloud and put you on the spot in front of the rest of the class. I had told Mr Ullmer about this and he readily suggested that if I couldn't face the class, he would have a word with the head teacher, saying that he could use my parents' separation as a way of justifying my absence. He would tell the head that the authoritative manner of the English teacher was throwing up certain issues for me with my dad and I should be allowed to miss the class. A few days later it was sorted. Term had just started and Mr Ullmer offered to help with my English A level.

He went off into his kitchen while I laid out my texts and notepad on his little round table. He came back in with a pot of coffee. I had been to Mr Ullmer's flat a few times before and it still felt like a privileged, grown-up thing to be doing.

The other kids went home to watch TV or play football in the park but here I was, drinking coffee out of a cafetiere and reclining on scatter cushions discussing Shakespeare. Mr Ullmer was awakening my interest in literature and writing. These sessions were used to discuss plays and books, and help me form analytical arguments. This night he had suggested that we would work and then he'd cook us a meal and we could watch a film.

I had called him the evening before to say I had been invited to a role-play game with my friends and so I would need to leave at 6 p.m. He became incredibly sullen, saying we had agreed we would spend the evening together too, not just the afternoon. It was ungrateful and if someone puts themself out for me, he explained, I should at least be courteous enough to respect the arrangement. I had now stopped him making plans for that night, so my behaviour had consequences. I made one last attempt to explain but he was so upset he could barely talk to me. I agreed to stay on for the evening, cancelling my friends.

We worked for about three hours and then he suggested we have a drink and go into the kitchen, where he had already done some preparation for dinner. I walked through the narrow little corridor to his classy all-white kitchen with illuminated windows in the cabinets, allowing you to peer inside at his posh bowls and glassware. He handed me a beer. Most of our conversation was easy-going and jokey, although a small part of me was anxious. I felt a little out of my depth. It was imperceptible to me much of the time, but then I would get a niggling doubt that I wouldn't know what to say or might appear stupid. It was how you might feel if Prince Charles started making small talk with you and you weren't quite sure how to keep it going.

Mr Ullmer took some plates from the cupboard and walked through a doorway leading off the kitchen into a fancy conservatory with a dinner table, complete with a cloth draped over it and thick, folded napkins. I watched him as he lit tea-light candles and then returned to make some finishing touches to the starter.

'Go and sit down,' he instructed me. I pulled out a chair and sat down in the darkened room, the candle-light flickering. The cutlery was lined up like a formal dinner, with small knives and forks set outside of the larger ones. I fiddled with the spoon, which had intricate metalwork on the end. I had never felt a heavier one in my life. He brought out a big plate of halved tomatoes with the insides taken out and filled with caviar and – I have a strong memory of this, but maybe it's wrong because it sounds odd – sweetcorn. Mr Ullmer had serrated the edges of the tomatoes, so there were little spikes all along the top. *This is how the educated, well-off live,* I thought. *Their spoons are heavy, they serrate their vegetables ornately and they don't think caviar is disgusting.* This meal was a big deal.

Mr Ullmer brought out the main meal, which was roast chicken. The gravy came in a gravy boat, there were sauces, each in its own receptacle, and loads of vegetables, again in separate bowls from which we could help ourselves. He had gone to a lot of effort. As we tucked into this feast we talked about the travails of John Major's government and he let me in on the political jostling behind the scenes at school, giving me the inside track on the current teacher romances.

I don't remember what we ate for dessert, but whatever it was, he had made it himself. He poured a glass of wine for me. 'How's it going with Vicki?' he asked.

'Good,' I replied, not knowing what answer I was supposed to give. These conversations made me squirm but they had been happening so often recently that they were now a normal part of the routine.

He started telling me how it was important to take relationships slowly. I was young and it was easy to get hurt, he said. Sex was a gift not to be given lightly. 'I've never had sex. I believe it's important to wait for marriage,' he said. He was thirty-three.

He sat back in his chair, and it creaked with his bulk. 'So, how far have you gone with her?' he asked.

I used my spoon to move around what remained of my pudding. 'It's private,' I said. No one had ever asked me anything like this before.

'Come on.' He laughed. 'We can have an adult conversation, can't we?'

'Yes, but …'

'Look, we're very good friends. Already. I trust you implicitly. But good friends tell each other everything. Tom, these things are embarrassing, but that's how you build deep, lasting friendships. You share stuff you don't share with other people.'

I wasn't comfortable but I followed his logic. Sensing his disapproval, I lied to him, saying we hadn't had sex but that I thought we might soon.

This expression of my intentions seemed to upset him. 'Sex deepens a relationship very quickly in a way you don't realise,' he said. I didn't think to ask him how he knew that if he hadn't had any. He implored me not to do it. I wished we could just keep talking about the books I was reading or the teachers at school, but this was part of the deal.

'Has she jerked you off?' he asked, arching an eyebrow and giggling. He could see I was reluctant to continue the conversation, so he carried on. 'I went out with my last girlfriend for four years,' he told me. 'And, you know, it was really difficult not to sleep with each other. She wanted to but we both knew it was important to only take the relationship further when we both knew we were ready.'

I admitted that we had gone further than just kissing. I hoped he could see that I was making an effort to develop our bond. Like a priest he took it upon himself to absolve me.

'That's natural, it's fine, but it's not a good idea to repeat it. You need to exercise self-control.'

I didn't agree with him but found myself out-argued. He furrowed his brow and pursed his lips. 'A couple of times my ex-girlfriend and I went further than we should and she jerked me off,' he said with the manner of someone who was admitting to small-scale fraud. 'When things get heated it's so much harder not to succumb. It's better not to get yourself in that situation.' I nodded.

He got up and retrieved a bottle of port from the back of his cupboard, as well as two special glasses for drinking it. He pulled out the cork and filled my glass to the rim. I think it was the first time I'd ever had it and I liked the sweetness. 'Do you know the game truth or dare?' he asked. I told him I did but had never played it before.

'Let's go through to the living room,' he said, taking his glass and the bottle and leading the way.

I followed him through. He took his place on the sofa and I sat opposite him on an armchair. I had imagined that this game would be fun to play if I was with a bunch of girls at school, and it surprised me that the first time I was going to play it was with a man in his thirties.

'I'll start,' he said. 'Truth or dare?'

I had no idea what we were supposed to dare each other in a small flat in Southend-on-Sea, so I opted for truth. He asked me which girl, if I had to, would I kiss in our drama class. I answered, and when it came to his turn he opted for truth too. 'Same question,' I said.

'Oh dear.' He looked stumped. 'I don't think I should answer that.' He seemed genuinely uncomfortable and started to mumble, 'Yes … I'm not sure … Umm … I think I would say none.'

'But if you had to?'

He answered that if he had no choice, it would be the same girl as me, but as her teacher it wasn't really a fair question. It was my turn again.

'Truth,' I said.

'Okay. Hmm. How many times do you masturbate a week?'

I laughed and he quickly joined in. 'Come on,' he chuckled. 'The rules are, you have to answer.'

'I don't know.'

'All right. We'll say this is my question and I'll answer.' This was a relief. 'There have been times when I have done it every day. I mean, not all the time. Sometimes I'm too tired.' He burst out in a fit of giggles.

It's difficult to know what to say when someone provides you with this information about themselves, but I came up with, 'What does the Bible say about it?'

He was a committed Christian. He had taken me to a number of church services and was keen for us to discuss theological matters. He would often talk about the Bible or quote apt parts of it to me. He'd tell me that the biblical characters David and Jonathan were the personification of platonic love between an older and younger man, and that's who we were like.

He would become very animated by this type of question. The morality of sexual behaviour would have been his specialist subject on *Mastermind*. He put his serious face on again. 'You know, I'm pretty sure the Bible doesn't say anything specific about masturbation, but it's very clear in other passages about the importance of moderation.'

Once he'd started he found it hard to stop. 'Jesus understood that we're all human with faults and imperfections, and that sexual desire is very natural. I think it's certainly better to masturbate than have sex outside of marriage. So what about you?' He had a look on his face that suggested he thought what he had just said was very thoughtful and, best of all, practical.

I gave him an answer to his question. Maybe he was right. He wasn't going to tell anybody. What was the harm in him knowing? He was being open with me, so what was my problem?

'Truth or dare?' I asked.

'Truth.'

I wanted to know if he'd ever run out of a restaurant without paying. He always tried to answer my questions fully, even though he had no interesting response. In fact, his replies would usually turn into a musing on the rights and wrongs of a situation and why he always behaved impeccably. He'd never run out of a restaurant without paying, but he understood the urge to do risky things.

After a while he insisted that I accept a dare. I got him to promise it wouldn't be anything difficult, so he suggested I drink a shot of port, which I did. The game went on. He had an inexhaustible supply of sexually probing questions about fantasies and wanking. It never occurred to me to tell anyone of this game, which we would come to play on many occasions. How could I? I didn't think it was wrong but I knew I couldn't casually mention this behaviour to a friend. It would have felt like I was betraying him. Out of context, how would this appear?

'I'll do a dare this time,' he stated.

I told him to drink a shot of port but he seemed disappointed. 'I can't drink much more,' he said, 'I'll have a sip.'

'No, you have to drink the whole thing,' I argued. He took another mouthful. 'That's enough, I'll be sick. Come on, you do a dare. You can't just pick truth.'

'Okay,' I said, my stomach tightening.

He thought for a moment before saying, 'I know, you have to take your clothes off and run from here to the kitchen and back.'

There was no way I was taking my clothes off.

'You have to do it.' He was almost petulant. Finally he relented. 'You're so stubborn. Okay, you just have to moon.'

'You mean show my bum?'

'Yep.' Another burst of laughter. 'Just your bum and then you can pull your trousers up.' This suddenly felt like a get-out clause. I could do that.

I got up in front of him, his eyes fixed on me. The amusement continued. 'It's such fun seeing you squirm!' I walked away towards the door with my back to him, undid my belt, unfastened the button on my jeans, pulled down the zip and yanked my trousers down to just below my bottom and pulled them back up straight away.

'Oh, come on!' he said. 'It has to be longer than that.'

'No, I did it,' I said, and pulled my belt tight.

'You have to keep your trousers down for five seconds at least.'

I sat back in the armchair, where I intended to stay, and took another swig of port.

Sensing that I wasn't going to comply, he settled for saying, 'Okay, but next time it has to be for an agreed amount of time.' It was approaching midnight and I told him I would have to go soon. I was staying at my dad's flat not far from Mr Ullmer's home, but it would still take me fifteen minutes to walk back along the cliff tops.

He conceded it was getting late but asked me to play one more round. 'I'll take a dare,' he offered. A quarter of a century later a fury rises when I think about this. His game was so clear but back then I didn't have a clue.

'Okay, you have to moon too,' I said.

Ullmer got up in front of me; he didn't feel the need to provide a bit of distance between us as I had done. He undid his trousers, turned round, pulled his trousers down and bent over, revealing his fat arse. He counted out, 'One … two … three … four … five …' He didn't stop: 'Six … seven … eight … nine … ten …'

He turned round, still with his trousers down so he was exposing his penis. He pulled up his trousers slowly. 'See, I did it for longer,' he said, as if he had triumphed in an endurance test.

'We should definitely end on a dare,' he said. The pressure to continue was relentless. 'Um … right … I've got one for you. Go out the room and come back with an erection.' He must have registered the shock on my face, so he added, 'You can wear your pants.'

I had to get through this or manage it the best way I could. 'No, I'm not doing that.'

'Go on, don't be so uptight.'

I refused again.

'Okay, I'll do it first.' He took his trousers off, keeping his pants on, and left the room. Two or three minutes passed by, during which I wondered if he was really going to return after arousing himself. Or rather I had no doubt that he would, but I couldn't quite imagine seeing it. When he appeared he had taken his pants off and he stood in the doorway with his shirt on but naked beneath, his penis erect.

I never took stock or looked at the situation objectively. Everything that happened felt like a small fire I had to put out. I had to be constantly vigilant and keep things under control. Resist, resist. I knew I didn't like it, but I didn't think it was untoward, just hard to deal with. Maybe the things I'd witnessed with my mum and dad had given me a fucked-up idea of normality. Maybe I let myself believe his assertions that it was all a way of developing our friendship because I so desperately needed the rest of what he had to offer. He put his pants and trousers back on in front of me but didn't do them up. He was upbeat and started making arrangements for next week. There was a film I might like and he suggested that we go to the cinema one day after school. I told him that would be great. He apologised for drinking too much and being unable to drive me back.

I didn't mind, although it was windy and cold outside and would be especially so along the cliff tops. I put my books back in my bag and told him I'd see him at school in the morning. He said he'd drive by my dad's flat at 8 a.m. and pick me up. I hated getting up early and asked if it could be 8.15.

'Oh go on, then, you cheeky so and so,' he said.

I closed the front door, leaving Mr Ulmer holding up his trousers on the other side of it.

Chapter 20

Mr Ullmer gave me everything I'd been crying out for. He'd buy me things, drive me places, fight my corner. When I got my English GCSE results I was disappointed with my C grade. Mr Ullmer reassured me, 'I've looked at your course-work and think it deserves a much higher mark. I'm going to get a friend of mine to read it and see whether he thinks it has grounds for appeal.' A week or so later he told me that his friend had said my work was worthy of a B. He organised the appeal, which came to nothing, but the act of support stuck with me.

He taught me all that life had taught him, encouraged my interests, telling me I was special. He told me I was his best friend, that I was smart. But most of all he listened. He seemed to put my interests first. While my dad sunk triple gin and tonics, Ullmer worried about my moral education. Was every act of his support premeditated to achieve his aims?

I now think that, back then, my vulnerability was not so hard to see. I think it was my defining characteristic. I wanted someone to look after me. To take my worries away, nurse my pain and watch out for me in a world I knew to be savage. My mum couldn't shield me, nor could my sisters, but I was proud to have this eccentric friend whose intelligence and care was obvious. I swept our weird games under a mental carpet.

Mr Ullmer encouraged me to attend his Baptist church. Life needed a purpose, he said, and he was keen to let me know that Jesus could provide it. 'I may not always get everything right. Life will throw me challenges, but if I can say I tried to live my life through Christ, then I think that's something.'

I thought it was all mad, but I could never tell him. Instead, I sought to please him, attending scores of services and politely telling any member of the congregation who asked if I'd enjoyed the sermon, 'There's a lot to think about.'

I spent hours with him drinking orange squash at church events. I even took Vicki, sitting squashed up together on the pew, surrounded by evangelicals swaying to hymns with fixed smiles, telling us Jesus had his eye on us.

Any form of confrontation, or the thought of expressing my own views, rendered me timid. I was frightened of what would happen in those moments. Would Mr Ullmer discard me for failing to respect his religion? Would he blow up and be furious? Would I have to become angry? I'd seen where anger went. I was fearful of it and kept it controlled, inside.

He'd lecture me on humanity, forgiveness and showing kindness beyond all else. He was a paragon of virtue, and he wouldn't shut up about it. I guess it's a smokescreen to talk about possessing morality and values when your own are wanting. He had sacrificed selfish pursuits and he encouraged me to take a leap in the dark. 'You're very analytical. But faith is a matter of trust,' he said.

I tried to believe in Jesus. I accepted that he existed and his teachings seemed benign, but I couldn't get over the fact that he thought he was the son of God. The kindest thing I could think was that he had been seriously deluded.

When choosing my A levels I had opted for English, the subject he had studied, drama, the subject he taught, and religion because I wanted to show him how seriously I took the matter. Now I was in the sixth form, one or two of the older kids in my year brought cars to school. They'd pull up in their battered old Fiestas or rusty Micras. I was jealous, not knowing when I'd be able to afford lessons.

'I'll teach you,' Ullmer offered one day, demolishing a Chelsea bun from the school canteen while slurping diet cola straight from the can. It was still a year before I'd be able to have a provisional licence, but I jumped at the chance. 'You'll let me drive the car?' I said, uncertain of his seriousness.

'Come round to mine tonight. We'll get a takeaway, then, when we can be sure the cars have left, we'll go to Leigh station car park,' he said, a piece of icing resting on his top lip.

Around midnight I sat behind the wheel of his car, pulled the seat belt round, and he instructed me carefully on how to release the clutch. It took a while, but once I was off, it was a thrill.

I spun round the tarmac, gaining in confidence with every circuit. His unease grew. 'Okay, okay, not too fast. Please,' he said. 'You're a little too close to the payment machine.'

'I'm nowhere near it.'

'Apply the brake when you turn.'

I kept going, practising the gear shifts.

'Okay, okay, now, Thomas, I think that's enough for today.'

'We've only been here fifteen minutes. We might as well make it worthwhile.'

'A few minutes more. I'll drive us to mine, that way we can have a quick drink.'

I felt a wave of disappointment. I had no interest in doing anything other than driving a car. I had school the next day, as did he, and I felt like I had nothing else left to say to him.

He sensed my reluctance. 'It's nice for me to be able to wind down at the end of the day, Tom,' he said. 'So a drink would be great. The whole evening's been devoted to you.'

'Sure,' I said, and put my foot on the accelerator.

Once home, he went to his bathroom while I waited for him in the kitchen. I could hear him spraying himself with deodorant. He came out and trundled over to where he kept his booze. 'Have you tried Advocaat?' he asked, grabbing two crystal glasses from his kitchen cabinet.

'It looks disgusting,' I said, as he poured two full glasses of thick, yellow liquid. He chuckled like I'd said something witty and pulled off his tie. I followed him through to the lounge, where he shut the curtains, put a Paul Simon CD in the hi-fi, slipped off his shoes and removed his socks.

'Argh!' he exclaimed as he lay back on the sofa. 'My back is agony.'

'I've nearly finished the scripts with Ian,' I told him, referring to my sketch show.

'That's good. Would you mind rubbing my shoulders?'

I'd never massaged anyone before, and why he thought I'd be able to ease his back pain by doing it, I had no idea. He shifted round on the sofa, so he was facing away from me, not waiting for my answer. 'Just here, for a minute. It would really help,' he said, reaching round to tap his upper back.

'Er, sure.' I got up, sat next to him and placed my hands where he'd indicated. It was odd, uncomfortable.

'Honestly, do it harder. I can't feel it.' I grabbed his shoulders and pushed in with my thumbs.

'Hmmm. Oh, that's it,' he said, leaning back into my hands. 'Ah, yes, just a little lower.' I followed his directions. His shirt was damp with sweat, although all I could smell was Right Guard.

'Hang on,' he said. 'I'm just going to take this off, because you can't get into the shoulder blades through the material.'

'It's fine with your shirt on,' I said, but he was already unbuttoning his top, revealing copious amount of hair all over his body. I held back.

'It's just skin! You're so prissy. You can touch another man, it doesn't burn, Thomas.' He chuckled away. His flabby back hung over his trousers and he edged towards me. It sickens me to write this down. His sighs of pleasure won't leave my head. I felt his back hair matted with sweat. Every touch elicited a soft groan. 'Just a little more, it's really helping,' he'd say.

I stopped after a minute or so.

'Is that it?'

He got up, lying down on the floor in front of me. 'It'll be better if I'm flat on the hard surface.'

I took a sip of Advocaat.

'You're really making my back better, thank you. It's important that friends can help each other out, isn't it? I might even drive you home if you're lucky. Save you walking.'

I continued with the massage. I knelt at his side and carried on with the task at hand.

'You're really good at this,' he said. 'I've had a few massages before, but you really know where it's stiff.'

After a while I decided to do it as well as I could, figuring that the more effective I was, the quicker it'd be over.

'Julie, my ex-girlfriend, gave massages, but she wasn't as strong as you. It has to hurt a bit,' he said. After a few moments he started to edge the top of his trousers down, revealing the top of his bottom cheeks. 'Right at the base, lower,' he instructed. He reached round to the front of his waist and unfastened his belt, shoving his underpants halfway down his buttocks.

I got up. 'Okay, I've got to get going,' I said. I expected him to protest but he agreed straight away. He turned round on to his back and lay there on the floor, looking up at me.

'Thank you. That's loosened me up,' he said.

I went into his bathroom and cleaned my hands with the soap. Now, it seems so obvious what was going on, but at the time I just thought it was a quirk of his I had to manage. Like pensioners you hear about, scammed out of thousands of pounds by dodgy double-glazing salesmen, I fell into a trap. I let myself believe his lies that all these games were just an expression of true friendship. I accepted his masquerade. He had become so important to me that I couldn't question the friendship because it would have pulled at the fabric of who he'd encouraged me to believe I was.

We'd watch videos at his flat in the evening. Mr Ullmer would often choose films such as *Basic Instinct*. One evening we watched a film called *Dirty Weekend*, about a woman who takes revenge on abusive men. After it finished, he said, 'I have something to ask you. Jackie is coming over next weekend and I have some old letters my ex-girlfriend wrote me. I don't want to throw them away, and I don't want her to find them, so I wonder if you'd keep them for me.'

'Er … okay.' I replied. Jackie was his new girlfriend. It never occurred to me to ask why he couldn't think of a better place to hide them.

He shuffled out of the room and returned with a brown envelope stuffed full of cards and bits of paper. 'I'd never let anyone else look at them,' he said, 'but I don't mind if you read them.'

I stuffed them into my school bag, assuring him that I'd take care of them. I had a look when I got home later that night. I quickly worked out that there was nothing interesting in them. They were pages long, with his girlfriend frequently complaining about his sullen moods.

'It was very sad in the end. But if you've been going out with someone for four years, the question is, Why aren't you marrying them? And I didn't want to marry her,' he said.

He frequently gave me advice about my relationship with Vicki. He would suggest romantic gestures for me to make. I took her to a restaurant he'd recommended for her birthday. He even told me to get the staff to prearrange glasses of champagne, so they'd be ready when we got there.

One evening I had plans with Vicki, but a rehearsal went on late. Mr Ullmer said I needed to work at school past ten o'clock.

'I put in the hours but I don't see why I should if you're not prepared to make the same sacrifices,' he mumbled, staring down at the floor. 'Vicki has to understand that. Compromise is what a relationship is all about.'

I called her and we argued. I was angry because she was upset but told myself it was because she didn't understand my dedication. Mr Ullmer took me aside and told me that despite being busy, we could drive out to buy some flowers and then pass by Vicki's house to give them to her. The whole thing was a palaver, taking well over an hour.

He'd click his fingers to get a waiter's attention. When talking to other teachers he didn't like (which was most of them), he'd look past them or ignore what they'd said. He was relentless in his pursuit of me. Very committed to the cause. And yet, looking back now, so much of it was hapless.

He instigated chummy wrestles at his flat after jokingly berating me for a missed deadline. I'd suddenly find myself pinned to the ground by this deviant Bertie Wooster. I'd dodge or shove my way out of it, but he'd try again, flinging himself at me, grabbing an arm or leg. He'd be breathless. He'd use all his weight, so I'd collapse under his heft. I'd wriggle out from underneath him, taking my hand and pushing it hard against his head. He'd get frustrated and I'd feel his hands trying to pull at the top of my trousers, at which point I'd become angry, kicking him off. He'd suggest a drink, sensing he couldn't take it any further. At the time I wasn't unhappy. Ignorance is bliss and I continued to navigate the choppy waters of the friendship because I understood that's what was required.

I never told Vicki any of what went on with Mr Ullmer. How could I? I didn't understand what was going on myself. By the time I met her he'd been part of my life for years. Where she came from, teachers kept a respectful distance, but Mr Ullmer wasn't like that. How could I explain the weird stuff that had gone on, seemingly of my own volition? It would all sound so seedy and that wasn't the truth. She disliked him. He made her feel like she wasn't smart enough.

I tried to tell Vicki about my upbringing, but I was incapable of being honest. I wanted to reveal to her the parts of me I had hidden, but instead I played it all down. I minimised the violence, making it sound like an aberration, resolved and in the past. I didn't want her to run, or to turn against my dad. She asked about my sisters and I just said, 'They're always drunk.' She thought I was joking and laughed.

I felt so raw that if something brushed past me it stung. Years of observing any sign of danger meant I was switched on all the time. It was like a super-power. I was highly sensitised to people's moods, like Spider-Man's spider sense. I'd ask people, 'What's wrong?' picking up on some small emotional change they had no wish to share with me. It was a tiring way to live.

Even if I tried to think of my past I switched the memories off before they arrived. I couldn't show my mum how sensitive I was because it would have hurt her to know how hard it had all been. My sisters had been crushed and wore their wounds without a dressing, but I made it my mission to show that everything was fine. I kept it all from my dad because not only was he the cause, he would have poured scorn on any tender side. I pretended I was tough like him.

My dad didn't question the amount of time I spent with Mr Ullmer. Sometimes Vicki would call the landline and my dad would airily tell her, 'Oh, he's at Ullmer's, try him there.' Why would my dad assume anything was awry? He couldn't admit to himself that he'd done anything wrong and so why would there be consequences of his behaviour? He told me he found Mr Ullmer strange and even laughed about how he was always suggesting we go away together. He had utter faith in my judgement. No son of his could be abused.

If I was going out with Mr Ullmer for the evening, he wouldn't want to come in for a drink first. He would tell me he'd wait downstairs in his car. On the occasions that he did meet my dad, he'd laugh nervously at everything my dad said and would wait for a break from my dad's monologue to cut in with, 'Okay, okay, okay. Well, we'd better be off.'

One night Mr Ullmer took me out for a meal. It was unusual because although it was still at an out-of-the-way place, it was in Southend. Usually we'd head to Basildon, a thirty-minute drive away, where there was no chance of bumping into teachers or students from our school. The waiter began to talk to us, asking what I did. I told him I was doing A levels. Ullmer's faced dropped. He stared down at his napkin, looking perturbed.

'What's wrong?' I asked, after the waiter had taken our orders.

He was silent for some time. 'You could have said something else.'

'Why?'

'Because people might jump to the wrong conclusions.'

Perhaps they would. I felt chastised.

'It doesn't matter,' he said, but I knew it did.

Later, back at his, Mr Ullmer placed his beer, untouched, on the small coffee table by the couch. He removed his black woolly blazer and returned to the tub of ice cream he'd bought us for pudding. He dug out five large spoonfuls, dumping them into his bowl. 'You're disgusting,' I said, concerned that my own share of the ice cream had diminished.

'You're the gannet, Thomas! Moderation is good for you.'

That afternoon Mr Ullmer had found a pamphlet on his desk at work, put there by another teacher. It was about inappropriate relationships at school. He made one of his long thoughtful sounds, 'Hmmm,' and said we had to be careful about people's perceptions. As far as I know that was the only time anyone ever questioned my intimate relationship with Mr Ullmer, even though I turned up with him in his car almost every day, leaving with him too. Not my mum or my friends, not Vicki or my dad or my other teachers. He pulled the wool over everyone's eyes, not just mine. He was hiding in plain sight.

He reminisced about how a Canadian friend had come to visit him while he was at his last school. His friend was good company but reckless. Mr Ullmer told me how his friend had come on to one of his sixth-form students. 'He ended up getting off with her and stuck his hand up her jumper to feel her breasts,' he said, shaking his head. 'I told him it was inappropriate, but he just said it was a bit of fun. I was extremely cross with him.'

At his suggestion we were writing predictions on pieces of paper for the year 2000. He said he'd put them in an envelope and we'd open them on New Year's Eve in five years' time. Earlier in the evening, when we came back from the restaurant, I'd noticed a bottle of baby oil on a sideboard near the television. I'd never seen it there before and my eyes kept being drawn to it. We carried on with our game. The only forecast I remember writing was that I thought Michael Jackson would be dead by the turn of the century. Once we'd finished our game he made the suggestion I knew was coming: 'Do you mind giving me a massage before you go?'

I agreed, and this time he stripped naked. He hesitated momentarily before walking over to the sideboard and picked up the oil. 'I bought this,' he said. 'It'll make it easier to get in between the joints.'

We went through the usual drill. As I finished, he said, 'I'll give you one too. It's only fair.'

We'd been doing this weekly, so I took my shirt and trousers off and lay down where he'd been. He sighed and grunted as he touched my young skin with his hands. It wasn't long before he worked his way down to my underpants and tried to push them down. This was the routine. I yanked them back up and he would go back to my shoulders, but soon he would try again. I counted down the minutes in my head until I felt I'd shown willing enough, then I broke off, grabbing my trousers and pulling them on.

He sat back on the sofa, naked, with one leg folded up onto the sofa and the other resting on the floor. He began to masturbate in front of me. This had become part of the routine now too. He'd begin to stroke himself after the massage had finished telling me it was a way for us to further our bond. He was moaning and panting. 'One more dare,' he said. 'Why don't you touch it, just for a second?' I refused.

'Just for a second,' he repeated. He went back to rubbing himself and leaned back on the sofa cushion. 'Come on!' he demanded. It disgusted me and yet I was contemplating if I should. How had I ended up sitting opposite Jabba the Hut while he wanked off in front of me? He grew frustrated with my inaction. The next few seconds are as clear as any memory I will ever hold. He snapped, 'Do it!' I reached out my hand, putting my fingers on it. At that moment he ejaculated, letting out an orgasmic yelp. I sat there stunned, staring at my hand as semen ran down my fingers. I rushed to the bathroom and began scrubbing my hand with soap.

He appeared behind me, leaning in through the open door. 'Sorry, I didn't know that was going to happen,' he said.

I told him I was going home and refused his offer of a lift. I opened the door of my dad's flat to the sound of him snoring. I went to the bathroom and washed my hands again, knowing that I'd never speak to anyone about this. I lay in bed, where the evening's event kept returning to my mind, but each time it did I shut it out.

My relationship with Vicki had come to an end. She had told me in a tearful late-night conversation that I was too complicated, too secretive, too judgemental, too hard to know. If she had delved more, I would have tried harder to hide. I'm sure we would have gone our separate ways anyway, most first loves do, but Mr Ullmer had inveigled his way into a position as my romantic adviser, guiding me with a feigned fatherly tenderness in how I should behave, what I should think. He soiled that relationship with his filthy fingertips, sowing division so he could get what he wanted: me all to himself.

Something in me clicked after that experience at Mr Ullmer's flat. It was not a path I could go down. I wanted to keep the friendship but, without admitting it to myself, I now knew what he was after. I started making excuses not to go round or to leave early if I did. School was finishing soon, and I hoped to make my own way in the world, free of this exhausting relationship.

Chapter 21

The words were written in big black ink on the newspaper board outside the shop: 'Ex-*Sunday Sport* editor hounds lover to Moroccan desert.' I knew it was him. I was twenty-four and returning home to visit my dad. I pulled the car over and picked up a copy of the local paper, the *Evening Echo*, where it was front-page news: WOMAN TELLS COURT OF HER PHONE PEST NIGHTMARE.

A former newspaper editor who pestered his ex-girlfriend with phone calls forced her into hiding after he tracked her down to a Moroccan desert. Austin Mitchelson, 52, hounded former lover Cheryl Bright after she walked out on him because of his tantrums, a Southend court heard. The well-known journalist who helped launch the *Sunday Sport* in 1986 said she had borrowed more than £30,000 from married lovers and accused her of threatening to tell the men's wives so she didn't have to pay it back.

My dad had met Cheryl when he shouted down to her from his balcony as she tried to manoeuvre her car out of a tight parking space. He ran down and, with a few turns of the wheel, set the car free. His impressive flat on the seafront gave her the impression he was a man of means. She didn't know the flat's rent was covered by housing benefit. When he returned with her telephone number, I asked him what she was like. 'Not as good closer up,' he replied.

I carried on reading the article:

Mitchelson denies making dozens of nuisance calls to the businesswoman after she moved out of his Southend flat and back to her own home in the same road. She told Magistrates that Mitchelson pestered her after their affair crumbled. Ms Bright said Mitchelson tracked her down to Italian and Moroccan hotels, bombarding her with calls. She told the court, 'It terrified me. It changed my personality. One night, at home, he kept banging on my front door. I thought he was going to come through it. It was frightening. Now I live somewhere difficult to find, away from rail links, and difficult to get to in one day from Southend.

She found him going through her private diaries, and she said he became very angry about past relationships and 'very disturbed' when he drank.

Mitchelson, cross-examining, did not deny making calls to her but claimed he was still seeing her. The trial continues ...

'I didn't want to worry you,' he said when I turned up half an hour later, holding a copy of the paper. 'She's completely mad. She's trying to ruin me professionally.'

She hadn't seemed mad to me but the echoes of his relationship with my mum resounded loudly. 'She's making it all up.' I knew that every word was true. I knew how terrified she would have been.

'Yeah, well, I never liked her,' was all I offered. The next day the court cleared his name.

He had destroyed his own career. He had been unemployed for years now. He'd been proud of a recent job application. The position was night editor of a small news gathering service. 'Why do you want the job?' he read out, proceeding to give me his answer. 'Two years as news editor of Radio Orwell, one year on Essex Radio and because … Yea, though I walk through the valley of the shadow of death, I will fear no evil, for I am the baddest motherfucker in the valley.' They didn't get back to him.

This wasn't the only story that appeared in the paper about him that year. He also took his former employers, Essex Radio, to a tribunal, claiming they had sexually discriminated against him. The paper reported him as saying, 'I asked the station if they had any vacancies and they wrote back saying they did but they had hoped it would be a female voice for their morning bulletins.' They knew about his behaviour towards my mum and the woman he'd had an affair with, and they were turning him down politely. The station responded by saying, 'There are always two sides to every story and we would love to give you ours. Unfortunately, legal reasons prevent us from doing so but we look forward to the tribunal hearing when the full story will come out.'

The story never did come out. They settled the case, giving my dad five grand. My dad split it with me, helping me pay off the overdraft I'd accrued while at university, and I thanked him for his generosity.

I'd see him regularly. I felt sorry for his lonely life. I set out to prove I was a good son. We'd go drinking in pubs and he'd start fights with strangers. It wasn't hard in Southend.

One evening we played pool in a local pub. It was the kind of place that was busiest during the day. The hardened drinkers had retired to their beds by seven o'clock. The pool was my suggestion, as games weren't my dad's thing. After a few goes, two men came over and placed a 20p coin on the table, which meant they were claiming the next game. My dad, pint in hand, cue in the other, glared at them as they made their way back to the bar.

'What's that about?' he asked. I explained the pub etiquette. 'Fuck them,' he said loudly. 'We're playing next.' He wasn't even enjoying the game. I explained that it was only fair they played too. We finished up as the other men approached the table.

'You're going next, are you?' my dad asked them, pumping his chest out and snarling at them.

'Yeah, is that a problem?'

I'm not sure what happened next but suddenly the man was squaring up to my dad. I rushed over, pushing my body between them, shoving the man away and saying, 'He's my dad and he's an arsehole. I'm sorry.'

My direct approach worked because the man's face softened. Still eyeing my dad warily, he said, 'I didn't know he was your dad. No problems, mate.'

I pushed my dad, who was posturing behind me, out of the pub. We were on the street as the sun was going down. Cars whizzed by on the busy road. I grabbed him by his coat lapels, throwing him against a wall. 'Fuck you!' I shouted at him.

'They were cunts,' he said, genuinely perplexed by my anger.

'No, they weren't. They just wanted to play pool,' I said. He made a dismissive sound. I pulled him forward and shoved him back hard into the wall. He looked scared. 'Fuck you!' I repeated. 'This is what you're like. You've always been the same.'

I wanted to let loose. I wanted to destroy him. I wanted to smash his head through the bricks. My mind was alive with the thought. I was so close to letting myself go, letting all the rage consume me. It was like having a sight of freedom from a prison cell. God, it would feel good.

I started to tell him I remembered everything he had done.

'What are you talking about?' he asked.

I told him about incidents from our past.

'Your mother has poisoned your mind.'

'No. You fucking did those things. I saw it. Don't you fucking dare deny it. I saw it.' I loosened my grip. He whimpered.

'Why are you doing this?' he asked.

'Because I fucking saw it,' I said, tears spilling out of my eyes.

He paused for a moment. 'And I'm sorry,' he said, looking me directly in the eye.

I leaned back against the wall of the pub as I watched him walk away, his shoulders hunched. I suddenly became tired; my energy drained away like I was a bottle being emptied.

He was sorry. He knew. Those words soothed me. He never owned up to anything, he denied our own reality. It was maddening but this offered me some hope. My body loosened, some knots untied. I almost crumbled. I had always wanted him to acknowledge what he'd done. To take responsibility for himself, so I didn't have to. While he refused, we'd forever be reliving the same fight. In that moment, outside the pub, I felt I could forgive him. I followed him home.

Inside, he sunk down onto the sofa, looking broken. I sat opposite him, wanting him to admit to his crimes, to understand what he was saying sorry for. Eventually he piped up: 'You were young, you think you know. Silly boy.'

With that the drawbridge was hauled back up. The light evaporated. The denial of the palpable truth felt like a knife in the chest. I roared at him with all that was in me. I stood over him with my fists raised. He cowered, with his hands over his head, just like my mother had done. 'Don't hit me,' he pleaded.

'Fucking listen to me. Hear me. What you did was wrong. It was wrong!' I screamed. And when my piece was said, and I was sure he wouldn't answer back, I went upstairs to bed.

Chapter 22

I pulled up in my rusty, pale blue Lada, not the classiest car but at least I had wheels. Due to an electrical fault, it had a permanently illuminated sign on the dashboard saying, STOP. I was scared about what I was going to do, but I'd get by. I always did.

It was a cold March morning and I made my way into the 1960s school building on Canvey Island, Essex. The old oil refinery loomed in the background and the only attempt at brightening the entrance was some rudimentary landscape gardening, presumably constructed in the belief that a couple of juniper bushes would make people feel less depressed about all the concrete.

There was a tightness across my chest, but I took a deep breath, knowing that once I walked through the heavy swing doors I'd have no choice but to deal with whatever was in front of me. I had asked around about the school and the consensus was, if you had a choice, you shouldn't send your kids there. It was not a shining example of academic brilliance. It was grim and the sky signalled imminent rain. It took me back to my old school days with Ullmer, and now I was to follow his line of work.

I had been to university to study drama. Ullmer had assisted me with my UCAS form, running mock interviews with me, advising me on subjects to talk about at the interview. While there I had drifted around and never spoke in my seminars, still feeling exposed when eyes were on me. I made friends, had girlfriends, laughed and joked but I held back from it all, watching at a safe distance. I enjoyed being in shows, garnering praise or attention, but raised a performative shield so people didn't see my real character. The texts of medieval theatre bored me. I didn't want to learn about the subtext in Shakespeare. Come to think of it, I don't think I was interested in drama. But I got involved in an alternative scene, where shows were devised and the rule book thrown out. It was fun and pretentious. Students putting on shows in which they rolled on the floor 'expressing' themselves, repeating the same sentence over and over again and miming actions that weren't even recognisable. Narrative was a dirty word and I once opened a show by taking twelve minutes to drag myself across the stage, moaning like an injured dog. I was pleased the government paid the tuition fees.

We were taken to one show called *Hamlet*, which was actually just an actor on stage alone, mumbling incoherent sentences for an hour before shitting in a bucket live on stage. At the end of the show, the lecturer got up from his seat and said, without any irony, 'Superb. I can't wait to see his *King Lear*.'

I had stayed in contact with Ullmer. I was a guest at his wedding, even performing a sketch. He came to see me in a show once and slept on the floor of my little room. His influence on me had waned: I no longer found his conversation stimulating, I found his views boring and his presence was an embarrassment to me. My friends at university laughed about him, saying he reminded them of Uncle Monty from the film *Withnail and I* and telling me that he obviously fancied me. And when I returned from university for the holidays I'd catch up with him for a drink. He'd suggest trips away or going back to his flat, but I'd refuse, making excuses. He would become sullen and talk about the importance of giving time to friendships even when there are other commitments. It didn't bother me now. I brushed his complaints away, feeling that once I'd seen him, that was it, my duty was done.

I presented myself at the reception of the school and was soon joined by a friendly, middle-aged head of year who looked a bit like Michael Palin. He made polite conversation and had a kindly manner. He showed me how the electronic register worked and directed my attention to what he called a 'panic button' at the base of the device. 'Don't feel bad if you have to press it,' he said. 'Most teachers do.' If I couldn't stand it, I told myself, I had the freedom to walk out.

Michael Palin led me along a corridor with the kind of blue laminate flooring you only find in schools, hospitals and other institutions people don't want to be in. Eventually we arrived outside a classroom. I could hear shouting. This all seemed to be happening a little fast. I mean, wasn't he going to give me a few tips? Or at least a blindfold and a cigarette?

He reached out to the handle of the door. Wanting to buy time I asked, 'It's an English language class?'

'Er … no. Maths, I think. Bottom set,' he replied, checking a slip of paper.

195

I'd told them I would teach drama and English. What were they thinking? Michael Palin pulled the door open, and I entered the classroom as half of the thirty or so teenage kids rapidly scrambled to find their seats, while the other half ignored my presence. 'Right, I'll leave you to it,' he said. I didn't want him to go.

'Has any work been set?' I asked.

He came into the room, which made a few more kids reluctantly get into their seats, and searched the desk. 'Doesn't look like it, but they'll have textbooks,' he said with an encouraging smile as he turned round and left.

The room smelled of disinfectant and pencil shavings. I walked to the front of the class and stood with my hands on my hips in what I hoped was a commanding stance. Few of the kids acknowledged me; they just carried on talking and laughing. 'I'm Mr Mitchelson,' I said, the words sounding hollow. If anything I was just Tom.

I told them to take out their textbooks and show me where they had got to. A group of diligent-looking girls sitting near the front indicated a page but some rowdy boys at the back suggested they hadn't got that far. I told them to start wherever they wanted.

'Are we allowed to talk, sir?' one of them asked.

'Yes,' I replied, not wanting to be undermined by them deciding to talk anyway and then have to try to keep them quiet.

A low mumble of chatter filled the next twenty minutes until a girl's hand shot up. I approached her desk. 'Sir, how do you work this out?' She slid the textbook over the desk towards me.

There are 720 boys and 700 girls in a school.
The probability that a boy chosen at random studies geography
is 2/3
The probability that a girl chosen at random studies geography
is 3/5
How many students study geography?
What is the probability that a student chosen at random from
the whole school does not study geography?

I needed to read the question again. 'Well,' I said. 'I think you have to work it out yourself.'

She was undeterred. 'But how?'

I reread it. My brain froze. 'You know, I don't usually teach maths, but let me have a look.' I returned to my seat, leaning back in my chair so it was balancing on only two legs, trying to keep the cacophony of chatter out of my mind so I could concentrate. It took me ages. Eventually I worked out that the answers were 900 and 0.37, and I went back over and proudly showed her how I'd done it. She looked at me as if I was the thickest man in the world.

In the dry, stale air of the staffroom at break, I mingled with the other teachers. It was the kind of place where if you laughed, several people would turn and give you a look. Suited men crumbled in the corner reading John Grisham novels and a couple of women were complaining in hushed tones by the catering-sized tub of instant coffee. There wasn't much of an effort to welcome me; in fact, there was a high level of uninterest: don't make bonds that will only get broken. I guessed that they saw temp teachers all the time and imagined I would be gone in a few days.

I chatted with a couple of younger teachers and asked them for tips about discipline in the classroom. 'Mmm, punch 'em!' a ponytailed man suggested. 'The problem is,' interrupted another, 'we can't expel the bad ones because where would they go? The kids that get chucked out from other schools come here.' I asked the guy with the ponytail how he felt about teaching. He told me he was hoping to sign a record contract with his band.

The kids were familiar to me. I knew the council houses they lived in, or the small terraced homes off the arterial road. I knew lots went to McDonald's three times a week and the chicken shop twice; that they went down the high street on a Saturday and watched TV five hours a day. That their mums gave their dads bumper boxes of cigarettes for their birthdays and they all just wanted to get by. Opportunities were limited and those who broke out of that mould were often viewed as having ambitions above themselves.

After finishing university I lived a hand-to-mouth existence. I was still notionally living at my dad's flat in Essex, but more often than not I was sleeping on friends' sofas in London. My dad, who had long since stopped applying for jobs, busied himself fighting with his neighbours (literally) and was a virtual recluse, apart from his trips to Sainsbury's. I spent time with him regularly, feeling sorry for how lonely he must have been. I saw it as my duty to look out for him, provide him with company when he'd burnt all his other bridges. There were one or two women in his life, although he told me nothing about them, and the affairs quickly ended for reasons I can only guess. The less active he was in his own life, the more interest he took in me. He thought that, with my interest in drama, I should become a movie star, which in a way flattered me, but the impracticality of his encouragement frustrated me. I had left university knowing full well what I was going to do with my life: make my own way. The feeling was ferocious.

Whatever I ended up doing, it would be by myself, for myself. I'd never have a boss. I'd never be reprimanded, held to account or beholden to anyone. This posed a problem, though, because without a job it was difficult to get money. I believed people who had jobs were fundamentally flawed. They had enslaved themselves to a master and I wasn't going to make that mistake.

I felt smart but didn't think I was clever in the way other people were. I didn't have opinions, and even if I did, I certainly wasn't going to share them. My intelligence was secret, observational, picking up on what people wanted and playing to it. I was still highly sensitised to people's moods and people reacted to me strongly. I responded to them in a way they liked. I'd reveal nothing. I'd give them a blank canvas and they could decide what to paint. *More fool them,* I thought, *because that's not what I'm really like.*

I had spent the years constructing myself. I felt I was a good piece of work. I accentuated my vowels and hit all my 't's and played up the self-deprecation. My dad had read the news on the radio and had a smart voice; I copied it and took it up a gear.

I aped everything and everyone. I imitated the way I thought intelligent people talked. I understood what it was to *look* thoughtful but the last thing I wanted to do was think. If you'd asked me who I was, I would not have known the answer, and even if I had, I wouldn't have told you. Where had I been? Where was I going? I didn't even want to tell my friends. For my whole life I had hidden everything and I wasn't going to give it up now. What was life growing up like? Good, thanks. Next question. I told strangers that I had been to Cambridge University. That made them sit up and notice me. A lot of my work could be done with that small lie. It was a nervy way to live: bobbing and weaving to other people's desires. A stream of pointless lies littered wherever I went.

I felt so strong, like an immovable boulder. But then sometimes I'd feel alone. Suddenly my heart would feel vulnerable and my legs so weak that they wouldn't support my body. I'd want to close the curtains, lie down and let the world pass by. Not because I was depressed, but because it was exhausting in the outside world. Just like our furniture when I was a kid, everything could be smashed to smithereens in a minute.

I couldn't see it at the time, but I armed myself to the teeth. If the world was going to try to rip me apart, I'd withstand everything it threw at me. I'd manage and navigate it all, using all the tools I had. Or I'd bring it all down in flames if I had to.

When you don't trust anyone – and I mean anyone – you don't think you're someone who doesn't trust anyone, you just think everyone you meet is untrustworthy. My head was plagued with thoughts. *What's your game? What do you want? What do I need from you?*

I'd analyse their thoughts, their words; I'd find out their schemes. I'd rationalise this voice away, but it was with me all the time. I looked at people who trusted each other and thought they were idiots. I mean, they would be, wouldn't they? They didn't know what I knew. Everyone has an ulterior motive, everything comes at a price.

Writing comedy was what I wanted to do. My sketch group at school had provided me with an escape. I wanted to turn everything into a joke. I'd written and performed my comedy sketches at school with my friend Ian, and we'd recently submitted some to a national radio show and earned ourselves a weekly commission for two minutes of material. We wrote jokes on spec for a topical comedy show on Channel 4 too, sending them in down a dial-up modem from home. We'd click 'send' on an email, have a cup of tea, and check back twenty minutes later to see if it had gone through. The big hope was that one of the jokes would be read aloud by the presenter so we could split the sixty quid payment. We made very little money but when we got something broadcast it felt like a sweet victory.

Becoming a successful writer was clearly going to take some time. Maybe a year, I thought, so when I saw an advert in my local paper asking for supply teachers and stating that a teacher training certificate was not required, it seemed like a great opportunity. I'd have to work five shifts in a pub to earn one day's wages, and that would involve someone telling me what to do. This would just be temporary, the odd day here or there in different schools. I would essentially be devoid of any real responsibility and I'd be my own boss.

Later on during my first day in the school, I found myself taking a German class, but it was a different type of language that caused me problems. 'Fuckers!' screamed a thirteen-year-old boy with a severe haircut who must have been about four foot three.

'Don't say that,' I told him.

'Fuckers!' he shouted louder.

He'd been saying this word ever since the bell had signalled the start of the lesson. 'He always does that,' a spotty-faced girl offered helpfully. I still avoided pressing the panic button. To me that would have been a failure. I escorted him outside.

'What's the matter? Why do you keep saying that?' I said.

He shrugged his shoulders. 'I don't know.'

'Can you stop?'

'Yes, but I don't want to do any work.'

'Okay,' I replied. 'Then don't.' This seemed like a sensible deal to strike.

The next day I found myself supervising a music class. An old television on a shaky stand had been wheeled in so the kids could watch *Grease*. I shouted myself hoarse trying to get them to pay attention to John Travolta quivering on the screen instead of pushing each other off their chairs. They were uninterested in a group of twenty-somethings in tight leather trousers pretending to be teenagers.

My home economics students were despondent when I told them they couldn't cook their Welsh rarebits even though they had brought in the ingredients. I didn't want to be responsible for thirty kids lighting small fires, but after a while I relented. I made a mental note of the two large fire extinguishers stuck to the walls.

As the kids were wiping down the work surfaces – and the walls – Michael Palin, the avuncular head of year, appeared at the door of the classroom and beckoned me over. 'How did you think it went yesterday?' he asked. His manner was inscrutable. There was something going on. I tried to reassure myself that if I'd done something wrong, I could just leave. He couldn't stop me.

'It was all right, I guess,' I said carefully.

'Would you consider taking on a role to the end of term?'

Christ, what? 'Excuse me?' I said. My reluctance to press the panic button was paying off, as they obviously had me down as someone who wasn't going to break easily. They were right. I told him I wouldn't be able to commit to anything long-term.

Back in the staff room an open-faced French teacher in her forties approached me. 'So, I heard they offered you a job,' she said with a flat Lancashire accent.

'Yeah, but I'm a comedy writer and there's a radio show I'll be working on next month.'

'Oh, right. Not going to carry on teaching, then?'

'The kids here are difficult. It's like being a riot prevention officer,' I told her.

She lifted her eyebrows a little and wandered off to make a cup of tea. *Snooty cow,* I thought.

I just saw sad-faced people shuffling from one room to the next, trying to regain control over chaos. I knew nothing about them, but I decided they were serving time, counting down the years till their pensions kicked in, like prisoners looking to their release dates.

The school was a place for kids to go during the day. If they got a bit educated while they were there, all the better. I didn't want to be part of it.

I got dressed and ran to the newsagent round the corner, picking up five copies of the *Daily Mail* and placing them on the counter in front of a woman doing puzzles in a magazine. She looked mildly perplexed, as if I had made some sort of mistake.

'I'm in it,' I told her by way of explanation.

'What have you done?' she asked.

'No, I've written a piece in it,' I told her. Outside, I hurriedly flicked through the first few pages. And there it was. A full-length picture of me in baggy jeans, checked shirt and cardigan with the headline A LESSON IN LUNACY. 'He's jobless, speaks no German and got a D in GCSE maths. But after a ten-minute interview, Tom Mitchelson was given a job teaching (you've guessed it, German and maths!) in an Essex school. Just what is going on?' And then the best bit: my byline.

After a few days of teaching in the school I had returned to London to tell my friends how ridiculous it was that I had become a teacher. One of them had suggested it would make a good newspaper scoop, and if I wrote up my adventure he would pass it on to a friend that worked at the *Daily Mail*. I hadn't hesitated. The school was trying to cope with chronic underfunding, a shortage of teachers and deprivation in the surrounding area, but it seemed like a good story. I started making notes each day after returning from school, planning my exposé. I had ended up following in my dad's career by accident.

I loved the thrill of being undercover, having a secret mission and making notes about the things people told me over what they assumed was a private conversation. This was a world I knew. Subterfuge and dissembling were second nature. I had grown up keeping secrets. And without knowing it, I'd learned from Ullmer the skill of manipulation. I could appear as one thing and be another. My vulnerability gave me a cloak to hide my deception.

If the staff and kids were to be collateral damage from my article, then so be it. I lied to them in order to reveal the truth. The pupils and teachers were characters in my story.

A couple of weeks later I was ready to write my article. Having no formal training in journalism, I tackled it in the same way I might have written a school essay on what I did on my summer holidays. I didn't understand what a subjunctive was or why you needed to conjugate verbs, so I focused on writing it like I told the story to my friends. I sent it to my dad, keen for his professional input.

I filed the piece and a little while later the features editor rang to tell me they wanted to run it the next day. I jumped in the air, rubbing my hands together. This was my big moment.

And now here it was in black and white. A whole page in a national newspaper. My chunky mobile was constantly ringing with requests for interviews and comments. There was one from the breakfast television show *GMTV*, which wanted me to appear early the next morning. For a man who wished to reveal as little as possible about himself, going on national TV was counterintuitive.

I was petrified of being asked questions I couldn't answer, yet somewhere in me I had to do it. I was thrilled that people were listening to me, taking notice of what I'd done. I wanted more of that feeling.

I warmed up with an appearance on a local radio station. After a jocular start the presenter turned the screw: 'But why did you keep returning to the school to teach there if you knew you weren't helping the kids?'

I was completely thrown. Why would I worry about not helping the kids? That wasn't my job. I felt defensive. 'I was only there ten days,' I said. 'It took a while to work out what it was like.'

The interview's change in tone took me by surprise. I was riding high from what I regarded a huge success. I was in the paper. The way this interviewer was speaking to me was like I was in some way the villain. I mean, fuck her, right? How dare she judge me? I was raising the issue of how shit everything was in school. She should have been thanking me.

Later in the afternoon Estelle Morris, the education secretary, was questioned by Jeremy Vine on his Radio 2 show about why someone like me had been able to teach in a school in the first place. She promised to put a stop to these agencies providing unqualified people. The government even brought in some new legislation to enact this. The whole thing felt exhilarating. On this show, it was even playing out like I was a truth-telling crusader rather than just a fly-by-night chancer. This was the ultimate reward for my ulterior motive – being praised for helping the education of the nation's children. The laugh was on everyone except me.

Early the next day I was waiting in the green room at the ITV studios on the South Bank, about to make my national television debut. I was too nervous to eat any of the array of pastries. I drank my coffee leaning forward so I didn't spill any on my pristine shirt. The *Daily Mirror*'s editor, Piers Morgan, was shown into the room and was halfway through defending himself to someone over printing a picture of Naomi Campbell emerging from a Narcotics Anonymous meeting. He glanced up at me, decided he didn't need to engage and continued talking loudly. I wondered how he could be so confident while at the same time being such an obvious dickhead.

Shortly after a news piece about Dudley Moore, who had died the previous evening, the call came and I followed a girl of about my age straight towards the pastel-coloured set where Eamonn Holmes and Penny Smith were waiting for me. 'Great story,' said Eamonn, and then, 'Penny wants to do a joke about you teaching German being similar to her teaching the offside rule. So just let her get that out, okay?'

I nodded and he shrugged his shoulders, theatrically exasperated. The bright lights were shining directly on us, making the rest of the room a darkened blur. Being myself in normal life was stressful enough, but having to think how I would come across to millions had sent my brain into overdrive. I sat down and was going to do everything I could to come across as relaxed. My fear of losing my train of thought had kept me up most of the night, but I was also thinking about getting my own jokes in.

A breezy jingle signalled the end of the commercial break and Penny looked into the camera: 'Let's talk about education. Which is never far from the news, is it? If you've got kids at school, you hope they're being taught by teachers who know their stuff. Well, that's not always the case. Meet Tom, supervisor in maths, home economics and German.'

She turned to me and gave me a breakfast-television smile. 'Good morning,' she said. 'Now, this wouldn't be so surprising if it wasn't for the fact that you got a D at GCSE maths, your degree is in drama and you have no teaching qualifications.'

'Yes, that about sums it up,' I said.

'So how did you get the job?'

I knew the story inside out so I kicked it off. 'It was very easy. I saw an advert in my local paper. It said I could become a teacher without a PGCE. I rang them up. I had a ten-minute interview in which they asked me a couple of questions: they said do you have any teaching experience and I said no, and then they asked me if I had a police record and I was also able to say no. And then two weeks later I found myself in front of a classroom with a load of kids looking at me.'

I was relieved to have got through this stage of the interview unscathed. This performance did not feel easy. When you see someone putting on an act with such intent, it makes you wonder what they're really like. The effect is intriguing. Who is this person really? What are they keeping from us? The thing was, I didn't know what I was trying to hide. Just who I really was, I guess.

'And when you say they were looking at you. How? Bemused?'

'As bemused as I was looking. It was difficult to get their attention. That was the first problem I had.'

'Well, that was the least of your problems. You had to teach German but you don't speak the language.'

'And that's quite tough teaching it. But it did give me something in common with the class, though.' I had wanted to get that line in, and Penny rocked with laughter. Ha!

'You're all learning together!' she said, joining in.

I'd gone from sleeping on people's sofas to being on the most famous sofa in Britain, and I was playing it well. This was the start of something. No one at the school had really expected me to teach anything but I was spinning it. It was stupid to have untrained people in the class, but the school didn't have a choice.

'But what made you think you could teach?' she asked.

This had never occurred to me. I didn't think I could. 'I didn't give it a lot of thought, to be honest. It was ridiculous. I shouldn't be allowed to do that really. They did have some work set. Work to copy out from the book. But it was tough getting them to do it.'

Penny nodded in agreement. 'I mean, it is an amusing story, but it is a bit like getting me to explain the offside rule, frankly.' She let out a large laugh and held on to the sofa cushion to steady herself. This was going *really* well. We were both making jokes. I could tell she was hoping her quip would have landed better but she regained her composure. She changed tone suddenly by putting a solemn face on. 'It's quite depressing as well?'

'Yes, it is. I mean, if I had kids I wouldn't want them taught by me.' This was another of my prepared lines and it hit the mark as both presenters nodded and giggled.

'What about the other teachers. How did they look at you?'

'They were okay. I wasn't unique for them. They'd had experience with people like me before, coming in and not having the qualifications. So they were quite used to it.'

'Did you enjoy it?'

'No, I didn't. I had no idea how to do it. You can't get any sort of satisfaction out of it. You're simply not teaching.'

And that was that. 'Well, thanks, Tom, for joining us. It is of course a serious situation in our schools.' She then read out a statement from the school: 'No supply teacher is expected to take practical lessons in subject areas in which they are not properly qualified … in each lesson the respective head of department will set appropriate work for the students and members of the department. Full-time staff will automatically provide support and assistance for supply teachers.'

I strode out of the television studio. I'd negotiated a £250 fee for appearing. That, along with the money I had been paid by the school, totalling over £1,000, plus the £1,000 fee for my piece, meant my immediate money worries had been alleviated.

I wondered what was happening at the school. I bet there was less John Grisham read that day. What had Michael Palin made of it all? What about the other teachers? What was done was done. The next problem I had, though, was now that my teaching career had blown up, I needed to move on to something else.

Chapter 23

I'd return to see my dad regularly. One night Ian and I were drinking gin and tonics with him, playing music loudly. Ian liked my dad, as did most of my friends, which infuriated me. They saw only one side of him and I never dreamed of giving them any information that would colour their view. I was happy they enjoyed the good qualities he possessed – after all, that's what I tried to do, but I was resentful that they couldn't understand the dark side. He was charming and made them laugh, but after a while they would realise that they weren't as important to him as he initially made them feel. He had good stories, was interesting company and had a wealth of knowledge, but it would often feel like he was just waiting for you to stop speaking so he could carry on talking about himself.

The downstairs neighbour rang the bell and asked us to turn the music down. My dad responded by shouting in his face, 'You can go and fuck yourself.' It made meeting on the communal stairs more awkward than it might have been.

My dad's flat was filthy, with bank letters, newspapers and circulars strewn across every surface. There were layers of grime across each kitchen appliance and the oven was so black it was beyond cleaning. His hands had become covered in psoriasis and the dead skin would cover the sofa cushions.

Frequently I'd arrive at the front door and hear the television blasting out from within. He would invariably have passed out in front of it, and I'd bang repeatedly on the glass until he opened the door, eyes glazed, and start an incessant monologue that was impossible to follow. He would often pass out in front of me while we watched a film. I'd hear a loud snort and look over to see him slumped, his head lying on the back of the sofa, his mouth wide open. I'd shout at him, push him, dare him to fight me. I wanted to obliterate him in those moments.

After the neighbour had left, looking shaken by the encounter, my dad sloshed back more gin. Ian could see how drunk he was but was unbothered by his deterioration. I despised it. He burbled on, reminiscing about his Fleet Street days as if I hadn't heard it all before. He told a joke about Italian tanks having five gears, all of them reverse. The repetition of this joke that he had told so often sent me into a fury. I spewed out the anger inside. Ian got up and made his excuses to leave, bewildered by my behaviour.

I was torn between screaming and subservience. I didn't feel there was a middle way. I had no capacity to explain to him what I felt, so I submitted to him and played the role of a devoted son, while wanting to rip his head from his shoulders.

He once encouraged Ian to take an unkind former employer to a tribunal for unfair dismissal. He became outraged on Ian's behalf for the way he had been treated, telling him justice must be served. He represented Ian, assuring him that he had everything taken care of. The verdict went against them. They were told to wait while the tribunal discussed whether a penniless Ian would have to pay costs. It was the longest ninety minutes of Ian's life. But my dad was baffled by his concern and instead blamed Ian for the defeat, saying he was 'fucking useless on the stand'.

His maxim was: show no doubt, exhibit no fear, front it out even beyond the point that your cover is blown. When the net was closing, he doubled down, claiming things were black when they were white. And yet I kept him close, determined to make the relationship work.

My mum was the only person I knew I could rely on, the one I truly trusted. I had learned love from her, what it should be. The love I received from her seemed to count double. I knew through my childhood that no matter what happened I would always have that. Without it I would have been a conman, taking people for everything I could, preying on their vulnerabilities. I held her so close. I saw what she went through and how she fought to keep going. I could see how much strain there was on her heart, and now I find it difficult to write about her because I feel so protective.

She was perturbed about my closeness to my dad but didn't question it. If I'd seen him, sometimes I kept it from her to spare her feelings. I once ate two Christmas dinners so I could spend part of the day with each of them. My mum flourished away from torment. She took pleasure in the things that had been denied her: peace, consistency, autonomy and even learning to drive a car.

I resented my continued association with Ullmer, but I didn't understand why. I responded to his emails, which he sent every six months or so, in a perfunctory way. They made me cringe.

How's things? Not heard for ages which means:

1. You're high on drugs and too embarrassed to say
2. You are filthy rich and discarding all your old friends
3. You are besotted by a woman and nothing else matters
4. You have split up and nothing else matters
5. You are rude
6. Life is moving fast and you are earning loads and not stopping
7. Life is moving fast and you aren't earning anything

He was now a principal of a sixth-form college in Canterbury. He told me his teenage son lived with just him during the week and they both returned to the family home in Southend at the weekend.

Do you know you are much older now than I was when you first met me ...? Amazing. How would you deal with a squeaky Tom who refused to get out of the car till he was taken home ... You're now even older and wiser than I was ... Food for thought ... Just chaired counselling service meeting and sitting having tea by the fire before I go home ... Got headhunted by international British school in China this week ... £140k and income tax in single figures ... shame I'm not ready to live in China yet.

I had no interest in the news from his life. A handful of times we met in London for a drink. He wielded control over me and I wonder if his desire to remain in contact was a way of ensuring it carried on. I had no idea that he had abused me.

No concept that I had been vulnerable. No idea how he had betrayed his position of trust. I didn't imagine he had tried to seduce other young boys because I didn't know that was what he had done to me. I thought back to that time and wondered if he had been secretly gay with a crush on me. Perhaps that was it. I knew he had looked out for me and that meant I owed him something, even now. I didn't want to meet him but was worried about saying no. I found that with people in general, I often agreed to things I didn't want to do. I was a secret rebel and grew bitter about what I saw as impositions. It was the same with my dad. I saw him and felt responsible but wanted to break away and follow my own line.

Chapter 24

I sat at the table with Daisy. The rain hammered down outside. Soho looked like it was washing away in a sea of umbrellas. She was obviously nervous and drank the glass of wine I gave her within minutes of us meeting. She looked furtively around but asked me if I was nervous.

'A bit,' I replied.

She leaned in, telling me how pleased she was that we'd met. We made small talk for a bit then she asked, 'What's the situation with your marriage?'

I stuttered. I hadn't given that much thought. 'It's complicated. We've been together a while, but there's no spark anymore.'

She flicked her hair from her face. 'I know exactly what you mean,' she said. 'That's how I feel about my husband. I love him, though.' She smiled with relief that we were on the same page.

A couple approached us, politely asking whether they could sit on the two vacant seats at our table. 'Sorry, we've got friends coming,' I said. There was something preying on my mind. 'If you love him, why are you here?' I laughed along with my question, to try to alleviate the directness.

'I could ask you the same question,' she said, looking a bit indignant.

'Maybe I don't love her. Anymore.'

She surprised me by reaching out across the table and touching my hand. 'That can happen.' I kept my hand there, but I wanted to pull it away.

'Do you have kids?' she asked.

'No,' I said. 'You?'

'Yes, two girls. Six and eight.' I didn't ask anything about them, so she moved on to my job. 'You're in property?'

When lying it's best to keep the falsehoods as near as possible to the truth. Throwing out lies here, there and everywhere leads to having to lie more. And it can get confusing. But I couldn't tell her what I really did. 'Yeah, I've got a few flats.'

'Where are they?'

I scanned my brain for possible locations, throwing out a few. 'Epping. South London.' I changed the subject back to her.

She told me she'd had an affair with a family friend a year ago. It hadn't ended badly but she had learned to make sure that when she played away, it was always well away from home.

She wasn't looking for someone to ride off into the sunset with, just some good old-fashioned fun. We ordered a bottle of wine. The only reminder that she was married was the ring on her finger. She asked me if I'd taken mine off. I told her I never wore one.

At the end of the evening we stepped out onto Greek Street. The rain had eased off but the air was wet. I gave her a peck on the cheek. She went to kiss me on the mouth. I moved back. I didn't fancy her, but I had given her signs of my interest all night.

On my way back I received a text from her to my burner phone: 'Had a lovely evening. Sorry if I ruined it at the end.'

I sent a message back saying I was worried about being seen on the street and I'd give her a call. I wasn't going to.

It was my third date with a married woman in a week. I had been led into this demi-monde by an explicit internet dating service established for the sole purpose of enabling married people to commit adultery. I didn't have a wife and I was undercover for the paper. They'd asked me to date women on the website Illicit Encounters, which was by far the most successful of its type, with double the members of the less seductive sounding Meet 2 Cheat. I'd gone on the site and the warning on the homepage made me laugh: 'Not all affairs have a positive effect on a marriage.'

I surfed my options. 'My preference is for a man who is much younger than me with rugged features,' said one woman on the site. Another warned, 'I prefer Asian men, as they respect older women,' but added, 'I'm not ruling out any nationality.'

One profile I came across acknowledged the dangerous game afoot. She cautioned, 'You must have a determination not to hurt your kids or partner.' What she meant, I guess, was someone who was good at covering his tracks and therefore hers. I spent hours arranging dates with these women. One turned my invitation down gently, informing me that she could 'sense' I should try again with my wife, while Julie22 only wanted to see me if I agreed to shave my head, which felt excessive.

When the piece came out in the paper I felt a little ashamed. There was a big picture of me, walking down the street with Daisy. Her face had been blurred and the head-line read WAYWARD WIVES CLUB. The piece I wrote had been substantially edited and a prudish, moralistic attitude had been added with lines like, 'I feel sorry for the husband that the mother of his children is pursuing cheap thrills with strangers.'

The only dating I did was for the *Daily Mail*. It allowed me to step out into the world protected by my double identity. I didn't have to have real relationships. I could just pretend.

These articles became my life. The first time I wrote one, a woman on the commissioning desk explained over the phone to me that she'd read in *Grazia* (that well-known journalistic source) that Britain was under siege from a regiment of Russian temptresses set on grabbing a rich British man and his British passport. She wanted to know if I'd be up for posing as a playboy and taking these women on dates. Brushing aside the xenophobic premise, I didn't really understand how it could be an article, but I agreed to do it.

'How does it work with expenses?' I asked. She explained that I had to buy things, but the paper would recompense me within two weeks. 'If I'm supposed to be rich and I'm out to lunch, what should I spend?'

She let out a thoughtful sound. 'I'd say try not to go crazy. Keep dinners down to seven hundred quid if you can.'

I gulped. How on earth would I ever spend that much?

The voice down the end of the phone added, 'And, of course, if you need to take them to a hotel afterwards, we'll get that too.'

I thanked her, but it was only after I had placed the phone down that I wondered, *If they were paying me to write a piece and expected me to sleep with the women, then what did that make me? And what did it make the* Daily Mail? *And what about the women?*

219

I didn't dwell on this for long because I was excited by the secret mission I had to execute. I looked at myself in the mirror. I certainly didn't shout money. I hardly whispered small change, so I went out and bought a Paul Smith suit on expenses. I saw myself as a shape shifter, slipping into identities like people do clothes.

I spent nights on my own hanging around in clubs in Chelsea, watching the ultraviolet light turn white dresses into glaring beacons while couples canoodled in the dark leather seating. The crowds were heaving. Sleek women of uncertain backgrounds danced round their handbags. I could hear the murmur of Slavic accents. I had no idea how to approach them, so I hung around, looking uncertain. I'd retreat to the bar and order a drink, where I'd steel myself for another attempt.

After a few nights it seemed clear that there wasn't a glittering army of glamorous, ambitious, sophisticated vamps descending locust-like on the world's leading financial centre in a mad search for merchant bankers and commodity traders. Or if there was, I wasn't looking in the right places. I called the commissioning desk to raise my concerns and was given short shrift. They really wanted the piece, and they were sure I'd find them if I kept looking.

I started taking my friend Pete out with me to haunts in Mayfair frequented by younger, minor members of the royal family. We drank expensive wine and chatted to women in upmarket hotels. I met Pete when he moved into a friend's house I was already staying at. He had left a girlfriend in a hurry, and we started going out for drinks together. He had constructed a bad-boy, working-class persona after being taken out of private school for a comprehensive when his mum left his dad. In some ways I'd done the opposite. We hit it off straight away. We both had a contemptuous attitude to authority and shared a similar bemusement at how many useless people had got into positions of power. He told me recently that he had the problems of a millennial without the advantages of youth.

I no longer cared if the women were Russian. I expanded my remit to include eastern Europeans. I made notes for my piece in the toilets while the women I chatted to waited on the dance floor. I heard a story about a gold-digging woman who had asked a man to buy her an expensive watch. When he said, 'But it's £50,000!' she had apparently replied, 'Is there a problem with money?' So that became my opening paragraph in the article, but I said it had happened to me.

I made a few dates. Lithuanians and Estonians mainly. It was easier with Pete there. It made the whole approach less awkward. I didn't feel they were after my imaginary money; they just thought it would be nice to go out with me on a date. I gave no attention to creating a second identity. I just told them my usual property empire story. The truth was that I could pack everything I owned into a rucksack in five minutes. The reality of these dates was that we had nothing in common. They were often hard work.

Natalia's high heels echoed over the marble. She had cool, pale skin and a pixie-like expression. Audrey Hepburn meets Björk. She asked for a glass of Chardonnay, but I insisted on Bollinger 1998 because I was worried how inexpensive drinks would look on my expense sheet. She kept telling me she was proud of her curves. 'Men are not dogs, they don't like bones,' she told me. I laughed and she shook her brown hair, asking me if I thought brunettes were more intelligent than blondes. I told her I didn't. She nodded enthusiastically. 'Yes, because if you were a blonde and dyed your hair brunette, how would that make a difference?'

I suppose it might have been tempting to take advantage of my secret life, but I wouldn't have dared. I couldn't tolerate the thought of making a move on someone who didn't know my real name. I found it hard to kiss girls I liked in real life. The idea of encroaching on someone's personal boundaries horrified me. I guess I knew how it felt. Instead, I led them on, playing my role, trying to charm them. I wanted them to want me, and I didn't care about the lies.

My friend Juliet would have a go at me over my less than salubrious jobs. She was just looking out for me, concerned about my walking this dubious moral line. It enraged me but I never said, 'You think I'm immoral? You don't know what immoral is.' The love and hate I felt for my dad had infected everything. It skewed my understanding of good and bad. It was the same with Ullmer: I had accepted the wicked in order to receive some benefit. Everyone was a potential enemy, everyone was on borrowed time. I was waiting for the moment when they would let me down or pass judgement on me. No one would involve themselves in my business in any way, ever again.

I'd regale my dad with stories of my journalistic exploits, and he'd lap them up. The more I had lied the more he applauded. He'd edit my pieces, buying a copy and keeping each article in a folder.

I told myself that my job gave me freedom. I could go wherever I wished, whenever I wanted. But it didn't. My work was so irregular I had no security. I wanted to do big things, make a splash, have my voice heard, but it was like I misunderstood the world. I felt like the umbilical cord that was wrapped around my neck when I was born was still there, pulling me back to where I felt safe. It took me back to my dad, kept me bound to Ullmer, and while I was tied to them I couldn't go anywhere.

It cost me fifteen quid to register with richsoulmate.com, which hardly seemed prohibitive. I sat up late into the evening surfing through the choices of women to ask out. My second date on the website almost didn't happen. The night before, I got a text message from Bella, the girl I was due to meet, calling it off: 'I can't meet you. I won't be messed around. I know someone you've been seeing.'

I rang her up. It turned out she'd had the site recommended to her by her friend Leah, who I went out with two days ago and who told her we were going to see each other again. 'I've got morals, and I can't do that,' she told me. I agreed, disappointed because now I'd have to set up another assignation and the paper wanted the piece by the end of the week. Fortunately, by the next morning Bella had put her scruples away and sent me a message saying we could go out after all if we didn't tell Leah.

We met at Nobu restaurant in west London, which I'd heard was swanky. The only way I could get a table was by calling them and telling them I'd give them a namecheck in my *Daily Mail* piece about dating. This ran a slight risk in that the maitre d' might mention it when I arrived, but I figured I'd just bluff it out. On arrival, I spotted pop singer Peter Andre on one side of the room and nearby was the actor who played Jim Robinson in *Neighbours*. I hoped their close proximity would show her I was no stranger to glamour.

Bella was perma-tanned with blonde frizzy hair. She kissed me on both cheeks and told me she'd been to Nobu a lot.

'Well, I didn't want to do anything special on a first date,' I lied.

'I have to tell you I'm not rich,' she said.

'How not rich are you?' I asked.

'I don't really have any money,' she said. She owned a small cosmetic manufacturing business that had hit hard times. She didn't know I was part of the hoi polloi.

'The thing is, I just want to meet interesting people and I thought it was more likely if they were rich,' she told me. 'I guess my idea of a good night out isn't a few drinks followed by a kebab. I want the opportunity to meet successful people.' She checked herself. 'Does that make me sound snooty?'

It didn't, and there was something about her I liked. Maybe it was her honesty. I had to remember I was on a job. I was digging for information for my piece. I poured us some water, ordered black cod and asked her if she had met anyone else from the site.

'I've hardly seen anyone I'm interested in,' she replied. 'A few really ugly guys have contacted me, but I didn't meet them because they were ugly.'

I came clean to her at the end of the meal, telling her what I was up to and that I wasn't a millionaire. She took it very well and we kissed outside the restaurant. I saw her off in a black cab and promised to call, knowing that I wouldn't.

Chapter 25

I was thirty-three years old. I rented a small room in the flat of a friend and my peripatetic career continued. I had no master-plan. I was hoping something would stick. Pete had a job as deputy travel editor of the *Sun* and sent me on occasional jobs in far-flung places. I took part in medieval battle re-enactments; I swabbed for cocaine in posh nightclubs; I trained as a life coach with a company where you handed over money to get qualified; I lived in Gatwick Airport for a week to see what it was like to sleep rough; I worked undercover as a shop model in Abercrombie & Fitch, revealing their bizarre working practices. I tried free running, took a Prince Harry lookalike to Buckingham Palace and applied for a job as a flunkie there a few days later. I learned how to hunt deer on the moors, assisted at a pet funeral parlour, and I was the face of *Take a Puzzle* magazine at Christmas. I was a joke writer on radio and TV shows. I took a leading role in a low-budget British romcom after I met the director by chance and he offered me the role on the spot. I took every job that came up but none of it felt right. The journalism appealed, though, because I kidded myself that when people didn't know who you really were, they revealed themselves in different ways. I thought it was only through deception that you could discover veracity. I was fixed on uncovering the Truth, but never my own.

My phone rang, displaying the word 'anonymous' on the screen. This usually meant a job and I put on a more serious voice as I picked up. It was the *Daily Mail* telling me they'd just got off the phone with a woman who'd called because she was desperate and had nowhere else to turn. And, of course, if she was calling them for help, she really was in trouble.

She told them that her husband had attended a strange training programme. It promised to help men regain their masculinity. There were no details about what the course entailed because it was shrouded in secrecy and her husband was keeping schtum. Ever since he returned to the marital home after the programme, he had been different. Instead of having dinner with his wife, playing with the children and going on holidays together, he now spent most of his spare time at the bottom of the garden, sitting under a tree and chanting. Now they were getting a divorce.

The main source of information was the website itself, which promised a 'process of initiation and self-examination that is crucial to the development of a healthy and mature male self', as well as helping men to 'confront their dependence on women' and move into the 'masculine kingdom', away from the 'comforting embrace' of their mothers.

The woman on the Femail commissioning desk asked whether I wanted to go undercover. I got a lot of work because the women on the desk knew I never said no. I leapt at the chance.

I had become very good at undercover work. I knew what it was like not to trust people, so I imagined what it would take for me to trust someone and performed that role to those around me. My creation was a character who was unbelievably trustworthy.

Around this time, I took a press trip to Turkey and ended up kissing the PR girl on the banks of the Bosphorus. 'Tell me something about yourself,' she said. I told her I was very good at lying. She went off me after that.

Being a secret operative gave me all the power. I was a chameleon. Fitting in with others but always being apart, observing unseen, disguised. I developed a line in sympathy without empathy. 'God, that must be terrible for you. Tell me more,' I'd say, while inside yawning and thinking, *I literally don't give a shit.* I would morph into a version of myself with a twist and people would get caught off guard by my tender nature. I couldn't comprehend my own pain, vulnerability or hurt, and I had no intention of getting to grips with anyone else's. I felt safe in this undercover world, where people couldn't take me at face value, but did.

I signed on for the masculinity course. I arrived on the train and a minibus took me and eight other men into the depths of the English countryside, far from civilisation and mobile-phone reception. The sky got darker, the woods got deeper and the air got colder. The bus rattled along and I could no longer see anything from the windows. Another group of men, dressed in army fatigues, greeted us as we arrived at the camp. The main one started shouting like a sergeant major, telling us where to go and what to do. He had long black sideburns and didn't quite have the solid authority of a military man. I thought he was probably an accountant from the suburbs. He pounded the ground with his boots as he walked up and down in front of us. 'Observe the sacred silence', he barked, and all the men fell quiet and looked at their shoes.

Under cover of a cattle barn they made us sign a confidentiality agreement that said we must never speak to anyone about what happened on the course. I remember feeling outraged that they felt they had the right to do things in secret.

I stood in front of the sergeant and emptied my bag onto the table. He picked up my mobile and wallet, and asked for my wristwatch. He lifted up my sleeping bag, feeling it all round like a child might feel a wrapped present. His attention was caught by a hard protrusion from the bag. He tipped out the Mars bar I had tried to smuggle in.

'Do you have a problem with authority?' he yelled. I said no, knowing that I did. We were kept in the pitch dark in a small room. After two hours we heard the distant sound of drumming. It was a tribal beat, sinister because of its unchanging rhythm. The leaders of the group came into the hut, blindfolded us and led us outside. The drumming became louder as I felt myself being led into another, bigger room. The door closed behind me, shutting out the evening air.

They ripped the blindfolds off. Standing in front of me and the group I'd arrived with were about ten men stripped to the waist, covered in warpaint and wearing feathers in their hair.

The man at the front was more adorned than the others. He had a headdress with different types of feathers sprouting out around him like a peacock's tail. He addressed us from a little stage, introducing himself as 'Eagle', and started talking about what it meant to be a man.

He made a series of statements as if they were a new set of commandments and he was Moses. All in a voice so deep that it seemed like a piss-take. 'Be responsible'. 'Be strong'. The solemnity of the occasion was undermined by the hall we were in, which felt like a scout hut. Eagle made each of us stand individually and tell everyone why we were there.

The first man who got up was hunched and unhappy. He said, 'I'm here because I'm a failure, I'm bullied by my wife, she dictates how I live my life,' and sat back down abruptly. The next got up: 'I'm here because sometimes I despise myself. I feel lonely all the time, I'm lost ...' He stumbled over a few more words before he burst into tears.

I sat watching all this with incredulity. What was the matter with these people? The man I'd just heard speak was genuinely sad, and I pitied his weakness. This display of vulnerability punctured me somehow. When it was my turn I talked broadly positively about myself for two minutes.

Eagle told us that when a group member shared something, the correct etiquette was to say, 'Ah-ho,' and make a gesture. He demonstrated this by raising both hands and waggling them in front of his eyes. He got everyone to do it. It felt ridiculous, but the atmosphere of the room had the intensity of an operating theatre.

We were up until the early hours of the morning, taking part in bonding exercises: carrying logs, sharing how we felt, doing visualisations and observing 'sacred' moments. We roared like lions. Middle-aged men crawled on the scout-hut floor, lashing out with their imaginary paws. We talked to our child selves. Or at least they did: I had nothing to say to my younger self. I was immersing myself in the experience without getting too involved.

We were told to choose our 'warrior' names by picking an adjective and an animal. I spent the rest of the weekend with Mighty Condor, Courageous Wolf and Intrepid Panther. I thought it was funny that no one opted for a sheep or guinea pig. I, however, became Relaxed Penguin.

This was my job. I took pride in telling the stories to my friends afterwards and would try to impress girls with my tales of derring-do. But I was like a magician using distraction, smoke and mirrors to avoid talking about anything personal. I would then fall silent, worn out with my performance and wanting to be alone. In a way I was undercover in my own life too, pretending I was something else.

In the early hours of the morning, with the moon still in the sky, we were ordered to strip and line up for a cold shower. I kept my gaze firmly on the shower cubicle as I waited in line behind the other naked men. We hadn't slept or eaten. Fortunately, having undergone extreme sleep deprivation for another article, it troubled me less than some. If we tried to talk to one another, the sergeant would spring into action, striding over to us to shout, 'Stop talking,' stretching the 'O' in the word stop. Owing to a few whispered conversations I managed to find out that most of the men were fortyish, married and had jobs in IT or finance. They were searching for something intangible. I liked them but the weirdness of the whole set-up meant I was determined to mock.

Most of the others took it deadly seriously. When I struck up a conversation with one man and referred to Eagle as old feather face, he reproached me. With sorrowful eyes he told me, 'That's Eagle. Don't call him feather face.'

After we'd been there for a day, we divided into three groups, each of which had a so-called 'sacred carpet'. It was interesting how many everyday objects had the word sacred in front of them. The silence, the carpet, moments. What I wanted was my sacred Mars bar. I was starving.

We stood around in circles, each man taking it in turns to step into the centre. Each was subjected to questions about why he was there. The first up, a balding man with jowls, started by saying that his dad had died when he was six. He added that his mother had told him he was worthless.

The sergeant whipped up the crowd. He got everyone chanting, 'You're worthless, you're worthless.' The aim was to transport this man back to his traumatic past. Once they'd done that, he was pinned to the floor by six men and had to wrestle his way out from under a blanket. Everywhere I looked men were drained, emotionally and physically. Lying on the floor or sitting propped up against walls, their eyes red and puffy from crying their hearts out. It was extremely disturbing to watch.

The men running the course weren't trained in psychology. The qualification they seemed to share was that they were graduates of the course, but some of them were very skilled at reading signs of hidden emotion.

Then it was my turn. I had been trying to work out what on earth I was going to say. What deep-seated emotional issue I could bring up. I scanned my mind for something to talk about from my own life but drew a blank. Of course, Ullmer and my dad might have made interesting topics, but I'd drawn a curtain around the troubling parts of their involvement with me. I settled on making something up. I walked to the centre of the circle, trying to finalise my story. I stood there with hundreds of eyes fixed upon me and told them I had cheated on my girlfriend.

Being cross-examined for an hour about cheating on a fictitious girlfriend was intense. They told me that I had to wrench the anger from my stomach by yanking a rope with five men pulling the other end. There were men all around, shouting, cheering, willing me along to I don't know what. I was lifted into the air like a cup-winning hero and spun round until the room became a whirl of colour. 'It's over! The pain is out! You are reborn. Your past holds no fear!' I scrambled back to my feet. I kneeled on the floor with my head in my hands, and just like I did the day I attacked my dad, I pretended to cry.

The night hadn't ended. Somehow I knew this was coming. We were instructed to take our clothes off, put our blindfolds back on and hold the hand of the man next to us. Most men were completely naked but, just as I had done with Ullmer, I kept my pants on. We all put our boots back on, grabbed our jackets and walked through the dark woods. The vision was obscene: the men in front of me trudging as a human chain down the muddy path, wearing jackets and shoes but naked from below the waist like Donald Duck. There was more chanting and some dancing, and we were given strange necklaces that looked like scrotums. We had become new warriors.

This was the life I had chosen. The weirder it was, the better it seemed. As the sun rose the next morning we congregated in a circle – everything had to be done in a circle – to cast off our previous identities. A giant wooden phallus was brought out and we passed it round, taking it in turns to talk about masculinity. I had to get another job, but in some strange way proving myself in challenging circumstances made me feel at home.

I was surrounded by all these men searching for some meaning. Trying to understand their place in the world and what it meant to be a man. The two significant males in my life had warped my understanding too. They were entirely different men. My dad was a fighter, refusing to conform; for him, conversation was a means to an end and feelings were for wimps. Ullmer lusted after status and recognition, aligning himself with the establishment; he thought of himself as a deep thinker, an explorer of intellectual ideas. But they were both incapable of being honest; they could think only of themselves and they refused to take responsibility for their actions. I turned to one when the other had failed me. Neither knew what it was to be a man. I was pretty sure the answer for me wasn't on the heather moors of Exmoor, either.

About a year later I saw one of the men from the course in a coffee shop in London. The story had been in the paper with a large photo of me and I'd detailed every one of the organisation's secret ways. He was with his wife and kids. I didn't know what his reaction to my writing about the weekend would be, but he was staring hard at me. I looked back. And then, very quietly, furtively, he raised his hands and mouthed, 'Ah-ho.'

Chapter 26

I met her at a party. There were tea lights everywhere. Someone got up and read a poem and then someone else started playing the guitar, accompanied by a curly-haired man on the bongos. Men with open white shirts and beads round their necks had intense conversations with pretty girls with plaits. It was the kind of thing I hated: people expressing themselves, being free and getting in touch with their feelings. I stood watching the proceedings with my friend. And then I saw her. I knew her from before. Not well, but she was doing an MA course while I was at university, and I'd seen her around. I always thought she was looking at me, but now that I think about it, maybe I was looking at her. My friend and I went over. Her big brown eyes ran into me, and she smiled a beautiful smile.

'Hello,' she said.

'I know you,' I replied.

She shook her head and kept looking at me.

I told her how we had been at university together. I mentioned some people we both knew. I told her the course she'd been on.

She looked up to the night sky, trying to place me in her memories. Her eyes landed back on me. Nothing.

I told her her name. I said I knew she was Brazilian. I reminded her about us bumping into each other on the Tube a few years after university. I told her where she had lived at the time. I sounded like a stalker. All the while she just kept smiling at me. Nothing was coming to her mind.

We talked more. The group of friends she was with were meeting at a restaurant the following night and she said I should come along. I thought about her a lot the next day, hoping that she would be as pretty as she was the night before. I also hoped that she would remember me.

I saw her through the restaurant window. Her hair was tied up and she greeted me like someone she'd known for ages, which in a way she had. At one point she looked at me across the table, tilted her head to the side and smiled. I felt like I had a slow puncture. She took the air out of me.

She was free, unconfined and didn't seem afraid of anything. She made me feel like a young boy and a man at the same time. She was successful at her work and it made me nervous. She mentioned a sold-out theatre show she wanted to go to, and I told her I could get tickets from a friend. The next day I called her and told her I'd got them, but she sounded surprised by my keenness. I hadn't even thought about so much as kissing her. I just wanted to be around her.

She wasn't interested in my anecdotes or the jokes I made. And stripped of those I felt unnerved. When we met again we talked about American politics. I told her everything I knew. Midway through my mini-lecture on Franklin D. Roosevelt's New Deal she said, 'What about you? Tell me something about you. What's your family like?'

Inside a small but manageable panic rose. What did she mean? She knew my job, I'd made her laugh. Wasn't that enough? *Don't ask me about my dad,* I thought. Anyway, what more information was there? I told her I had triplet sisters but we weren't close. My mum and dad were divorced and it hadn't been happy. That felt like enough for now.

She was the opposite. She told me everything about herself. She said what she felt, told me what she wanted. A few weeks later I told her that I loved her and it felt like a small defeat – like someone signing away his fortune – but it was true. I wanted to reveal everything too, but I didn't know how. She loved me too. She took a sledgehammer to my fortified walls and it hurt like hell, but it felt good. She had her own traumatic past, a childhood of loss and despair, and somewhere, as different as we were, we recognised it in each other. And it soothed us and excited us at the same time. I kissed her and kissed her and haven't stopped.

We disappeared together to a different realm of the earth for a while, trying to possess each other entirely. It hit me like the ocean. It was peaceful, deep and vast at first. And then waves would crash into us, knocking us off our feet, but we were used to storms. We found some comfort in that. I returned to Portugal with her, where many of her Brazilian family lived, and we visited old haunts of my childhood. We returned to the old farmhouse, finding that the roof had collapsed and the walls had crumbled. I travelled to Brazil with her, meeting people who hugged me a lot and seemed to mean it.

I knew that at some point Diene would have to meet my dad. I had told him very little about her, struggling to talk to him about anything that mattered to me. I eventually arranged a lunch in my local pub. He arrived breathless, before she did, wearing a bright red blazer, which accentuated the reddish hue of his skin, and sporting a new haircut. He gave me a hug. He was now in his late sixties. His health had deteriorated in the last few years. Heavy drinking, years of smoking and a diet of apple turnovers, oven chips and processed meat had taken their toll. I used to berate him for how unfit he was becoming, and I would be annoyed when it fell on deaf ears. He ordered a double gin and tonic and I was immediately in a bad mood. I felt that every sentence he uttered carried with it a risk of revealing his monstrous side, and I feared he might say something that would so incense me I'd be unable to hide it.

My dad turned his charm on for Diene. Because he didn't get out much, he enjoyed the human contact. He didn't drink excessively and he clearly liked her. She hadn't heard his stories before and he was reluctant for the afternoon to end, suggesting puddings and more drinks. He picked up the bill on one of his many credit cards, and as I waved him goodbye at the Tube and watched the Docklands Light Railway shoot off, carrying him away, I realised that my two worlds colliding hadn't caused an explosion.

That night my dad had a heart attack. He called me from the Southend hospital where he was recovering. He told me how the pain had seared through his arm to his chest, but he'd called the ambulance himself. I felt winded. He had seemed untouchable. I understood, in the way that lessons are only really learned through experience, that no one escapes death. Diene joked that, given he was returning from meeting her, maybe she had caused it. I half-laughed and then thought it was quite possible, given his excitement about his trip to see us. I went straight to Southend, where I was annoyed to see him in such good health, chatting away to the nurses, enjoying the attention. I had rushed to see him – the only person who did – worrying all the way there, and now he was treating it like a joke. The reality of life evaded him, or he evaded it, at every turn.

Diene and I decided to have a baby. What better way to show our love than to make something from it? My mum had always gently encouraged me towards fatherhood, but she never pushed. It hadn't been on the cards. I couldn't imagine what it meant to be a father. The thought of having a child of my own almost overwhelmed me with sadness. I never knew why. I ignored the feeling. I guess I could only relate it to my own sorrow. I imagined it had to be the same for any child of mine. My sister Emma once said that she couldn't look at fathers playing in parks with their kids because it made her too unhappy. I know what she meant. The thought of taking my son or daughter to school made my stomach ache. I would never bring a child into this painful life.

Yet things were different now. Falling in love had grounded me, making me feel more settled. My defences had slackened. I knew that if I thought too much about having a baby I wouldn't do it. So I agreed. It was my birthday and we told ourselves that a year from that day, we'd begin to try.

One year later we were at a family party in Portugal. Chairs and benches had been placed around the side of a large room, and wrinkled old aunts wearing dark mascara and bright lipstick sat chatting with each other, eating stuffed olives and *pastéis de natas*. I took a third glass of vinho verde as I wandered around, trying to find someone who spoke

English, because although I'd learned to ask people how they were in Portuguese, I couldn't understand their answers. I eventually ended up talking to a family friend. 'I understand you begin trying for a baby today,' he said, slapping me on the back.

A few cousins nearby joined in the conversation. 'Hopefully you'll have some good news for us in a few months,' they said.

The wife of the friend came over, handing me a brown paper bag. 'It's a good time to give you this, I think,' she said. Inside was a scientific-looking book about how the food people eat can influence the sex of a baby. 'Asparagus is good for boys, apparently,' she said, giving me a wink.

'That's a lot of pressure to put on yourself, everyone knowing. You'd better deliver now, don't you think?' the family friend said.

I nodded in agreement. Unsure of how everyone knew my business, I found Diene out in the garden. 'Everyone knows we're trying for a baby,' I said.

'I mentioned it to my dad. I think he might have told some people. Why are the English so English about everything?' she asked. As we left that evening, several guests shouted out, 'Good luck!' I'd gone from resisting revealing anything to anyone to letting the world know the most private of details.

Chapter 27

My dad called me to tell me he had been arrested. I knew that the drama in his life would always become my drama too. His version of the story was that one afternoon he heard someone attempting to pick the lock of his front door. He raced over to find a burglar fiddling with the keyhole. 'What the fuck are you doing?' he demanded, to which the man had no explanation. He shoved him down the entrance steps, causing him to stumble and drop his mobile phone, which smashed on the floor. The police arrived, informing my dad that the man was in fact an estate agent who was trying to gain access with his key to one of the rental flats in my dad's block. He had simply got the wrong flat, and called the police after being attacked.

The estate agent told the police that he had tried to explain his error but a drunk and aggressive pensioner ignored his explanations. My dad was adamant that the man was trying to rob him, although he admitted that the police had confirmed he worked for Bairstow Eves. The charges were dropped because there wasn't enough evidence.

He had left his old flat when a dispute over the timing of a rent increase led him to stop paying the rent entirely, pocketing the money the government gave him for it. It was a year before the landlords managed to give him notice to leave and he was ordered by a court, who took into account his penury, to pay the sum of £1,000, a fraction of what he owed, in monthly £5 instalments. He delivered it in person every week. He'd take out a crisp fiver, screw it up, go outside, tread it into the muddy ground and piss on it. He'd then put it in an envelope and post it through the door of the estate agent. To my dad this was victory in its clearest form.

He'd bought his new flat by pressuring his mother to front up a deposit and telling lies on the mortgage form. He repeated his trick of signing off the dole and then, once the purchase had been completed, he signed back on and the government took up the mortgage repayments. He was a sophisticated benefit cheat.

Six months after we'd started trying for a baby, Diene, who had decided to visit a Chinese acupuncturist in order to help with conception, came home from work and handed me a pregnancy test.

'The acupuncture worked,' she said.

I looked down at the plastic stick that showed we were going to have a baby. The one person who didn't know our plans was my dad. I found it impossible to tell him. Once we'd seen a scan and found, to our relief, that we weren't having triplets, I took my dad out with Pete for a drink. I had planned to tell him before Pete arrived, but I was unable to find a moment in between the stories I'd heard many times before. I got up to go to the toilet and whispered to Pete to do it for me. As soon as I walked off Pete interrupted my dad and said, 'Tom's having a baby.' According to Pete, my dad made a 'mmm' noise, took a sip of his pint and picked up exactly where he'd left off with his anecdote.

241

When I returned to the bar there was no acknowledgement of the news, so I asked him if Pete had told him anything while I'd been away. 'Oh, yes. He did. That's good,' he said. I offered to show him the photograph from the scan, but he simply said, 'No, thanks,' and delivered the punchline to his story. I took a breath in and then a swig of my pint.

Around this time, having not seen Ullmer for a couple of years, I attended a party with Diene that he was holding in celebration of being awarded an MBE in recognition of his services to education. I laughed and joked with his Christian friends, talked to his wife and kids, and what had passed between us remained unsaid. I was his former pupil, returning to celebrate his success, and I told myself that my presence would mean a lot to him. I viewed it as payback for his influential role in my life. After some time Diene and I stepped out from the gathering and found ourselves in his office. Diene looked at the photos dotted around the room. 'It's creepy,' she said. 'There are three photos just of you. None of his other students.' I brushed it off.

Diene's labour was tough. Our plan for the birthing centre, surrounded by candles and a playlist of soothing music, had gone out of the window when, just like my own birth, the umbilical cord was found to be wrapped around the baby's neck.

Thirty-six hours after we went into hospital, he arrived. A boy, Leo. From the moment I held him, a minute after he came into the world, I determined that this boy's life would be different. I cradled him in my arms, staring down at him, taking him in. I loved him but I didn't know him. I felt the responsibility and it made me sit up straighter. He needed a dad, and I was going to be a good one.

I would be firm with him when I had to be, but I wanted him to feel heard. I threw every ounce of love I had towards him, like nothing I had ever known. He deserved every part of me, and my heart felt relieved to give it. As the next couple of years passed, I could feel that I was repairing myself by loving him.

My dad visited once a month or so. He held Leo and bought him little presents. Once he read him a bedtime story but put on such a deep, ominous narrator's voice that Leo looked at me and asked me to take over. He didn't need my dad in his life. I was sure of that, yet still I felt I had to give my dad the opportunity to be part of our lives.

He came one time with the news that he had been diagnosed with bladder cancer. He was perturbed enough to give me the news, and he asked if I'd attend a hospital appointment with him. But, just as with everything else, he didn't seem to grasp the full gravity of the situation. Once his treatment had ended he decided to move to Portugal, near Lisbon, further north from where we'd been as a young family. He was living off his state pension and wanted more readily available cash, so he'd hit upon the idea of selling his flat, capitalising on the gain, paying off the mortgage and buying a small studio apartment in Portugal for about £50,000. He'd done all this and had about £25,000 left for the rest of his life.

I told him over the phone, 'You need to be careful with that money. You can live cheaply in Portugal but if you just blow it, you'll struggle to get flights home and life will be tough. Please look after it.'

'Yes, yes,' he said. Two days later he rang to tell me that he'd bought a speedboat.

A month after his move signs of the cancer returned. He'd made no provision for medical treatment in his new home and planned to return to the UK for check-ups. It was while I was visiting him in Portugal that I took him to the hospital. He stayed there and I flew back and forth to visit him every couple of weeks. His only other visitor was Nuno, the taxi driver. The hospital staff weren't authorised to make calls abroad so they took Nuno's number and promised to notify him. He would in turn call me if there were any developments.

I lay in bed at night worrying about his demise. The muscles in my back were rocks. He was facing death alone in a foreign land. He was losing his mind. My phone conversations with him were bewildering; he barely made any sense at times. What did I owe him? My life was in England. I had responsibilities. I would go when I could but I dreaded it each time. He would grasp me by the hand and tell me, 'The doctors have captured me. Tom, something is going on here. They are torturing me. Don't let them do it.' I would calm him down, reassuring him that I would make the appropriate checks. In other moments he'd repeatedly ask me to buy him new shoes, convinced that the ones he had were no longer any good.

The cancer, or the drugs he was on, had affected his brain. He had turned the people who were trying to save his life into adversaries with evil intent. His paranoia came to the fore, and every night he pulled the drips from his arm, trying to escape. He would be ushered back to his bed by the nurses. 'You will die if you leave, sir. You must go back to bed.'

At night he shouted abuse at them, but he was calmer during the day. A nurse explained to me on one of my visits, 'He gets very angry at night, maybe you could have a word with him. Help him to understand we're trying to help. I do understand he is confused.'

'He is also a …' – I stopped myself from saying 'bastard' – 'a very difficult man.' It was as if his demons had come to haunt him in this lonely place. I was there when they put a catheter into him. He begged me to stop them. They drew the flimsy curtains round the bed. I heard him scream that he couldn't bear the pain.

The doctors decided that for him to have any chance they'd have to remove his bladder. He made frequent calls to me when I was in the UK. 'Can you not ring me at six o'clock?' I'd say. 'I'm always giving Leo his dinner.'

Yet each day he'd call at six. 'This is not a hospital. You have to get me back to England,' he'd say.

'You can't fly. They won't let you. They need to operate first.'

I'd spend hours on the phone calming him down, telling him that the operation would work, but then night time came around and it would start all over again.

He had a fifty-fifty chance of survival, the doctors said. I returned to be with him. The night before his operation I cried alone in a restaurant. I kept my head down so the waiters couldn't see that my *bacalhau* seemed to be making my eyes run. I couldn't stop but it was having a restorative effect. With each tear that fell I felt calmer, knowing that everything was going to be better. I've never cried thinking about him since.

After his operation I arrived at the hospital unsure if he'd survived or not. I saw the doctor drawing on a cigarette outside. I approached her, steadying myself for the news that he'd died. She saw me, inhaled a lungful of tobacco, turned her head to blow it away and said, 'It was successful. He's in intensive care but awake. You can go and see him.'

It was some time before I was allowed in, so I sat outside the unit reading Mike Tyson's autobiography. I was halfway through a passage where he was rolling around in sewage trying to persuade a street hooker that he didn't have to wear a condom while high on morphine, having drunk a bottle of Hennessy, when the automatic doors whooshed open and the doctor beckoned me in.

'You've got two minutes. And two minutes only,' she told me. The low hum of medical machinery and the hushed, respectful tones of confidential chatter filled the air. He looked remarkably well considering he'd just come round from a life-threatening operation. Healthier than he had done in months, in fact.

'Surgery agrees with you.' I said. 'You're strong.' He looked pleased. I reminded him several times to keep his mobile phone with him, as it was our only means of contact. He asked me to buy him some shoes when I had the chance. I told him life would be better now and his colostomy bag wouldn't impede his life too much. I was flying back to the UK that night but would return in a few days.

'Thank you for taking care of it all. And for being here,' he said.

'Always.' The word left my mouth almost thoughtlessly. The word felt heavy. It was true. I was always there.

Chapter 28

I was having lunch with Diene, her brother Sandro and his partner, Monica, when I heard a text message ping. I casually reached over, picking up my phone. It was Nuno. I'd never received a text from him before, so my heart pumped hard as I opened it. 'Good morning Tom!! Your dad is dead. Nuno.'

If you've got bad news to deliver, get it over with. That was obviously Nuno's motto. I think I shouted out, although I don't remember. Hearing the news felt like an electric shock but the pain was over in a second. Different thoughts hit me quickly. I'd never see him again. Ever. This part of the story was over and nothing more could be said. Was there anything else to say? What would happen next? Did I have to bury him? I was right not to buy him those shoes. I was vaguely aware of the others at the table, asking what was wrong. 'My dad's dead,' I replied, and by uttering those words out loud I understood it a little more myself.

Monica hugged me and it felt good. I could have lost myself for a while, but I pulled away because I wanted to do what I saw as my duty. I called my mum to tell her the news. She asked me how I was; I told her I was fine. A strange calmness had come over me. The sun was shining and I sat out in the garden, absorbing the heat. I called my sisters, whom I hadn't spoken to in over a year.

I think Victoria cried when I told her. Not for long. I said I'd be in touch when I knew more.

My second call minutes later was to Emma.

'He's dead?' she said incredulously.

'Well, he had cancer. I think it was coming.'

'Right. Okay. Thanks for letting me know,' she replied.

My third call was to Kate, who went quiet, so I explained a little more about what had happened. It was all matter of fact, like telling a friend a mildly surprising football result.

I sat beneath an apple tree and relief washed over me. This was for the best. What would the future have held? A hard-drinking, obnoxious, bladderless man, living in a foreign country without any friends, frittering away his last remaining money and calling me every day, scared and confused? Thank God that wasn't his future or mine. I imagined what it would be like to sit in the sun, outside his Portuguese studio, having one more drink. He'd tell me his plans to buy a motorbike and I'd make fists under the table. I could live without that.

I arrived in Portugal and entered his dirty little apartment. The view was of a car park but behind that you could see the ocean. I went through his possessions, setting aside the things I thought I might like to keep. There were hundreds of bills from loan companies threatening legal action. One was for £7,333, which I saw he had managed to settle for £240. It was an achievement of sorts.

There was the picture of the girls wearing stripey T-shirts, taken when they were sixteen. Next to that was a picture of Bobby Moore, my dad and George Best. Taken some time in the 1980s, all three were grinning for the camera. My dad had told me that shortly after the photo was taken, George Best tried to start a fight with him. It only calmed down when Bobby Moore got George Best in a headlock. There was a DVD of *The Crimson Pirate* starring Burt Lancaster sitting open next to the TV. It wasn't much for a lifetime. There was a box full of old newspaper articles, frayed at the edges, some of them ripped and turning yellow. I stayed there reading them till the early hours. I was struck by how much the tone of the pieces was similar to my own.

Chapter 29

I carried the large, green plastic urn by its handle, swinging it gently as I walked along a rocky path scattered with wild yellow flowers. The sun was beating down and the wind was bracing. I didn't have a plan for exactly where I'd scatter his ashes, but I headed down towards the cliff tops, overlooking the Atlantic Ocean. There was no point in flying his body back to the UK. There was no point in a funeral. There was no one to come. With the help of Diene's dad, I arranged his cremation, and now his immolated remains hung by my side. I rang and explained to my sisters that we wouldn't be having a funeral. They all said fine but I told them we could all meet up and hold our own private ceremony if we wanted. They said that would be fine too. We never did.

Now that he was gone did they care? Why should they? Why hadn't they called to see how I was after his death? Why was I doing this walk alone? They had no need to see him off. He had left them long ago.

I wish I had seen them for who they are years ago. I wish that time hadn't passed and left us wary, mistrustful and not knowing each other. I never spoke with them about anything that occurred, a bit like witnessing with a friend a horrific car crash and never mentioning it to each other. My father would have his violent rages, smash our furniture, spit his ire, and we'd just silently retreat upstairs when it was over. They to their room with their music and me to mine and my action figures.

Why did I not turn to them for comfort and solidarity? They were my sisters. We were victims of the same man, yet I never contemplated turning to them. I kept my focus firmly on my dad. I believed that he loved me and I needed him and he needed me. My sisters were dispensable.

Every year in adulthood they would send me thoughtful, sweet presents for my birthday or Christmas, and when Leo was born he was the recipient of equally carefully chosen presents. I had been annoyed by it. I never reciprocated. Why did they think a present made up for their absence? What was the point of a card if they didn't visit or call and ask me how I was? I now see that it was their way of showing me they cared. It was all they could manage, but I didn't understand.

I was outraged by them. Sometimes I thought I did not care if they lived or died. Until not so long ago, if you'd met me at a party and asked me about my family, I'd have told you that I grew up as an only child. Telling anyone would provoke a lot of questions. Are they close? Do I see them often? Do they have kids? Where do they work? And, occasionally, are they telepathic? I wasn't comfortable with answering any of those queries. I didn't want to talk about my family.

I never thought of them and when we met I was ready to take offence at the slightest provocation. We'd all rub along okay but it was awkward, and then they would be chippy and refer to me as 'the golden boy' under their breath. I'd be seized with fury. Fuck them. They're against me. Just because I sometimes had that man's favour.

A few years back, when my mum was ill, they didn't visit her at all. Why was I the only one to go to her side in the hospital, pick her up, take her home and look after her? And why do I remember sitting on the stairs alone while my parents fought and my teenage sisters hid away in their attic room, music on, door closed?

Their insularity extended to never travelling abroad. Kate and Emma didn't work, and a trip to London would have to be planned for weeks and involve all three of them going on the train together. Even making a phone call was a step too far for them most of the time.

They were hard to know, reticent and unworldly. They morphed into a collective in my mind and sometimes I don't know what to say to them. It's stilted on the rare occasions that we meet. But somewhere along the line I made a choice. I chose to discard them and side with my dad. I was his ally. He was the last person on earth who had earned it. I stood by him, the only person to be with him when he died his slow, painful death. Like a loyal dog I stood by him to the end, offering him kindness and care, and all the while my sisters had made their choice: to cut themselves off from the poison that he dripped into their lives.

Yet I took pleasure in my dad's company. I visited him every week, sometimes spending days with him, watching films, talking, asking for his help with my work. I chose to spend time with the man who beat and raped my mum. He would make comments about the girls underachieving and being lazy, and I'd agree and tell him how pathetic I found it.

Don't Ask Me About My Dad

I'd share with him how let down I felt by them. He'd nod and say he didn't understand why they were so disengaged from life. No one ever offered me any explanation for why they cut themselves off and it never occurred to me to ask the questions. My mum had stuck with my dad for so long it seemed natural that I should follow suit. No one else condemned him so why did it fall to me? My sisters sent him Christmas cards and still called him dad.

Perhaps I learned my antagonism towards them from him. He didn't trust them, so why should I? When my dad's mother died, I stood with him outside the red-brick crematorium waiting for them and joined in with his complaints about their lateness to the ceremony. It was as if I was more bothered by time-keeping than rape. I don't have an answer. I don't feel that way now.

I climbed down to the precipice, the wind blowing my hair. It was cold then hot, and I kept removing my jacket and putting it back on. The waves crashed onto the rocks. I wasn't the first to make this journey; there was evidence of a campfire littered with beer cans. I opened up the urn to see it was full to the brim with ash. Was that all really him? Or was it the ashes of others too?

He had told me once what he wanted for his funeral: 'When I'm dead don't worry about paying for a funeral, don't get a coffin or a hearse or any of that. Put me in a big black bag, hire a van and get Ian to help you load me up.' It wasn't a practical plan but he was sold on the idea. This little ceremony wasn't that far off it.

Here, by this abandoned vagrants' campsite overlooking the vast ocean, was where I would say goodbye. It felt about right.

In the absence of mourners, I didn't need to stand on ceremony. This was just for me and him. I said out loud, 'Bye, Dad,' and stopped there. That would suffice.

I threw the ash from the urn like you would a bucket full of water. It was carried by the wind a little way and tumbled down to the rocks below. It took about three goes and he was gone. My duty had been fulfilled and I was glad it would be the last one. I looked at the urn and wondered for a moment if I should keep it, but I couldn't see a reason why. I tossed it onto the rubbish nearby and made my way back up the hill.

Chapter 30

'That sounds like grooming.'

While having a conversation with a friend about old teachers I mentioned Ullmer. No details, but I said we'd become close at school, went away together, and he tried to move the single beds next to each other.

And now that word: grooming. Grooming. I kept saying it. It stopped me in my tracks. I wasn't groomed, was I? What would it mean to have been groomed? The serious way my friend said the word, his concerned expression, went right through me. No messing around. My friend didn't like what he heard. It sounded serious to him. Groomed.

I had spoken to Ullmer twice on the phone in the years since his party. Once when he called me to tell me he was moving to Kazakhstan to teach in a private school, and another last year when he emailed me to ask how things were and I rang him to tell him of my dad's death. I was surprised by how he reacted, just a cursory, 'Oh, sorry to hear that,' before he moved on to talk about his own career successes. I finished the call wishing I had never made it.

My head whirred. A low whoosh reverberated in my brain. My friend was still looking at me. His jaw clenched. Vulnerable people are groomed. I'd never thought of myself as vulnerable. It was hard to concentrate above the whooshes. Maybe I was vulnerable as a kid. I mean, growing up had been pretty tense. I sat dazed on the Tube afterwards, staring at adverts without taking them in. I almost missed my stop.

If … that *friendship* with Ullmer wasn't a friendship at all, what would that mean? What if it was something else? He was my teacher, after all. What if he had abused his position and I wasn't responsible for what had occurred? What if he was the one who was responsible?

It would be quite a different story from the one I told. In my world I was a hero. Indomitable, streetwise, cynical, capable of anything but just biding my time. Un-bloody-breakable. But maybe I wasn't. Maybe I'd been broken and didn't even know it. How vulnerable was I? I had never had these thoughts before. If I had been groomed … that changes things, right?

I paced the front room. Breathe … breathe … it helps to breathe. I felt like I was almost hyperventilating, just like I had as a kid when my dad rampaged around the house. It was wrong, wasn't it? Someone tell me I'm right. I googled a child-abuse support line and talked to a woman. 'If this happened …' I said, giving her more information about Ullmer than I'd ever told a soul, 'that would be wrong, wouldn't it?'

'Yes,' she said. 'That's sexual abuse.' Breathe. Fucking hell. The woman at the end of the line carried on in the most sympathetic of tones, which for some reason irritated me. 'It must be so hard for you,' she said. 'We have a programme where victims meet with the perpetrator and that sometimes helps with healing.' She seemed to be jumping a little ahead.

'I'm not sure he's going to admit it,' I told her, and barely listened to the rest of what she said. But she had said what I needed to hear. It was abuse. I became calmer. Good. That's clearer. Now I know what I'm dealing with.

That night I lay awake, staring at the ceiling. Replaying every part of my life. My dad had made me vulnerable. The love and hate I felt for him had overwhelmed me. His behaviour had contorted my understanding of the world. I had searched for a good father but instead Ullmer had appeared. A line from *Macbeth*, a play that he'd taught me about, popped into my mind: 'Look like the innocent flower, but be the serpent under it.' No wonder I lived my life on edge. I had been betrayed by people who should have offered love.

But now that my dad was dead I was released from his curious spell. I could see things a little clearer without his presence clouding my mind.

I turned over in bed, and then back again. I was back in my childhood home. The shabby gold curtains in the front room, the peeling ceiling roses around the lights, an empty plastic litre bottle of wine my dad had consumed. He was there now, screaming at my mum. Then a vision of Leo appeared. He was sitting on the stairs in our flat, just like I used to in my old home. He was crying and observing something I couldn't see. Watching something terrible happen. I couldn't see what it was but I knew it was me, screaming, shouting, fighting. Leo was desperate. I saw the panic in his sweet face. He was unable to understand why his dad was behaving this way. My beautiful boy driven out of his mind with panic and fear. He was convulsing. His legs were banging together. I couldn't bear it. I saw the anguish in my son's face. And then Leo was no longer there. He became my younger self. I was seven years old. I was cowed, petrified.

In that moment I saw the child I was. I could see that the chaos my dad wrought had made me defenceless. I was manipulated. You only know you were manipulated the moment you know. I understood. What happened should not have happened.

It wasn't as if I had amnesia. I remembered all that Ullmer and my dad had done. I had just viewed it differently until that moment. I ran from all the hurt, refusing to acknowledge it because I was afraid it would break me. But now I was there and I could see it for what it was.

There was no sleep. My eyes refused to shut. I was overwhelmed by the secret I had kept being revealed to me. My life wasn't what I thought it was. I wasn't the man I thought I was. I realised my actions had been clouded by all that went before. My life was soaked with confusion and hurt.

It was like getting glasses – everything rushed into focus. I could suddenly see all my inadequacies, deficiencies, foibles, sins and weaknesses at once. That night I took the full force of my past and for the first time understood its severity. I cried for my mum, I cried for my sisters, I cried for the little boy I was. And I forgave myself. And then I was back in my fantasy, staring at myself on the stairs. The boy I had always dreamed of rescuing. I climbed the first two steps, reached out and the little boy ran into my arms.

Chapter 31

'And where exactly did he touch you?' the policewoman asked. I got the feeling the conversation was more embarrassing for her than it was for me. We were sitting in my flat on a hot summer's day. There was birdsong drifting through the open window. I was twice her age and it felt like she was about to bring out a little doll for me to point to, so I didn't have to name body parts. The police had seemed the obvious place to start. I called the local station, told them in the broadest possible terms about what had happened, and they sent a constable to take some details.

She was doing her best and was applying all the training she had been given to show sympathy. I appreciated her effort but still, it felt *weird*. 'This must be *very* hard for you,' she said. 'Take your time. If you need to stop just let me know. We can always take a break. Even if I have to come back another day …'

I told her the details and she said someone from the sexual offence unit would be in touch.

A few days later I received a call from a detective on the Child Abuse Investigation Team. He had a breezy manner and a seen-it-all-before tone. 'Yeah, well, the problem with these cases is that it's just your word against his. It was all such a long time ago,' he said.

This wasn't the reaction I'd had hoped for. He continued, 'I dealt with a case recently where a girl said her teacher abused her when she was fifteen, but she was in a relationship with him for five years after she left school.'

'Right, so what do I do?' I asked.

'We're in the business of getting convictions. That's what I can tell you. And this will be hard.'

'Is it worth arresting him and seeing if he admits it?'

'I will arrest him if that's what you want. I can bring him in for questioning, but in my experience they never confess. I couldn't guarantee that we could then investigate it. You see, if it got to court his defence would point out the fact that you've been in contact with him for all these years.'

I wondered if the police did this to everyone who called up. For some people it could be the hardest call they ever make in their life. It could be their first time telling anyone, and the man on the end of the phone isn't going to help. They could be sitting with a bottle of gin and a hundred sleeping pills, hoping that someone takes them seriously. I was telling this detective there was a child groomer, a molester, out on the streets and he was turning the other way.

If the police weren't interested, I'd do their job for them.

I wanted to hit back at him. I would show him I was the wrong person to have messed with. I would exact revenge on him. It would be swift and painful. I would hurt him like he had hurt me. The only thing to do was work out how. He was a highly paid head teacher of a British private school in

Kazakhstan, and I wondered how many other kids he had tried to abuse. The answer seemed obvious. I would expose him in a journalism sting. I'd write a story for a newspaper bringing national shame and opprobrium upon him. I'd humiliate him by revealing to the world exactly the type of man he was. I'd spent most of my career exposing dating sites or dodgy holiday companies, but now I'd unmask a molester.

The advantage I had was that he didn't know I knew. I'd have to be patient and wait until he returned home in the holidays. I'd arrange to meet him to get proof. I'd wire myself up before the meeting, lull him into a false sense of security by pretending nothing had changed, and get him to talk about what had gone on. He'd manipulated me and I would manipulate him. The tape would convince a newspaper editor to publish.

Once I had his confession, I'd punch him in the face. Some old-fashioned justice, just like my dad would deliver. I'd say my piece and then break his nose. No one could blame me for that. Or maybe I should get him to give me compensation. He was a wealthy man with a small property empire. *Money would go some way to reconciling this,* I thought. *I'll take something from* him *this time.* I could tell him I had the tape and ask for a hundred grand. Then I could print the story anyway. If you are going to fuck someone over, fuck them over, then make sure to fuck them over again.

How would he react to my turning the tables on him? Was it possible he could take his own life? Maybe he'd feel there was nowhere left to run. Pete suggested he might hire a hitman to try to kill me and keep the story quiet. I couldn't see that happening, unless there was a hitman he knew from church. But it was possible there would be consequences I couldn't predict.

I wanted someone to know exactly where I'd be and what I was going to do. I arranged to meet Kane, an old school friend of mine who was now a policeman. He'd been in one of Ullmer's first productions. I'd tell Ullmer at the end of our meeting that a policeman knew about it, which would make him think hard about any action he might take. I'd not told many people about Ullmer but I somehow knew that Kane would understand. He had been in the army for years and was now in the Metropolitan Police's armed-response unit. Not much surprised him.

I emailed Ullmer, suggesting we meet when he was back in the country. He responded straight away:

Great. I am in Astana another three weeks on holiday with children. You around after 8 July? Free till mid-August.
Jonathan Ullmer MBE

The last time I had seen him was at his party to celebrate him. Prince William had just pinned a medal to his chest. This time would be different.

'Fucking hell, mate,' Kane said, rubbing his lumberjack beard after listening intently to my story. 'What a fucking nonce.' There was something dependable about Kane. He hadn't changed since school. He swore just as much at thirteen, which was also the time he started growing the beard. I told him that what I really wanted to do was beat the shit of

Ullmer but I'd come round to the conclusion that it might be unwise.

'Fair enough, old son,' he said. 'The wanker deserves it. If you're meeting in St Pancras there's a little alley round the back. Don't do it in a bar. And don't touch his face. Fuck his body up.'

I told him I was worried it would complicate the issue.

'All right,' he said, in a suit-yourself way. He told me he would be on shift the night I was meeting Ullmer and offered to stop by if I needed him. I told him that, given he was armed response, it might look a bit over the top.

He shrugged. 'Let us know how it goes, pal.'

Chapter 32

2018, July, London

'Our friendship,' I said.

'Ah-hum.'

'What do you make of it, looking back now?'

'Interesting question,' he mumbled, shifting in his seat.

I said nothing.

His eyes darted up to my face and then back to his own hands. 'I guess it's kind of … ummm.'

He fell into silence again and I could see his jaw muscles twitching. Another long pause. 'At the time … It did cause me a lot of …' He didn't finish the sentence. He looked as if he had just received the news he had six months to live and was doing his best to put a brave face on it. Another twenty or so seconds passed. 'But I guess, we were, erm … quite close friends, early on.'

It all felt very different, sitting opposite him now. The imposing bar was filling up with commuters grabbing a drink before dashing for a train. I could smell the faintest trace of diesel or oil wafting in from the open doors. The waitress arrived. For a moment Ullmer switched back to his old self, ordering a coffee rudely. The waitress decided she didn't need her pad, flipped it closed and spun on her heel to go and deliver the order. My phone lay on the table. I hoped it was picking up every word.

He looked me up and down, as if to check I was still the same person. There was a long pause. I stared directly at him.

'Ummm. I guess it's kind of, ummm … Good question,' he repeated, falling back into silence. He started again, determined to make a point. 'It did make me think a lot. Particularly when, um …' He was unable to finish the sentence. It seemed like each thought was beyond his ability to express.

The waitress arrived with his coffee. Ullmer shuffled in his seat, waiting till she was back by the bar.

I wanted to push him on the exact timing of when everything had happened. I suspected he would try to deny everything. 'What do you mean about us being good friends early on?' I said.

'Well, I guess it must have been getting towards the end of the sixth-form period.'

I remained quiet. I could see the mental calculations he was making about where this conversation was headed.

'We had lots of conversations,' he continued. 'About, um … er … I guess me being concerned whether you, we were … because of the age difference between us, I guess.'

I nodded. His shoulders lifted slightly and he raised his head. 'I enjoyed working with you a lot,' he said with a thin-lipped smile, which quickly disappeared when I cut in.

'I meant sharing beds.'

He let out one of his favourite, 'Hmmm,' sounds.

'Because now I'm older I look at it in a different way,' I told him.

'Yeah. Hmmm. I guess …' he wet his lip with his tongue, furrowing his brow. He stared down at his coffee cup like he was encountering one for the first time. 'Yeah, I mean er … I remember the first time … we kind of had a lot of deep conversations … and …'

I was losing patience with his inarticulacy. 'We used to have deep conversations pretty early on, from when I was fourteen. Didn't we?' I said.

'I mean that was … yeah … we did. It was a …' He gulped a breath of air. 'You were a very … very mature guy for your age.'

'What do you mean?'

'I guess, um … you were very, um. I don't know … we'd talk about things that were quite, you'd ask quite detailed questions about stuff and, um …'

'Detailed?'

'I suppose, kind of, um … er … you know … you'd talk to me. It was Vicki at the time, um … and er … and er …'

I resented his suggestion that it was me with all the questions. 'You asked a lot of questions,' I said.

'Yes. It was kind of … I mean er … how … how you were getting on. How things were developing … um …'

'What about sharing beds? And the board game you made.'

He once presented me with a homemade cardboard game. It was a wheel of fortune, with a cardboard arrow attached to a paperclip, allowing the arrow to be spun round to choose a category. The categories were all dares involving showing parts of our bodies to each other or sexual questions he wanted to know the answers to.

'That was in the sixth form,' he said. I could see what he was doing. He wanted to make it clear that everything had happened when I was sixteen. Before the Sexual Offences Act in 2003, grooming wasn't a crime. He'd have been sacked for gross professional misconduct if anyone had found out, but I knew that he had waited to make his move because he knew the law.

He made another humming sound.

'You're not really saying anything,' I said, growing frustrated with his dithering.

'Well, no …' He laughed. 'I suppose partly because, you know … um … you know I do feel … you know, that the friendship did move quite … fast, and I guess … when I look back it did make me feel uncomfortable.'

'What about when we shared beds?'

'When you stayed over a number of times?' he asked. 'We used to, um … you know, you used to sleep in a sleeping bag in my bed, um ….' He smiled wistfully.

For a moment I was lost. What sleeping bag? Suddenly the memory raced back. I had taken a sleeping bag to his flat so that I could fulfil his wish to sleep in his bed but run no risk of his flesh touching mine.

'It was in my house for ages afterwards. I think I threw it out in the end.' He neighed with laughter. 'I was a little surprised the first time when you didn't want to sleep in it.'

'Sorry?'

He repeated himself. I felt a rush of anger. He had teased me for using the bag, but it was my cocoon to protect from any advance. He would pretend he'd tidied it away and couldn't remember where it was. I would search his cupboards to find it.

He carried on, 'But I didn't say anything … but, um … I suppose with time passing and you look back, um …'

I swallowed and focused on the task at hand. He had brought up the sleeping bag because it preyed on his mind. A boundary from him and my body. A source of frustration to his desires. Let the bastard reminisce if he wanted to.

'Things were very different then. I would have …'

I interjected: 'What was different then?'

'I suppose, you know, the, um … In … you know … I hesitate … I hesitate to say things … because … because I don't think I really agree with it. Well, I guess things, you know … you know in … in those days it wasn't. It was a … um … it was a friendship, um … it was, um … er … I think in the … it's not, you know … um. Perhaps things are just an awful lot clearer … today than they were then.'

I asked him what he meant.

'I couldn't conceive of a situation of having a … er … close friendship with someone in the sixth form today. It's a different world.'

It was a different world. One where people weren't as aware of grooming and the coercive powers of child molesters. A world where Jimmy Savile enjoyed years of freedom abusing kids as he pleased while people turned a blind eye.

'Are you gay?' I asked.

'No, I'm not gay. I'm … I'm, you know, a fairly heterosexual guy and … very happy … in the life I've had over the years.'

'Why did you want me to touch your penis?' It seemed an obvious question.

'I don't think I did.'

'You were masturbating and you came as soon as I touched it.'

There was no reply. He wiped a bead of sweat from his brow.

'You can understand why I'm confused by it, can't you?' I continued.

'Yeah,' he replied, and stared at the table this time as if he expected it to move. He carried on: 'Yeah that was ... um ... yeah, I'd be very ... I'd certainly be very upset if I thought, if I ... you know, caused you grief or anger. Over anything that's happened, and that would never have been my intention. And, um ... It's, um ... you know, I ... I suppose because I look back and think I ... um ... I'd never be that close to a sixth former or, you know, someone of that age again ... um ...'

Suddenly he seemed to find a thread he was confident of pursuing. 'It was unusual ... I mean I've never ... I've never worked with a student before who was ... you were ... incredibly bright ... you were very ... very perceptive ... um ... it was a ... er ... one of my strongest memories ... um ... was of, um ... you ... it was on a piece of work you did. I think I'd given you a B for it or something, and I went through and explained exactly what you had to do to get a top grade and, you know, it took me aback ... You listened really carefully to what I said and you did it. And you achieved it. And that's unusual for a student to do that ... and be perceptive.'

His praise for me centred around the fact that I was able to do what he had advised. He'd put a lot of work into getting me to do things his way. 'You were my teacher, asking me to touch your penis? And asking me to give you naked massages?' I asked.

'I think ... you know ... if I remember rightly, you massaged my shoulders.'

'I didn't just massage your shoulders.'

'No, no, the first time. It was a kind of … I think we both … gave each other massages. I don't particularly remember being, um … you know … er … a driving force in it. I remember being very much … reticent about things at the time … um … um …'

The insinuation that I had wanted to rub his body made me want to tip the table over. I knew it would be a mistake. I wondered what my dad would have made of my confrontation with Ullmer. He wouldn't have understood how I came to be in that situation in the first place. It would have blown his mind to think I allowed such things to happen. He'd have wanted me to thump him, though. I gave Ullmer a second chance.

'You mean I drove it?' I said.

'No, I don't think any … no … I would say … um … it came from both of us or, erm … ah.'

'From both of us? I think it was coming from one direction.'

'I don't recall it quite like that.'

'One of us was thirteen years old. I came from a difficult childhood …'

'Hmmm. Hmm.'

'And you did everything you could to help me, in so many ways that were important. Especially with what was going on at home.'

'Hmm. Hmmm.'

'I think the naked massaging, the board game, the dares, going out the room, coming back with an erection strike me as very inappropriate.'

'Mmm.'

I could see he had justified every single act. The stark facts of the matter frightened him. Laid bare, he had no answers, just a sense that I had played an equal part.

'Would I make friends with a thirteen-year-old, bending over backwards to help them and then, when they were sixteen, share a bed with them?'

'Mmm.'

I continued: 'Would I play games of a sexual nature, drinking with them? Would I do that? No. I would not do it. I would not do it.' My body trembled as I made my point. 'I want to ask you that question again. Are you gay?'

'No, I'm ... I'm not gay.'

'But why did you want me to touch your penis then?'

'Was it a single occurrence?'

'Yeah.'

'I think, you know, maybe we talked about it at the time, you know. I was ... yeah ... I'd married comparatively late in life. I was pretty nervous about, um, er, you know, um ... sex. I was a virgin when I got married, um, and, er, having, you know ... I was, you know. Things are very different now. I mean, that's why I was with Jackie, because it was all about the nervousness of being married and being in a sexual relationship that I was about to embark on.'

'I'm not someone to test stuff out on. What was more regular were the massages and pulling my pants down. That was regular.'

'Mmm.'

'Giving each other massages happened on a number of occasions.'

271

'Yeah, it happened a lot.'

'Yeah,' I replied, glancing around the room to check if anybody had tuned into our discussion.

'Yeah. Um … and um … I look back and, er …'

'But why? What was the motivation? I mean, I don't get my friends naked and massage them.'

'I suppose, kind of … I enjoyed massage … I always had a stiff … bad back … for many years.'

I could have asked why he hadn't gone to an osteopath. 'What about asking me to touch your penis?'

'Well, on that one occasion I can't remember … I don't remember it in detail … I can't, um …'

'Looking back at it now, would I do that? It would be wrong.'

'Yeah, yeah, yeah.' He nodded his head like he was malfunctioning.

'And what would I do if a teacher was doing that with Leo? I'd beat the shit out of him.'

'Yeah, yeah. Hmm. I … you know, to be honest I think things are incredibly clear … today.'

'What's clear?'

'Well, in terms of the level of appropriateness. And, er … you know I wouldn't, certainly I was very conscious that I … um …'

'You think that in the nineties it was appropriate?'

'I think, um … you know … I'm not saying there's a parallel at all because I don't think it is, but, you know … um … the head of Ofsted, you know, had … had a relationship with a sixth former and … it was a different world … um, and perhaps you can take from it the fact that, you know, I'm finding this conversation difficult, the fact that's how I feel about it, um … I think if, um … er … You know, it's not an easy conversation and it's a good one to have, um … and, er … I was very conscious when you were under sixteen, very conscious of, um … boundaries and the limits to any kind of friendship.'

He stuttered his way through some more non-sequiturs until I got fed up of the burbling. 'I've got a problem,' I said. 'Because I can see it very clearly now. I don't think it was right.'

'Yeah.'

'I think it was inappropriate.'

'Yeah.'

'I think it has in many ways formed and changed the way I am as a human being.'

'Mmm.'

'It was an important relationship. It had an effect on me. I am curious that you say you're not gay because that would make a bit more sense. When I look back at it, I don't think it was right. And I have to ask myself, what do I do about that?'

Each time I told him that it had been wrong, my mind became clearer. Everything rushed further into focus. If I didn't know it before, I knew it now. I was doing the right thing.

He murmured away while his coffee sat getting cold.

'Does your wife know about the sexual side of the friendship?'

'No.'

'You've never told her?'

'I haven't really discussed that. And I … yeah, I … bearing in mind, you know, what you say and your views on it, you

273

know, and my feelings, I … you know, have to give a really, you know, I'm really, really sorry.'

'You're sorry?' I didn't believe it.

'Yes, you know, the fact I feel uncomfortable about, um, discussing it, um, is a very clear indicator for both of us that, er … yeah, I am uncomfortable about it, um …'

'What would you do in my shoes?'

At this moment he seemed to regress to his role of my teacher. He pondered the question like he would when I asked him advice as his pupil.

'I think I'd do what you've done,' he said. 'And I'd talk about it and, um … it is a friendship that we had which was close and, you know … perhaps too close and …'

'Don't you feel there was a level of manipulation behind it?'

'I … I would be horrified to think that I … I would not have wanted to do that. I would not have …'

'You spent a lot of time talking me into stuff, Jonathan.'

'Hmmm. It's not completely … well … um … we're going back in time a long way … um. And … I would be really upset if you thought I'd manipulated you. Umm … it was a good friendship we had, um … and, um … I'd feel really, really bad … um … and, er … it's not, you know, something that … um, and, um … it was more, I think, about how, how we clicked at the time.'

'I didn't like the sexual stuff. I was uncomfortable with it.'

'Yeah.'

'I felt like it was a situation I had to manage. I was thirteen, fourteen. I had to navigate it and try to avoid it. Stop it from going any further … and that's a lot to put on a kid. It wasn't on. Do you get that?'

'Yes, I do.' He became animated. 'And, um … yes, and you talk about thirteen, fourteen, fifteen, you know. There was nothing inappropriate at those ages.'

'I wonder why you helped me as a young teenager. Why you invested that time in me. It's weird that it then had a sexual element as soon as I turned sixteen.'

He moved from side to side in his chair, leaning forward slightly. 'Well, that I'd be very clear about. I helped a lot of kids I got on well with and put myself out for. I would be, you know, absolutely clear there's no element of, er … I think what you're talking about is grooming … and there was absolutely no element of that.'

'So you weren't grooming, you're not a paedophile and you're not gay.'

'No.'

'Yet you still asked me to touch your penis?'

'No, yeah. Um … I … um …'

I felt I had all I needed. I told him, 'I'm going to go.' I picked up my phone and turned the recorder off. 'I've told a policeman that I'm coming here to meet you today. You should know that.'

'Right, yes,' he said without batting an eyelid. I got up and walked to the door. He called out from behind, 'Oh, no, Tom. Tom!' I kept walking out into the concourse of St Pancras, past the ugly, enormous statue of a kissing couple that dominates the hall and out onto Euston Road.

I walked briskly towards King's Cross station and could see a number 73 bus that would take me home. I was being powered by an invisible force. My legs were working as usual, but it felt different. Nothing could get in my way. The crowds around melted and the buildings and cars faded away, and I can't be sure but I think I was smiling. FUCK, YEAH! I felt good. I could feel my blood pumping. Bigger strides, chin up, chest out.

I jumped on the bus and bounded up the stairs, sat at the front in the best seat. I glanced around. There were only ten or eleven people there. I took out my phone and saw that the recording was there. I pressed play and held it up to my ear. Ullmer's voice rang out crystal clear. Every word. My shoulders softened a little more. He might deny what he had done but he would never be able to explain discussing it with me for thirty-four minutes. For a split second I imagined Ullmer sitting alone at that table. His evening hadn't panned out the way he'd thought. I wondered what he would tell his wife about his night out when he got home. I closed the app carefully and put my phone in my pocket. I leaned back in my seat and gazed out to Upper Street in Islington, not really taking anything in, just breathing. Enjoying the bus ride. Feeling good.

Chapter 33

I addressed my email to the chair of governors. I had come to the conclusion, as much as I wanted to hit Ullmer, or as useful as a chunk of money would be, I needed to put my personal wish for vengeance aside. Everything I had read about child molesters told me that they didn't only try it once. I began to see things, or feel things, more clearly. I wanted to protect other people from going through what I had, or if they had already, at least give them a chance to reconcile it. Otherwise no good would come of any of it. That had to come first. I didn't want his money anymore. It would have repulsed me to take it. It was only when I understood what had happened to me – that it had been bad – that I could properly differentiate between good and evil. It was the first moral decision I'd ever knowingly taken in my life. And it felt good.

> I would like to give you some information about the headmaster of Haileybury Astana, Jonathan Ullmer. It concerns his time at Cecil Jones High School in Essex, where I was a student between the years of 1988–95.
>
> When I was sixteen, Jonathan Ullmer sexually abused me. It was the culmination of three years of a close relationship between us both, starting when I was thirteen.

I have confronted him with this and he does not deny it. I have taken legal consultation as well as speaking with the police and have decided pursuing this in court is not what I want to do.

I do not know if Jonathan Ullmer will deny this to others but, if he does, I would be prepared to talk to you and provide you with evidence. You will realise that this matter has been troubling me deeply and I am very concerned to safeguard any other children from what happened to me. I believe that as chair of governors you have a duty of care and must act on this information.

I would be grateful if you would confirm you received this and let me know what action you take.

I hesitated before pressing send. This was the beginning of a journey and I didn't know where it would end. I clicked the mouse and the email whizzed into the ether.

The bursar from Haileybury met me in the grand bar of St Pancras. I figured I might as well be consistent. It was the middle of the afternoon and the place was all but empty. Mr Watkinson gave me a firm handshake. He looked like the CEO of an oil company, slick suit, sharp haircut and a direct way of talking. We perched on stools at a table. He thanked me for meeting him.

'Just to let you know I'm not recording this conversation,' he said.

'Neither am I,' I responded, unlike the last time I'd been in this bar. I got down to business. I told him what had happened. When I explained how it had all seemed so complicated at the time, he interrupted and said with absolute conviction, 'You don't have to explain, Tom. I absolutely understand.' I was moved by his intervention and took a few seconds to carry on.

I told him how I had confronted Ullmer. He looked surprised.

'I did record that conversation, though,' I said. 'Would you like to listen to it now?' I handed him my phone and a set of headphones I'd purchased from a station shop, especially for the occasion.

He sat in front of me and listened to all thirty-four minutes of the recording. When he'd finished he carefully removed the headphones, winding the thin cable into a neat loop, and placed them back in the box.

'It's an interesting conversation, isn't it?' I said.

He paused. 'That man cannot continue to be the headmaster of Haileybury, Astana.'

Chapter 34

I could blame my dad for this trip to Coventry. He was the one that had made me susceptible to Ullmer's advances. Apart from the occasional emotional outburst, I hadn't been able to confront my dad in his lifetime. But I had a chance with Ullmer. He wasn't dead.

The train pulled into Coventry, a city that at first glance seemed to be constructed entirely of roundabouts. It was bleak and seemingly all concrete, but I wasn't here for the sights.

The Teaching Regulation Agency, a government depart-ment, had been notified by Haileybury of my complaint against Ullmer. The school had removed him from his posi-tion soon after our meeting, telling Ullmer that they were convinced by the veracity of my story and compelled by the recording. Now the TRA had decided to prosecute their own case to ban Ullmer from teaching. He had denied everything. I had been called as the main witness.

I made my way to the Premier Inn, where my friend Harjeet was waiting. I didn't want Diene at the hearing. I wanted to protect her from the anguish she'd feel for me. This was my job. I wanted to be fully focused on the task. I walked into the pastel-coloured lobby and there, standing at the reception desk was Ullmer. I let out a laugh as the ridiculousness of the situation struck me rather than feeling any horror at seeing him. Of course, he had to stay somewhere. He was greyer and fatter than the last time I had seen him. His shoulders were hunched. He turned to me, his face expressing little surprise. I must have looked shocked. I could feel my face harden. Weren't there two hotels in Coventry? *What should I do now?*

'Hello, Tom,' he said quietly, giving me a sideways glance and taking a couple of steps away. The receptionist looked up, scanned us both, picked up on the awkwardness and scanned us again. Then he found something more important to do. I kept my eyes fixed on Ullmer. I knew I shouldn't say anything. Ullmer slowly turned around, skulking off to the bar.

I checked in, went to my room and called Harjeet. He came down from his own room, a floor above. 'I think Ullmer is in the bar,' was the first thing he said. I told him he was.

'How did you know it was him?' Harjeet had never seen him.

'I just knew,' he said. 'He was sitting in the lounge when I arrived. A waiter came in. Ullmer waved him over and told him to turn the volume down on the television. The way he did it was so arrogant, somehow I knew.'

In the morning we passed Ullmer again in the corridor. This time I didn't look. We took a cab to the TRA building. The driver chatted away merrily about Coventry City's prospects for promotion to the Championship and I joined in, although my head was full of what was to come. The government's lawyer had told me little. Not a word on what I might be asked, what might be said, what Ullmer's defence might be. It struck me how unfair this was. Ullmer had my statement. He and his lawyers had heard my tape, but I was in the dark.

The lawyer had explained that I could have a screen brought into the hearing and put up between me and Ullmer, so I didn't have to look at him while giving evidence. It seemed superfluous given that he was now staying in the same hotel. I rejected the offer. I wasn't hiding from anything anymore.

I could feel the same nervous energy that made me pace up and down as a kid, so I told myself I had been asked to testify, to explain what Ullmer had done, and that's what I would do. I was not on trial. I was not being judged.

We arrived at a newish-looking building that screamed administration down to every last brick. The receptionist breezily signed us in, directing Harjeet and me to some chairs in the middle of the foyer, and told us to wait. I saw Ullmer again passing by. It felt like a dark farce where all the main players keep opening and closing doors and discovering people they don't want to see. Ullmer's wife was with him now, as well as a man in a sharp suit and waistcoat, who I assumed was his lawyer.

We were led to another room to wait until I was called to testify. A bare table was placed in the middle, the windows had those municipal vertical-slat blinds drawn to give us privacy. The room had more plug sockets than I'd ever seen in one place before. The light pink walls and green carpet reminded me of a nursing home. I wanted to get started, but no one came to get us. I paced the room, drinking water from those squidgy white ringed cups that are bad for the environment.

The government's lawyer was young. She was followed into the room by an assistant who looked even younger. The lawyer greeted me, her strong Liverpudlian accent bouncing off the

walls. They were both a little shy and didn't radiate confidence. The lawyer's eyebrows were carefully sculpted and she
had what seemed to be false eyelashes. Her long hair was tied
up in buns on the top of her head, giving the impression of
animal ears. Her long fingernails were like talons. The whole
get-up made her look like a sort of human cat. She told me
the panel would hear my audio recording first and then I'd
be next.

I wondered what this process would be like for someone
younger than myself. A seventeen-year-old boy or girl who
had suffered abuse, turning up to face their teacher, being
booked into the same hotel. Relying only on themselves,
hoping that they could find their voice, worried about getting
tangled up in dates or inconsistencies under cross-examination.
The pressure they would feel, the upset of facing their abuser.
Not a word about what they would be confronted with.
Running the risk of not being believed.

Due to a technical glitch, they couldn't play my audio
recording and it delayed the whole proceeding for nearly three
hours. With the heightened tension, Harjeet and I ran out of
things to say to each other, so I just circled the room and he
looked into the distance, occasionally adjusting his scarf,
which he had kept on because the room was so cold. Eventually the glitch was resolved and the human cat returned,
telling me the hearing would reconvene after lunch. The panel
had heard the recording and wanted time to absorb it. I asked
her if Ullmer's wife had listened to the tape, but she said that
she had left the room of her own volition before it was played.
She didn't return for my evidence either, although she came
back when it was Ullmer's turn to speak.

After a dry sandwich, which I forced down, I made my way into the sterile, airless room. The tables were arranged in a horseshoe. The panel, comprising of two women and one man, sat at one side, joined by a legal expert at the end, to make sure all procedures were followed correctly. The lawyers and Ullmer were opposite, and I was at the end, in the middle. A large stack of papers sat in front of me, containing everyone's evidence. I was told that I would be referred to as Pupil A throughout the proceeding. They could have used my name for all I cared.

The panel introduced themselves and asked for a clarification on part of my evidence, about the date of Ullmer's marriage. I had mistakenly said in my statement that Ullmer was married a year later than was the case. I told them I had got this wrong, saying I was sure Ullmer knew when his own wedding took place. There was a smattering of laughter from those present. In the past I would have joined in with this ice-breaking moment, smiling along to try to lift the tension. Now I looked down, unsmiling, to the bundle in front of me.

Ullmer's lawyer had pale skin, largish spectacles and receding hair. His waistcoat was the smartest thing about him. I can only recall the woman on the panel closest to me, who had rosy cheeks and a mumsy vibe. The other two appear as judicial smudges in my mind, blank faces in Marks and Spencer clothes. I took comfort in their kind, professional tones.

They asked me if I wanted to swear on the Bible or make a legally binding oath. I opted for the latter. Ullmer would choose the Bible and I wondered what would go through his mind when he was lying to God. Did he actually believe in Him? And if he did, surely it's hard to lie to Him.

The affirmation was placed in front of me to read. Every eye in the room turned to me. I looked at Ullmer, who was shuffling some papers. I felt exposed, raw, open. I felt defenceless but that was because I had chosen to drop my guard. It was like the boxing videos that my dad and I used to watch. The boxing ring is an unforgiving place, and you only drop your guard when you know they can't hurt you.

I wanted nothing to get in the way of my words. No artifice. The character I had created had left the room. He hadn't even come to Coventry. I was Tom mark II and I liked this version better. This was the first time in my life where I would apply no filter to my voice. There would be no built-in edit, no pre-planned speeches. No jokes.

I felt no shame, no embarrassment, no anger. I would speak the truth. My life had been an act, a painstaking performance, but now I'd walked off the stage and thank fuck for that. I would let them see me for who I was. Every cut, every bruise, every fucking scar. I had nothing to hide.

I read the words in front of me. 'I do solemnly, sincerely and truly declare and affirm that the evidence I shall give shall be the truth …' At this point my voice broke. I could feel a well of tears spring into my eyes. This was a little too early to lose it. I stopped, took a breath, and the tears retreated.

I had tried so hard to escape it all my life. I had lied to myself for years, and the word *truth* hammered home like a nail into wood. Each time I said the word it almost overwhelmed me. I had been shackled to my past and my desire to bury it, and I could feel the chains falling away. I continued: 'The whole truth and nothing but the truth.'

The human cat began asking me questions, unsure and shakily. What had happened and when. At this point I noticed that she had a pencil case with cats on.

As I gave my answers, Ullmer started scribbling away on a piece of paper. He would shake his head, letting out an inaudible sigh as I explained what he had done.

He acted like the proceedings were an irritation. I was a silly child playing a tiresome game. He believed he was the most powerful person in the room. I wondered how he rationalised it all. Was he convinced by his own performance? He knew how he got his kicks. You can't hide that from yourself. Had he justified his own behaviour? What was it that stopped him taking responsibility for his actions? To admit what he had done would mean losing everything. He was the one running now.

The rosy-cheeked panel member gasped at points throughout the day. She recoiled when I told them how Ullmer had said we were like David and Jonathan from the Bible, and flinched when I explained how he had shouted at me to touch him.

Waistcoat smiled uneasily and peered down at his papers. He gave me a quizzical look. 'You stayed in contact with Mr Ullmer for many years after you left school,' he said. 'You exchanged emails. You met up occasionally for meals. You were friends, weren't you?'

Nothing Waistcoat said concerned me. Nothing would be reconciled in this room. The wrongs would not be redressed but a balance was to be restored. I was no longer a victim.

'No, we weren't,' I told him. 'I was a vulnerable kid. Very vulnerable.' My voice shook as I spoke. 'My mother was brutally attacked by my father in front of me for years.' I stopped to compose myself. 'That man …' I said, pointing to Ullmer, 'took advantage of me. Pretending to be my friend but he had an ulterior motive. He sexually abused me. It caused me deep confusion and I felt complicit in his actions, like I had played a part. I couldn't face what has been done for years because I didn't understand it. It caused me turmoil.'

I stared at Ullmer, with his pen poised to make his next note. 'Some kids are so hurt by being abused by someone they trusted they can't ever talk about it,' I said. 'Some people can only do it years later. He had control over me. That's what sexual abuse is. That's manipulation. Now I can see it for what it was. We were never friends.'

'I see,' Waistcoat said, his elbows on the table, holding both his index fingers to his lips. My voice had become lower. I spoke slowly, clearly. I wanted him to ask me his next question. I wanted everyone there to hear what I said.

'You were actively involved in the drama department,' he said. 'You took part in plays. You were quite happy, it would seem.'

'Yes, it felt good to be encouraged at school by Mr Ullmer. I threw myself into drama. I liked being listened to. The interest and the enormous amount of time he gave to me meant a lot. But what he offered me came at a price. I think I paid it because I needed it.' I felt more assured, fluent, concise than I had ever been. To say I was enjoying it wouldn't be quite right, but I could feel myself changing. I had an energy I'd never felt before. It drove through my body. My chest, my limbs, my head. I was discovering who I was.

Waistcoat turned in his chair. 'You were doing very well at school,' he said. 'You may have seemed destined for big things. You made plans for a television show for your sketches. Are you sure you're not bitter about not achieving those things? You're not as successful as you thought you'd be. And now you're angry at Mr Ullmer?'

The legal governance woman grimaced at this question, shaking her head and sitting back in her chair.

'It depends what you think of as successful,' I said. 'I've had an interesting career. But coming from where I did … growing up how I did …' Tears fell from my eyes and landed on the official documentation. 'I have a good relationship with my partner. We have an incredible little boy. I live in a nice flat in London. I think I've been successful.'

Our age tends to suppose that informality is conducive to honesty: that truth-telling flourishes when we're most relaxed. Perhaps, though, we overlook what can be revealed in the gravity, severity and focus of a formal cross-examination in an official setting. Maybe the suits, the depersonalisation, the sense of words being chiselled in stone can be a sharper spur to the truth than the kitchen table. Lies can be told on sofas that would not survive the witness box. I knew the panel believed me and that Ullmer's lies would be revealed.

The legal woman at the end nodded along as I spoke. I liked her for that. Waistcoat didn't pursue this line of questioning. 'Okay. Okay.' His voice was calm. He lifted up a photocopy of an article I'd written fifteen years ago. 'You do make things up for a living though, don't you? Here you say just that.' He waved the paper around in a theatrical manner.

'Well, this is real life,' I said.

'But you wrote stories undercover, where you had to lie to people?'

'Yes, I did. I think I went into that career because I was comfortable in a world of deception. My whole life I had to keep secrets. I lied about my dad, I kept the truth about what Ullmer did. I did manipulate people in those articles, pretending to be one thing and being another. I think I learned it from him.'

The panel sat quietly, observing, making notes. At the end they asked if I had anything else to say. And for the first time ever, I found that I did. I turned fully to them. 'My motivation for being a witness has been questioned so I just wanted to tell you what it is. I know what Ullmer did to me. I know the danger that he poses because he caused me damage. I can see it very clearly today. I wanted to take revenge on him for what he did, but then I decided what was important. No more children should be hurt by him. That's why I confronted him and recorded him because I thought he might try and deny it later. That's why I wrote to the school he worked at, played them the tape, and that's why they knew he couldn't continue to teach there. I am here to tell you what I know. This man should not be teaching in schools or be around young people.'

The panel thanked me. I got up and the human cat scurried behind me, asking if I wanted to stay and hear the rest of the evidence. But I didn't. I had no interest in what Ullmer had to say. I didn't need to be there. I had done my bit. Now it was up to them.

I walked out into that bleak little waiting room. I wasn't the same man. My shoulders were pushed further back and my head was high. I understood myself, my failures, my triumphs.

If I could pick one moment in my life when I was proud of myself this would be it. I felt fearless. I had nothing to hide and it was magnificent. I remember reading the quote, 'The truth will set you free.' I didn't understand it then. Now I do.

It was as I flicked through the pages of the bundle of documents in front of me while I was giving evidence that I saw my first girlfriend, Vicki, had been called to give evidence after me. Once I was out, I asked the human cat if I could say hello. It had been twenty-six years since I'd seen her, and now we were both in the same building. The human cat slunk off to get her, with her assistant scampering after her. I stood in the middle of the room waiting. Ten minutes later the human cat reappeared, leaning her head through the doorway. 'She's here,' she said, like she was announcing the arrival of an ambassador. In walked Vicki. It was as if the past was walking into the present. She looked the same. And when she spoke, I instantly remembered how she sounded back then. We threw our arms around each other and held one other for a whole minute. I took her hands in mine, smiling like this was a happy day. And maybe it was.

She lived in Cornwall with her partner, had three kids and presented a radio show. She was nervous about appearing, so I looked her in the eye and said, 'You don't have any reason to be. Speak the truth, say what you know, don't say what you don't. Tell them how you felt. There's nothing to fear.'

'Why are your hands shaking, then?' she asked.

It was true, they were. She had driven three hundred miles to tell the panel her memories of Ullmer, how she'd call my dad and he'd tell her I was at his. It was beautiful to see her again. I was reminded that part of that time was good. And that goodness had survived, was here now and was on my side. It still abides – we have become good friends now.

A few weeks later the verdict broke in the press. The *Daily Mail* ran the story.

A married teacher has been struck off for pleasuring himself in front of a pupil he lured into bed.

Jonathan Ullmer, 59, also 'begged' the boy to touch his penis and massage him with lubricant. He preyed on the teenager in his time at Cecil Jones High School, in Essex, where he worked from 1989 to 2002.

Grooming the boy, he suggested the two of them discuss sex and go out for meals to become closer, a tribunal heard. Ullmer even took the boy to his Kent flat where they shared a bed and the sick teacher started masturbating.

Mr Ullmer had abused his position of trust and taken advantage of a vulnerable pupil who Mr Ullmer knew came from a turbulent family background.

The *Daily Mirror* went with:

Prince William unwittingly honoured a depraved school head at Buckingham Palace. He gave an MBE to head teacher Jonathan Ullmer who had secretly groomed a pupil. Ullmer won the gong for services to education but a tribunal this month found he had sexual activity with a vulnerable schoolboy 25 years ago.

Married Ullmer was found to have been guilty of sexual misconduct with the school boy from the age of 16 and to have had an 'inappropriate relationship' with the lad from the age of 13.

The BBC ran the story too and it made it into the French press. He had been struck off for life. The decision was signed off by the Secretary for State for Education. It was done.

I wasn't the only one. A few days after the story broke, I got a text from R, a younger brother of a friend of mine at school. R asked if I was free to meet up. I knew it was about Ullmer. He told me that similar things had happened to him. I was anonymous in the news stories, but R knew it was me because weeks before the hearing, Ullmer had contacted him to be a character witness for him. It's quite a delusion. Ullmer must have been sure he wielded the same power over R as he had over me. R refused and told me he was sorry he hadn't come forward for the hearing but that it had been too hard. I understood. Much of what happened to him had been when he was fourteen, and he was thinking of going to the police.

Chapter 35

We are made in childhood. Our reactions, fears and dreams stay with us. They become themes in our lives. I wanted to break the chain of secrecy and the lies that had run through mine. Not just for me, but for Leo too.

When I stopped running from the truth and showed people who I really was, I was met with love and understanding. I saw a new world. Not the harsh, scornful place I had imagined, the one my dad had tried so hard to join. It was full of warmth, tenderness and acceptance, and it was there, all around me. It had been there all along but I couldn't quite see it. It was at the same time disconcerting and heartening: compensation for all that had happened. Humanity was brighter and lighter than I knew.

And I drink it all in these days. And it's beautiful. I am happy. I am a good father. And I know that change can happen because I have lived it and it wasn't too late. I know who I am and I know what I want to say. Finally, I have understood the power of the truth. I was always waiting for the moment when someone was going to try to screw me over. It was printed into my core like the message in a stick of Blackpool rock. I was at every moment ready to fight like hell. It was an exhausting way to live. I knew who was on my team: me. And I was as loyal as they came. I couldn't trust the love I received because it was meant for someone else. The person I had created.

I could listen to reports about molestation or domestic abuse and think, *Poor them. That must be hard.* I couldn't see the parallels with my own life. I just knew to look after myself because I was the only person I was sure wouldn't hurt me.

My mum has blossomed in the years without my dad, although, perhaps not surprisingly, she steered clear of a relationship again. It is one of the greatest pleasures I have known, one that I never knew existed, to watch her with Leo and see all the love she gives to him and the love he has for her.

It was only when I faced my own pain that I was able to feel it in others. It made me think of my sisters. I had felt the burden of their brittle souls and it reminded me of my own fragility. Somewhere inside I knew the pain I had was theirs too and I wanted to run from it. The idea of a relationship with them seemed to have gone for good, and revisiting the past in hope of resuscitating it, as I have in this book, was taking a dangerous risk.

I no longer blamed them because what they had to endure was horrifying and cruel. They were broken by the time they were fifteen. They got through it by supporting each other and it is their achievement to have made such a strong connection, building lives for themselves. Once I realised, my anger dissipated almost overnight, and what was left was warm. If it's possible to miss something you've never had, I miss them.

I don't suppose they will forgive me for writing this, but I hope they will see that I understand now, and did not then.

It's hard to say what's left to salvage. Forty years of silence and estrangement are not easily remedied. We are still different tribes and they've been so outside my life that it's hard to know where they'd fit in now. They probably feel the same about me, but perhaps it can be repaired. I recently started a WhatsApp group among the four of us and shared some photos of Leo. They responded with photos of their pets, emojis and kisses.

I want to talk to them and care for them and feel the connection of our blood ties. They are my allies. They're not ghosts. They're real. They are my sisters.

As for my dad, I'm glad I can see him for who he was. Nothing he did will be forgotten. He lives within me still. Writing this now, I wonder why I don't feel regret for living all my life till now in some kind of blinded funk, giving love to a psychopath. But I don't feel regret for keeping the relationship with him. Why not? Now he is dead I do not miss him. The only thing I can tell myself is that if I had cut him off for good, I would not have had the thing I wanted most: a dad.

He wasn't the hero I thought he was when I was five. Whose father is? Could his rage ever have been fixed, in the same way that an alcoholic might go to meetings? If he were capable of being treated, I don't think he would have been rageful. Like Androcles' lion with a thorn through his paw, my dad roared at anything that touched his broken sense of why he was as he was.

He lives in my head; he's part of me. I can see his smile, hear his laugh; I can still sense his enthusiasm for his mad schemes and I can feel the love he gave, for what it was worth. I can see too the demons in his eyes as he throttled my mum and the flare of his nostrils as he shouted abuse. It's all there. The good and the bad, even if one outweighed the other.

In a way, talking to you, my reader, has been part of my release. I'm no longer confused by the love and hate I felt and received. I have learned to understand that they both existed, side by side, and accept both. Once I understood that, as I have in writing this, I pushed the pain aside. I began to walk with my head held high, not ashamed of my past, not frightened of the future, but more free than I ever imagined.

Postscript

At the time of writing, Ullmer still has his MBE. My friend Ian became aware that he was trading off this, offering his services as an education consultant and as a volunteer for charities, including as a mentor to young people in vulnerable families.

Ian took it upon himself to alert the Forfeiture Committee to the fact that Ullmer had been barred from his profession in a decision signed off by the Secretary of State for Education in December 2019.

The Committee were evasive and non-committal about any action they might take. Eventually Ian got an undertaking that, at some unspecified time in the future, it may be looked at.

It was also Ian who spotted that Ullmer, only a couple of months after being banned, had taken a job with the National Citizen Service (NCS), an organisation that primarily works with sixteen-year-old-kids. David Cameron is its patron. Ullmer should have been listed with the Disclosure and Barring Service (DBS) and prevented from working with children, but here he was, doing just that.

I called the NCS to warn them and found them unresponsive, with little idea of the severity of the situation. Eventually someone there promised they'd look into it. A few days later they wrote to me telling me that, 'We comply with all safeguarding rules and best practice: a recent external assessment was undertaken on our safeguarding procedures which were found to be exemplary,' but asked for time to investigate.

They wrote again a week or so later, admitting that Ullmer had been employed by one of their providers but saying he hadn't any direct contact with young people and had now left his position. They again boasted about their exemplary result in a safeguarding audit. All they needed to have done was a Google search and they'd have seen Ullmer's prohibition order.

It seemed that due to a systemic failure of the system, the DBS had delayed putting Ullmer on the list by a few weeks. I spoke to them and they, too, said they had followed all the procedures correctly. It seemed no one wanted to take responsibility for something that shouldn't have happened.

We think that we've advanced, living in a world where people no longer turn a blind eye to evil, but maybe in the same way that I ran from my own demons for so long society runs from its own. It's easier to tell the world how seriously you take things, rather than take them seriously.

Once I finished my book, I sent it to my sisters. I was worried that raking over the horrors of the past would anger them. I thought they'd fight back against the things I had said and be scared of the exposure. They weren't. They told me it was hard to read, that they cried and seeing it all written down made the awfulness stark.

They had thought I was on my dad's side. They said they were sorry for their meanness towards me and for leaving me to deal with my dad alone. I told them they had nothing to be sorry for. We all did what we had to, to get by. They said the book had shone a little light on their own difficulties in life. They told me they loved me and always had. Years of hurt fell away, just like that.

Acknowledgements

Thanks to Kelly Ellis at HarperCollins for believing in my book. To my agent, Rowan Lawton, who calmly sealed the deal. To Harjeet Johal who told me when I was hiding from the truth and guided me like only a true friend can. To Dr David Wood who helped me see things I could not see. To Alistair Beaton who contained his frustration over my grammar and read everything I wrote. To Victoria Leigh, who appeared from the past offering understanding and a smile. To my pal Jake Mintrim who told me home truths with kindness at 4 a.m. To my mate Pete Bell who made me laugh by joking about things that probably weren't funny. To Matthew Parris for a hundred reasons. To my beautiful friend Juliet Maingay-Cooper who was with me every step of the way, right from the moment I met her. To my old friend Ian 'Champ' Hawkins who doggedly made my fights his, and to my mum, who understood why I had to write this book. But most of all to Diene and Leo, who give me joy.